WEBSTER'S
CHILDREN'S
VISUAL
DICTIONARY

PUBLICATIONS INTERNATIONAL, LTD.

Louis Weber, C.E.O.
Publications International, Ltd.
7373 North Cicero Avenue
Lincolnwood, Illinois 60646

Permission is never granted for commercial purposes.

Manufactured in U.S.A.

8 7 6 5 4 3 2 1

Library of Congress Catalog Card No.: 95-68461

ISBN: 0-7853-1109-2

REFERENCE MATERIALS

Ambesi, Alberto. *Oceanic Art.* Feltham, England: Hamlyn, 1970.

Arts of India, 1550–1900. London: Victoria and Albert Museum, 1990.

Bacharach, Jere L., and Irene A. Bierman, eds. *The Warp and Weft of Islam.* Seattle: Henry Art Gallery, University of Washington, 1978.

Baechle, Thomas R., and Barney R. Groves. *Weight Training: Steps to Success.* Champaign, Illinois: Leisure Press, 1992.

Berliner, Paul F. *The Soul of Mbira.* Chicago: University of Chicago Press, 1981.

Billingsley, Hobie. *Hobie Billingsley's Diving Illustrated.* Portland, Oregon: Taylor Publishing, 1990.

Branson, Oscar T. *Fetishes and Carvings of the Southwest.* Santa Fe, New Mexico: Treasure Chest Publications, 1976.

Campbell, Stu. *The Way to Ski!* Los Angeles: The Body Press, 1986.

Colwin, Cecil M. *Swimming into the 21st Century.* Champaign, Illinois: Human Kinetics Publishers, 1991.

Douglas, Paul. *Learn Tennis in a Weekend.* New York: Alfred A. Knopf, 1991.

Espejel, Carlos. *Mexican Folk Ceramics.* Barcelona: Editorial Blume, 1975.

Fassi, Carlo. *Figure Skating with Carlo Fassi.* New York: Charles Scribner's Sons, 1980.

Ferrier, R.W., ed. *The Arts of Persia.* New Haven, Connecticut: Yale University Press, 1989.

Furst, Peter T. *North American Indian Art.* New York: Rizzoli, 1982.

Glassie, Henry. *The Spirit of Folk Art.* New York: H.N. Abrams, 1989.

Good, Merle. *Who Are the Amish?* Intercourse, Pennsylvania: Good Books, 1985.

Grehan, Ida. *Waterford: An Irish Art.* Huntington, New York: Portage Press, 1981.

Gwon, Pu Gill. *Taegeuk: The New Forms of Tae Kwon Do.* Burbank, California: Ohara Publications, Inc., 1984.

Hoad, Al, and Abdul Latif. *We Live in Saudi Arabia.* New York: The Bookwright Press, 1987.

Hobson, R.L. *Chinese Pottery and Porcelain.* New York: Dover Publications, 1976.

Ikat. Victoria and Albert Colour Books. New York: H.N. Abrams, 1989.

Insight Guides: Peru. Singapore: APA Productions, 1991.

Leonard, Anne, and John Terrell. *Patterns of Paradise.* Chicago: Field Museum of Natural History, 1980.

Liu, Laurence. *Chinese Architecture.* New York: Rizzoli, 1989.

McCarthy, Mark (with George R. Parulski, Jr.). *Taekwon-Do: A Guide to the Theories of Defensive Movement.* Chicago: Contemporary Books, Inc., 1984.

Mitchell, Jan. *The Art of Pre-Columbian Gold.* Boston: Little, Brown, and Company, 1985.

Murphy, Brian. *The World of Weddings.* New York: Paddington Press, 1978.

Ochiai, Hidy. *Complete Book of Self-Defense.* Chicago: Contemporary Books, Inc., 1991.

Pauletto, Bruno. *Strength Training for Coaches.* Champaign, Illinois: Leisure Press, 1991.

Petkevich, John Misha. *Sports Illustrated Figure Skating: Championship Techniques.* New York: Sports Illustrated Winner's Circle Books, 1989.

PGA of America. *PGA Teaching Manual: The Art and Science of Golf Instruction.* Palm Beach Gardens, Florida: PGA of America, 1990.

Radice, Barbara. *Memphis.* New York: Rizzoli, 1984.

Schedel, J.J. *The Splendor of Jade.* New York: Dutton, 1974.

Shimizu, Yoshiaki, ed. *Japan: The Shaping of Diamyo Culture, 1185–1868.* New York: George Brazziler, Inc., 1989.

Willett, Frank. *African Art.* New York: Praeger, 1971.

Williams, Peter. *Wedgwood: A Collector's Guide.* Radnor, Pennsylvania: Wallace-Homestead, 1992.

TABLE OF CONTENTS

WHAT IS A VISUAL DICTIONARY?

YOU ARE LOOKING AT A VERY UNUSUAL reference tool. It's a *visual* dictionary, and it's really not like any other dictionary you've ever seen. Instead of teaching you about words and language, it presents information to you with illustrations. In fact, it has information about almost every subject you can think of.

Some illustrations cover the basic science and nature topics you study in school. You'll find information about plants, animals, outer space, and more. Others deal with some of the complex things that people have created, such as architecture, communication devices, culture, and music. The book also covers sports, heavy machinery, and other fun subjects that might be of special interest to you. Finally, you'll find information about some familiar things that you probably never studied very carefully. The illustrations of clothing, furniture, and kitchen appliances may show you a new way to look at these everyday objects.

The hundreds of illustrations in this book can teach you a great deal. As you spend more time looking through them, you'll find several different ways that you can use the information they hold.

You'll notice right away that this book is organized by subject. Each major subject, such as Astronomy or Music, gets its own section. The sections all have short introductions that give you an idea of what you'll find on the subject.

Suppose you want information about a specific topic—say, cats—for a school report. You can start by looking at the Table of Contents at the front of the book. There is no section called Cats, but there is an Animals section. If you flip through the Animals section, you'll find three pages that contain pictures related to domestic cats. You'll also find several more illustrations of large cats; these illustrations tell you where cheetahs live, how lions' jaws are built, and what animal group these cats belong to.

If you want to learn about engines, again you can turn to the Table of Contents. You might think that engines would be included in the Heavy Machinery section, but if you turn to those pages you'll find no engines. Another section you might think of is Transportation; in those pages, you will find drawings of several different kinds of engines.

Another way to find the information about engines would be to look in the Index at the back of the book. The Index is arranged in alphabetical order. It contains a list of all the pictures in this book. It also includes some big subjects that you might be looking for. If you looked up *engine* in the Index, you'd see several different page numbers listed. If you turned to all the listed pages, you'd find the drawings of all the engines in the Transportation section. You'd also find that the drawings of some spacecrafts in the Astronomy section include engines.

As you use this book, pay attention to the way the illustrations are organized. Sometimes you may be able to learn even more than the pictures show you by themselves. For instance, the Fish illustrations in the Animals section include drawings that show the insides of Jawless Fish, Cartilaginous Fish, and Bony Fish. This tells you that those are the three major types of fish. If you look carefully at these drawings and compare them to each other, you will probably be able to tell what the differences between the three types are.

The information in this book will be helpful to you for schoolwork. You'll also enjoy looking through it even if you're not searching for anything in particular. The illustrations are colorful, exciting, and fun to look at. You're sure to find new information about subjects you've always been interested in. You may also find some new subjects that you'd like to learn more about. As you look through these pages, you'll find out where things come from, how they work, and how we group them together to study them.

ASTRONOMY AND SPACE

IN ASTRONOMY, SCIENTISTS study planets, comets, stars, galaxies, and other objects in space. People have been interested in astronomy for thousands of years. It wasn't until the invention of the telescope in the 17th century that people were able to study distant objects. Today, scientists are still working to understand how stars and planets form, what other galaxies are like, and how the universe is changing. This section will show you our solar system, distant galaxies, and the workings of stars. It will also give you some information about the equipment we use to do work in space and to study astronomy.

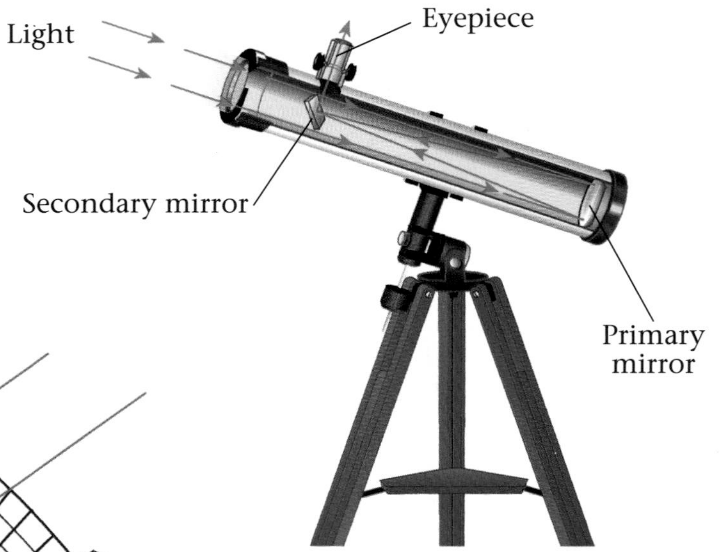

Light

Eyepiece

Secondary mirror

Primary mirror

REFLECTING TELESCOPE

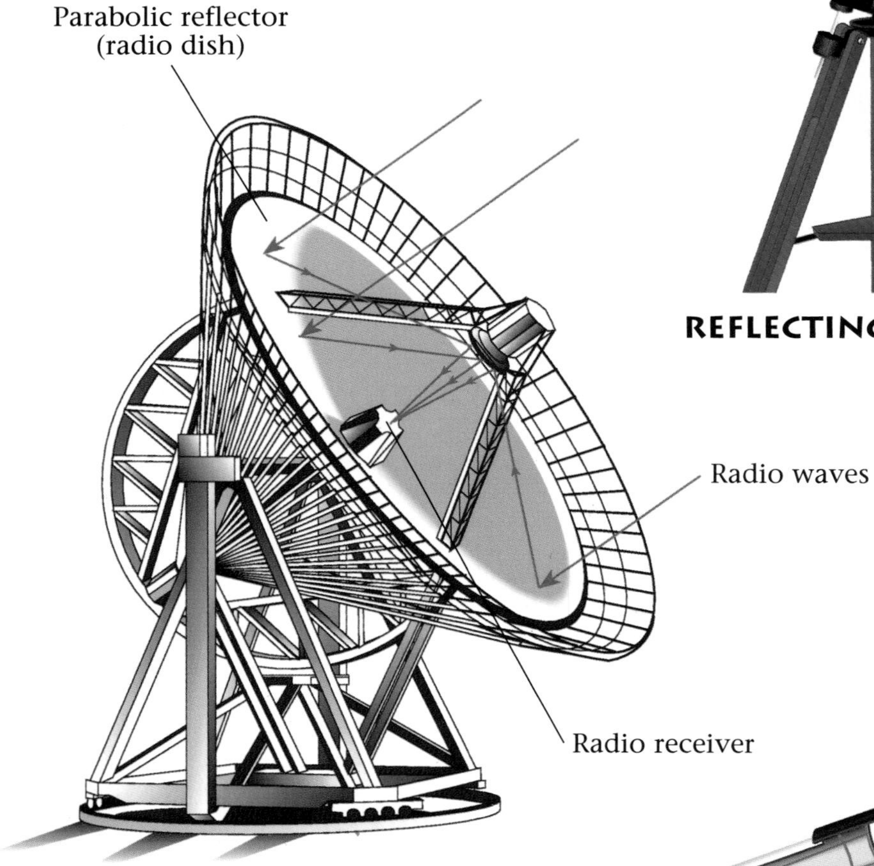

Parabolic reflector
(radio dish)

Radio waves

Radio receiver

RADIO TELESCOPE

Light

Objective lens

Eyepiece

REFRACTING TELESCOPE

HUBBLE SPACE TELESCOPE

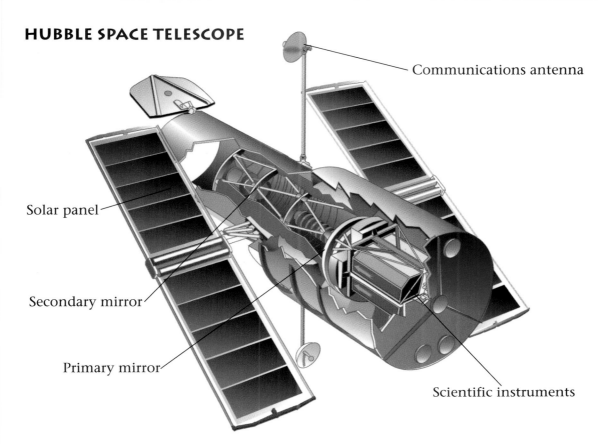

Communications antenna

Solar panel

Secondary mirror

Primary mirror

Scientific instruments

IRAS (INFRARED ASTRONOMICAL SATELLITE)

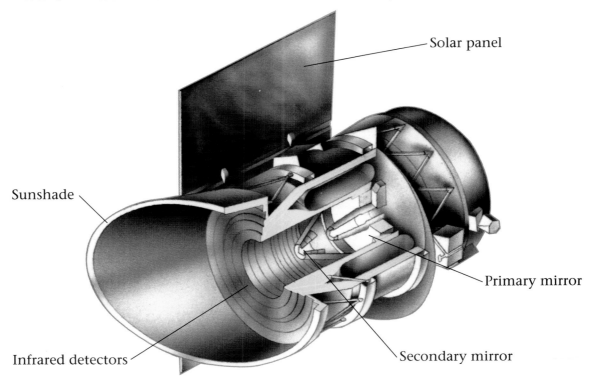

Solar panel

Sunshade

Primary mirror

Infrared detectors

Secondary mirror

ASTRONOMY AND SPACE

SATURN V ROCKET

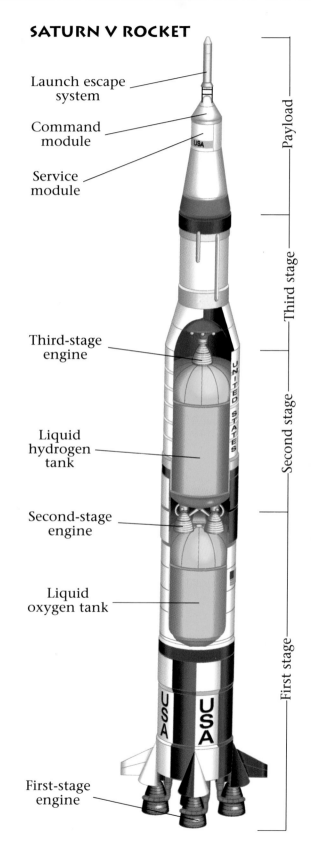

Launch escape system

Command module

Service module

Payload

Third stage

Third-stage engine

Liquid hydrogen tank

Second stage

Second-stage engine

Liquid oxygen tank

First stage

First-stage engine

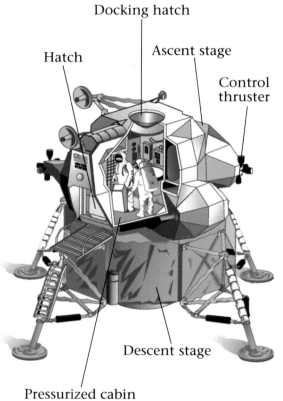

Docking hatch

Hatch

Ascent stage

Control thruster

Descent stage

Pressurized cabin

APOLLO LUNAR EXCURSION MODULE

MIR SPACE STATION

Soyuz
space craft

Solar panel

Multiple docking adapter

Mir work module

Kvant laboratory

VOYAGER SPACE CRAFT (DEEP SPACE)

Extendable boom
with magnetometer

Communications
antenna

Planetary radio
astronomy and plasma
wave antenna

TV cameras

Radioisotope
thermoelectric
generators

Plasma detector

Cosmic ray detector

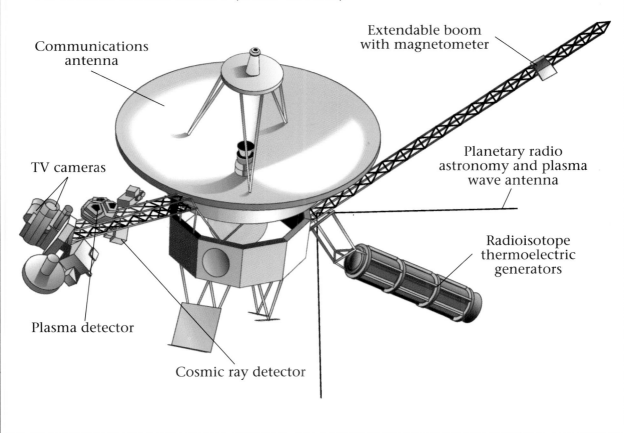

ASTRONOMY AND SPACE

SPACE SHUTTLE AT TAKEOFF

External fuel tank

Solid rocket boosters

Shuttle

USA

Main engines

SPACE SHUTTLE IN FLIGHT

Rudder

Main engines

Scientific instruments

Remote manipulator arm

Flight deck

Cargo bay

Wing

Maneuvering thrusters

Tiles

SPACE SUIT

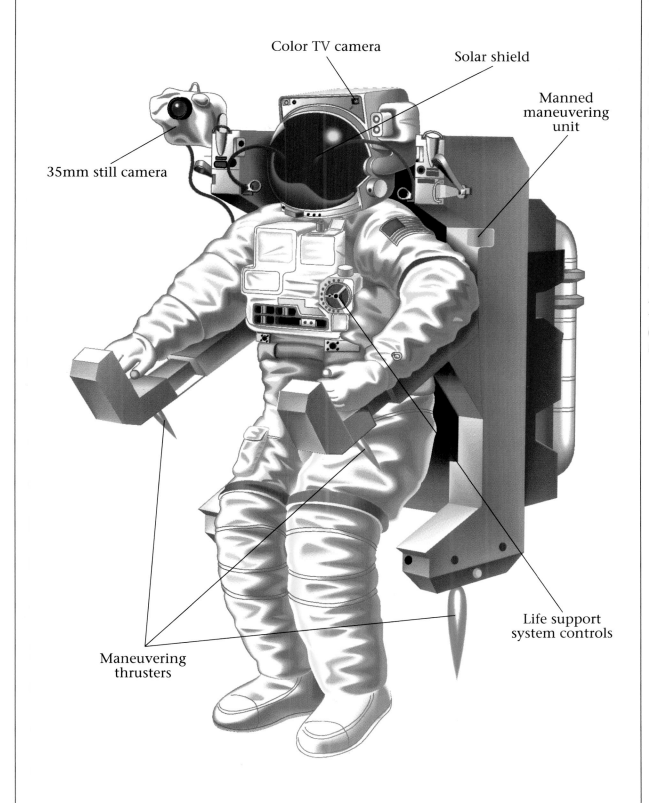

Color TV camera

Solar shield

Manned maneuvering unit

35mm still camera

Maneuvering thrusters

Life support system controls

ASTRONOMY AND SPACE

SPIRAL GALAXY FORMATION

|———— 500 million years ————|———— 1 billion years ————|

Overdense
cloud of gas

Collapse of gas
into rotating disc
of radiant matter

Further contraction
into spiral shape

CLASSIFICATION OF GALAXIES

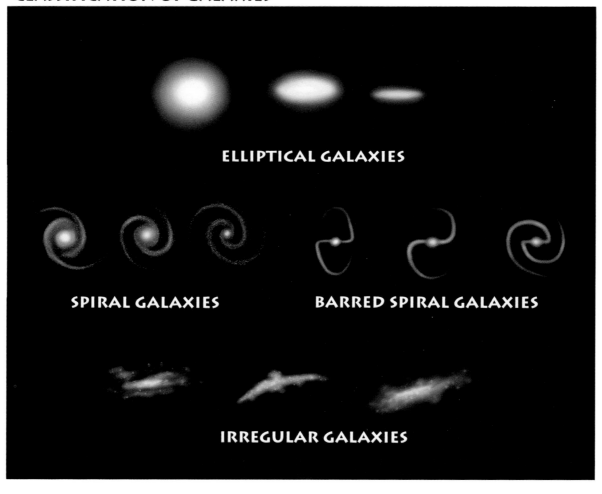

ELLIPTICAL GALAXIES

SPIRAL GALAXIES

BARRED SPIRAL GALAXIES

IRREGULAR GALAXIES

VIEW FROM EARTH

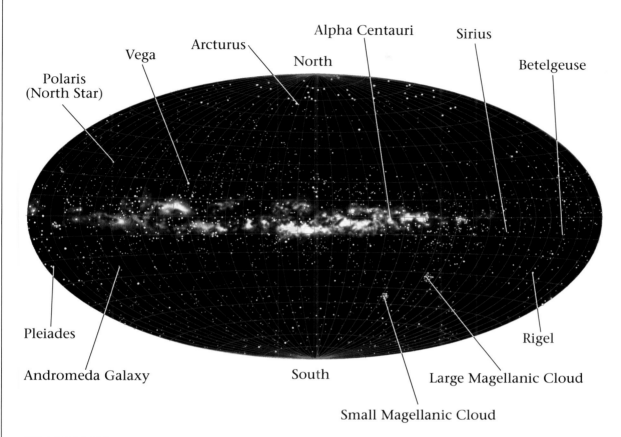

Polaris
(North Star)

Vega

Arcturus

North

Alpha Centauri

Sirius

Betelgeuse

Pleiades

Andromeda Galaxy

South

Small Magellanic Cloud

Large Magellanic Cloud

Rigel

FEATURES

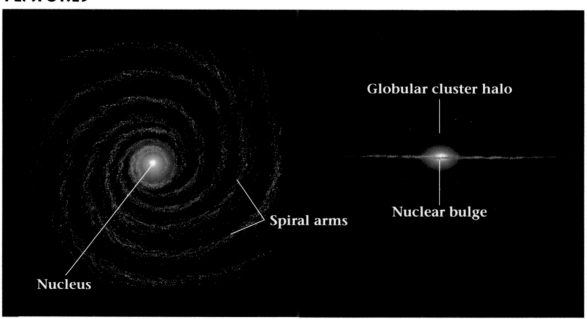

Globular cluster halo

Nuclear bulge

Spiral arms

Nucleus

FACE-ON VIEW

EDGE-ON VIEW

ASTRONOMY AND SPACE

SPRING SKY

North

Cepheus

Draco

Cassiopeia

Hercules

Perseus Pleiades

Little Dipper

Corona
Borealis

Auriga

Taurus

East

Big Dipper

Gemini

West

Boötes

Cancer

Orion

Serpens

Canis
Major

Leo

Virgo

Canis
Minor

Ecliptic

Corvus

Hydra

Milky Way

South

SUMMER SKY

North

Milky Way

Cassiopeia

Little Dipper

Cepheus

Big Dipper

Pegasus

Draco

Corona
Borealis

Boötes

East

Cygnus

Lyra

West

Leo

Delphinus

Hercules

Serpens

Virgo

Ecliptic

Ophiuchus

Aquila

Corvus

Sagittarius

Libra

Scorpio

South

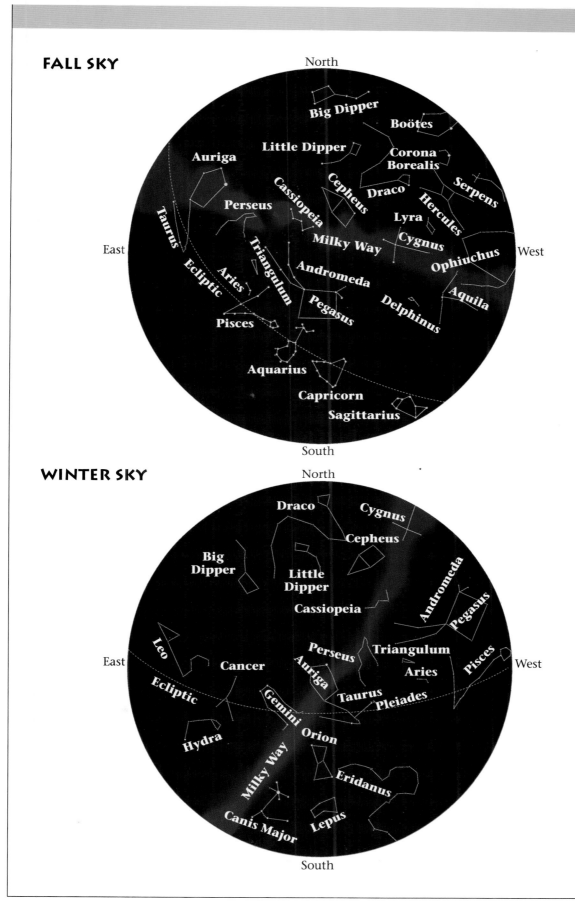

FALL SKY

North

Big Dipper
Boötes
Little Dipper
Corona Borealis
Auriga
Cepheus
Draco
Serpens
Cassiopeia
Hercules
Perseus
Lyra
Taurus
Milky Way
Cygnus
East
Ecliptic
Triangulum
Andromeda
Ophiuchus
West
Aries
Aquila
Pegasus
Delphinus
Pisces
Aquarius
Capricorn
Sagittarius

South

WINTER SKY

North

Draco
Cygnus
Cepheus
Big Dipper
Little Dipper
Andromeda
Cassiopeia
Pegasus
Leo
Perseus
Triangulum
Pisces
East
Cancer
Auriga
Aries
West
Ecliptic
Gemini
Taurus
Pleiades
Hydra
Orion
Milky Way
Eridanus
Canis Major
Lepus

South

PLUTO

NEPTUNE

URANUS

SUN

MERCURY

EARTH

VENUS

MARS

ASTEROIDS

JUPITER

SATURN

COMPARATIVE SIZES OF SUN AND PLANETS

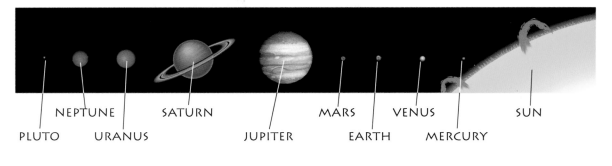

PLUTO NEPTUNE URANUS SATURN JUPITER MARS EARTH VENUS MERCURY SUN

COMET

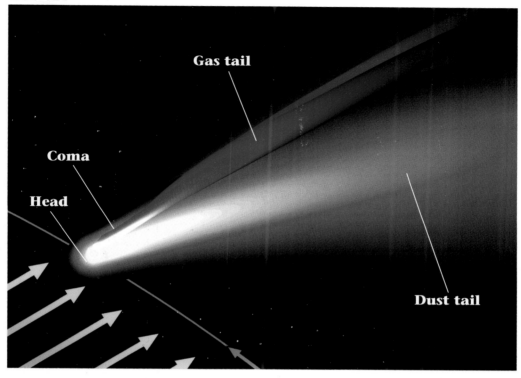

Gas tail

Coma

Head

Dust tail

Rays from sun

ASTEROID BELT

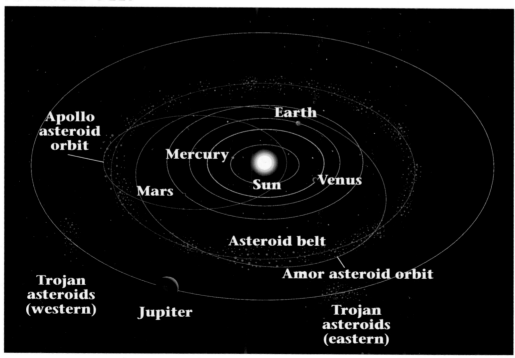

Apollo asteroid orbit

Earth

Mercury

Sun

Venus

Mars

Asteroid belt

Amor asteroid orbit

Trojan asteroids (western)

Jupiter

Trojan asteroids (eastern)

ASTRONOMY AND SPACE

Dense carbon
dioxide atmosphere

Land mass

Nitrogen/oxygen
atmosphere

Ocean

EARTH

VENUS

MARS

Rocky, cratered
surface

MERCURY

Faint
rings

Great
Red
Spot

JUPITER

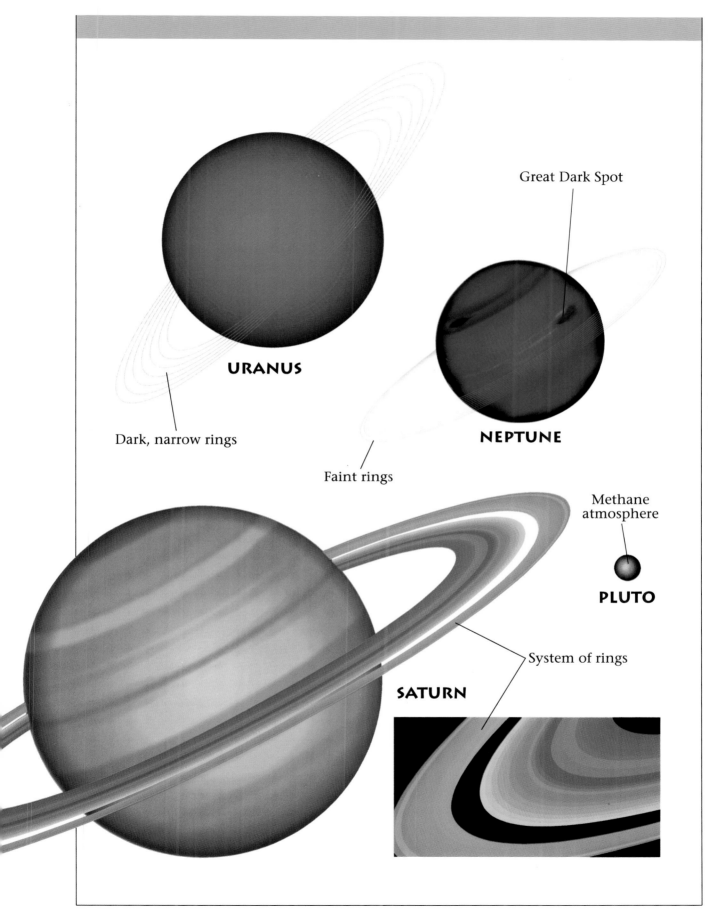

y

Great Dark Spot

URANUS

Dark, narrow rings

Faint rings

NEPTUNE

Methane
atmosphere

PLUTO

System of rings

SATURN

ASTRONOMY AND SPACE

SUN

STRUCTURE

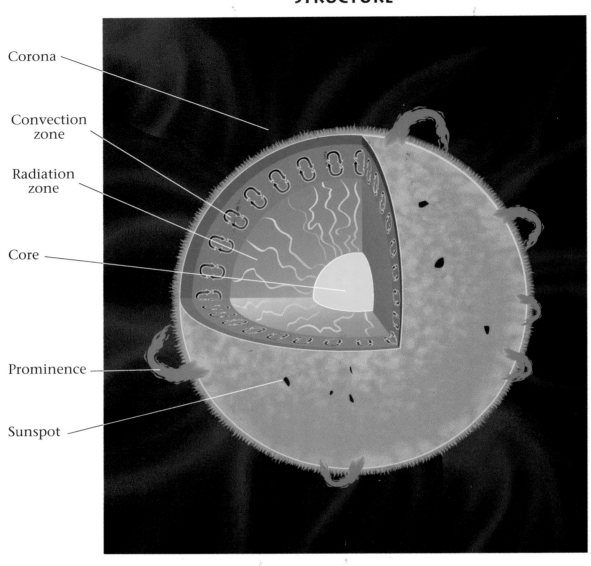

Corona

Convection zone

Radiation zone

Core

Prominence

Sunspot

SUNSPOT

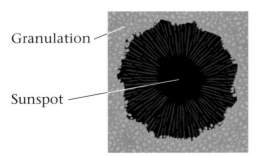

Granulation

Sunspot

MAGNETIC FIELD LINES OF PROMINENCE

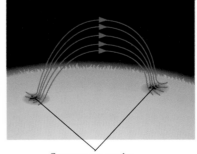

Sunspot pair

PROMINENCE

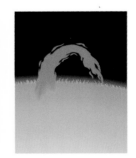

ASTRONOMY AND SPACE

LUNAR FEATURES

Crater

Sea

Lake

Ocean

LUNAR PHASES

WAXING CRESCENT

FIRST QUARTER

WAXING GIBBOUS

FULL MOON

WANING GIBBOUS

THIRD QUARTER

WANING CRESCENT

SUNLIGHT

THIRD
QUARTER

WANING
GIBBOUS

WANING
CRESCENT

6

7

5

NORTH POLE

NEW
MOON

4

FULL
MOON

EARTH'S
ROTATION

1

3

2

WAXING
CRESCENT

FIRST
QUARTER

WAXING
GIBBOUS

ASTRONOMY AND SPACE

SOLAR ECLIPSE

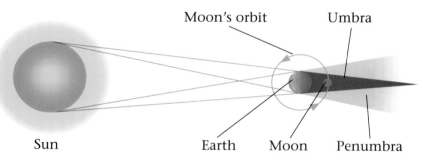

Umbra Moon's orbit

Sun

Moon Penumbra Earth

TOTAL
ECLIPSE

ANNULAR
ECLIPSE

PARTIAL
ECLIPSE

LUNAR ECLIPSE

Moon's orbit Umbra

Sun

Earth Moon Penumbra

**TYPES OF
LUNAR ECLIPSES**

PARTIAL
ECLIPSE

TOTAL
ECLIPSE

1991 SOLAR ECLIPSE

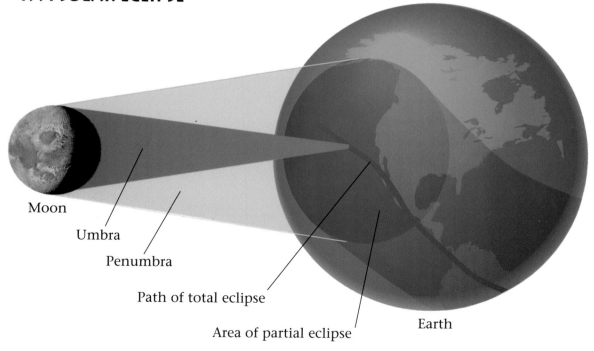

Moon

Umbra

Penumbra

Path of total eclipse

Area of partial eclipse

Earth

EARTH

THE EARTH IS ALWAYS changing. Continents drift and oceans become wider. Mountains push upward and valleys deepen. Wind and water wear away at the Earth's 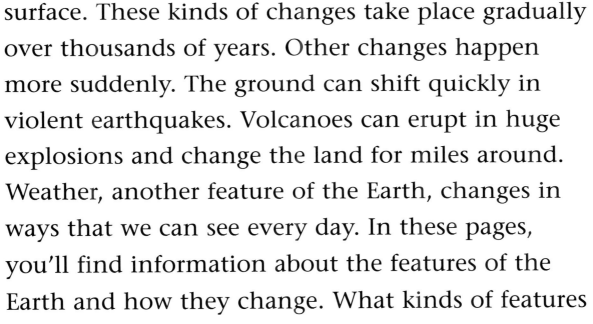 surface. These kinds of changes take place gradually over thousands of years. Other changes happen more suddenly. The ground can shift quickly in violent earthquakes. Volcanoes can erupt in huge explosions and change the land for miles around. Weather, another feature of the Earth, changes in ways that we can see every day. In these pages, you'll find information about the features of the Earth and how they change. What kinds of features does the Earth have where you live? Are you near any oceans, lakes, or rivers? Do you live near mountains or in open country? Have you ever experienced a tornado or other natural disaster?

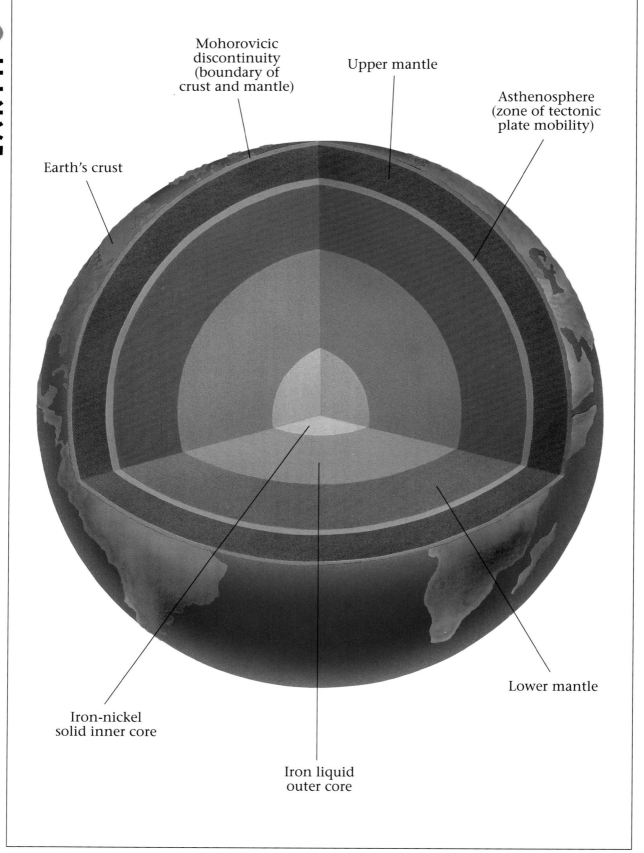

Mohorovicic discontinuity (boundary of crust and mantle)

Upper mantle

Asthenosphere (zone of tectonic plate mobility)

Earth's crust

Iron-nickel solid inner core

Lower mantle

Iron liquid outer core

VOLCANO

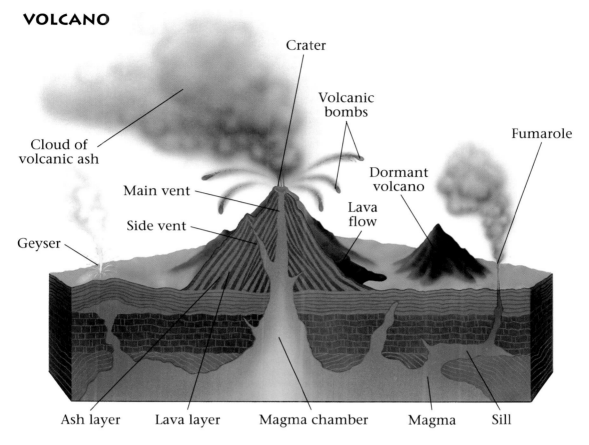

Cloud of
volcanic ash

Crater

Volcanic
bombs

Fumarole

Dormant
volcano

Lava
flow

Main vent

Side vent

Geyser

Ash layer Lava layer Magma chamber Magma Sill

UNDERWATER FORMATIONS

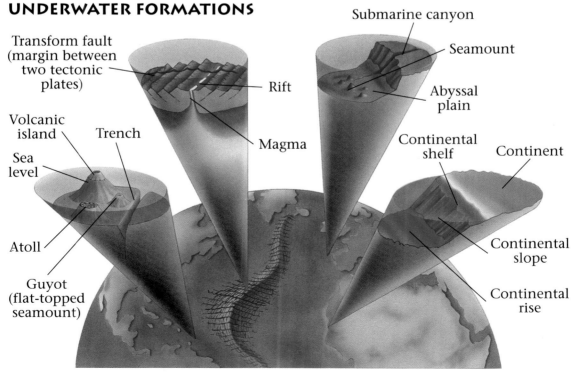

Submarine canyon

Transform fault
(margin between
two tectonic
plates)

Seamount

Rift

Abyssal
plain

Magma

Continental
shelf

Continent

Volcanic
island

Trench

Sea
level

Continental
slope

Atoll

Continental
rise

Guyot
(flat-topped
seamount)

THE EARTH'S CRUST

Mid-ocean ridge
(spreading center)

Oceanic
crust

Lithosphere

Molten basalt

Asthenosphere
(zone of tectonic
plate mobility)

TYPES OF FAULTS

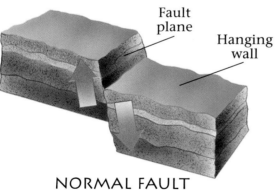

Fault
plane

Hanging
wall

NORMAL FAULT

REVERSE FAULT

THRUST FAULT

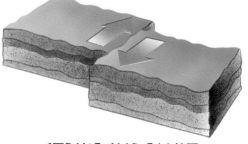

STRIKE-SLIP FAULT

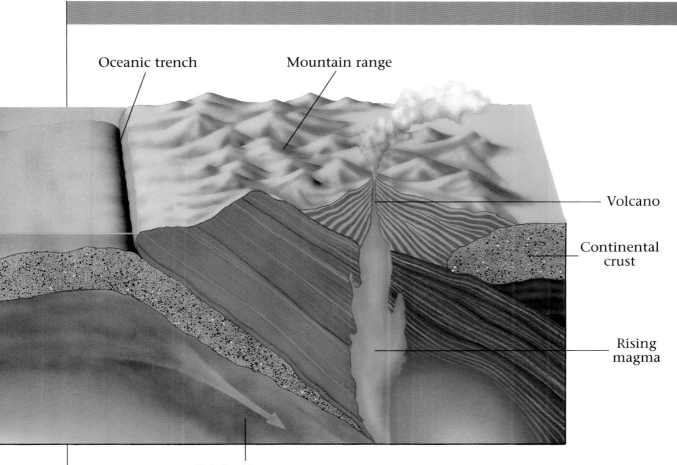

Oceanic trench

Mountain range

Volcano

Continental crust

Rising magma

Subduction zone

LOCATING AN EARTHQUAKE

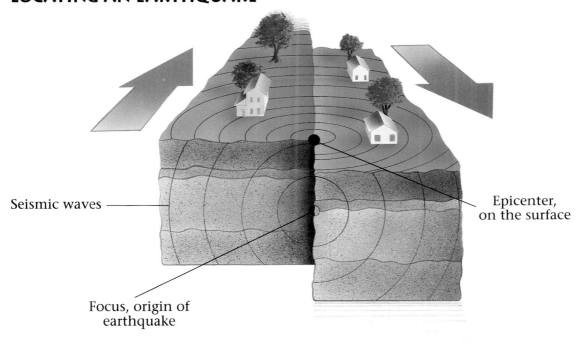

Seismic waves

Epicenter, on the surface

Focus, origin of earthquake

COAST

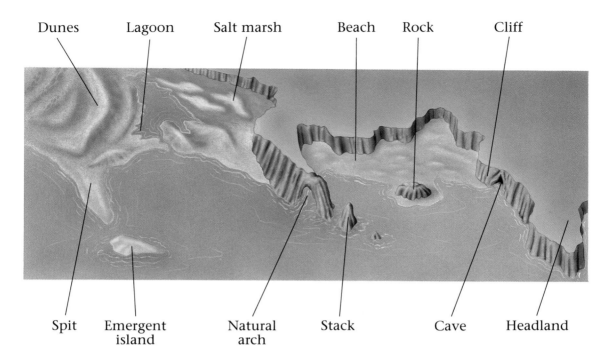

Dunes
Lagoon
Salt marsh
Beach
Rock
Cliff

Spit
Emergent island
Natural arch
Stack
Cave
Headland

GLACIER

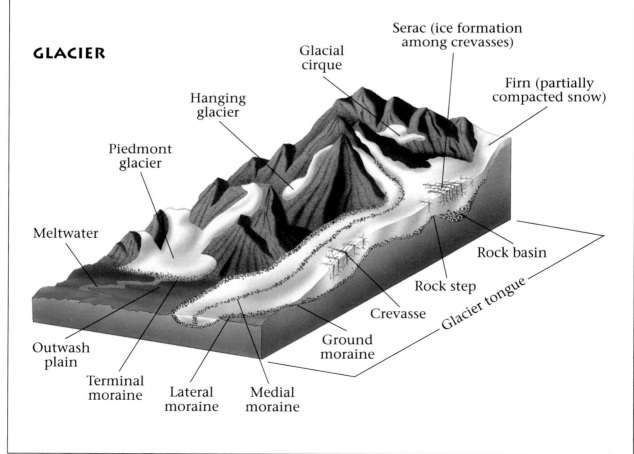

Serac (ice formation among crevasses)

Glacial cirque

Firn (partially compacted snow)

Hanging glacier

Piedmont glacier

Meltwater

Rock basin

Rock step

Glacier tongue

Crevasse

Outwash plain

Ground moraine

Terminal moraine

Lateral moraine

Medial moraine

CAVE

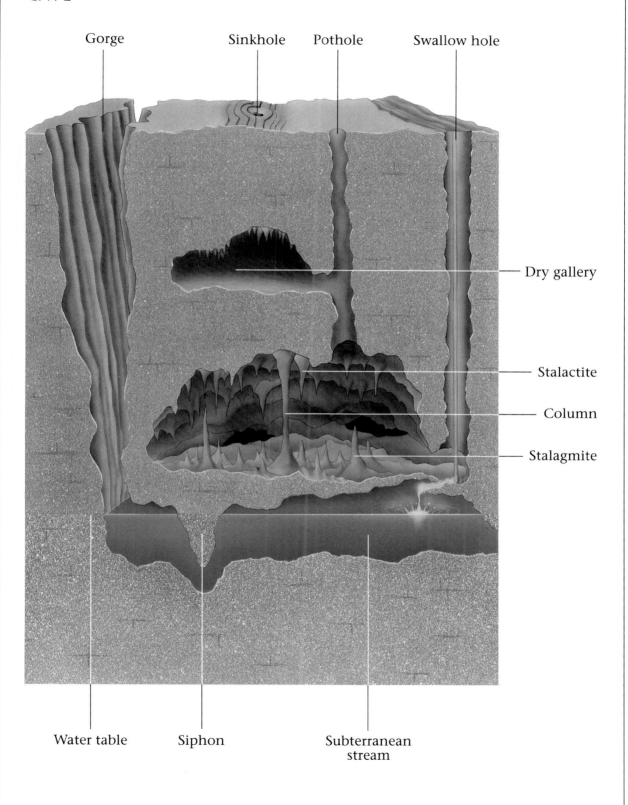

Gorge

Sinkhole

Pothole

Swallow hole

Dry gallery

Stalactite

Column

Stalagmite

Water table

Siphon

Subterranean
stream

RIVER

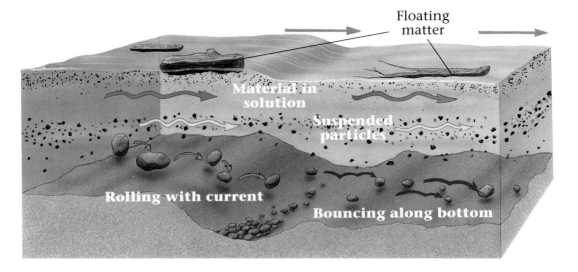

Floating matter

Material in solution

Suspended particles

Rolling with current

Bouncing along bottom

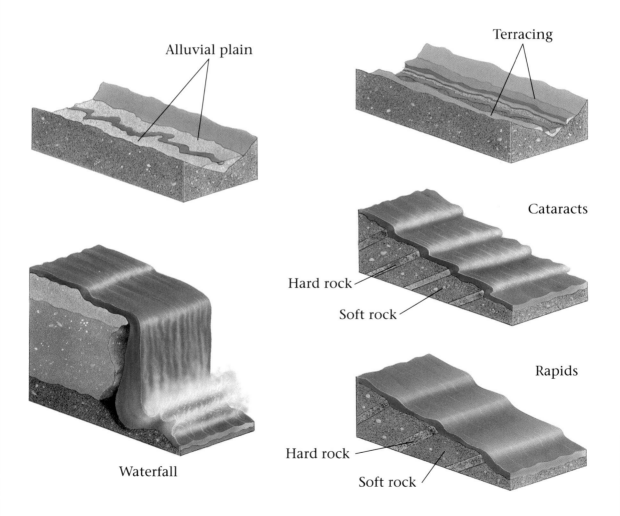

Alluvial plain

Terracing

Cataracts

Hard rock

Soft rock

Waterfall

Rapids

Hard rock

Soft rock

THE SEASONS

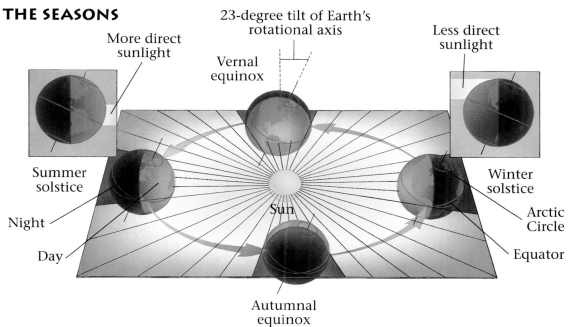

23-degree tilt of Earth's rotational axis

Vernal equinox

More direct sunlight

Less direct sunlight

Summer solstice

Winter solstice

Night

Arctic Circle

Day

Sun

Equator

Autumnal equinox

HEMISPHERES

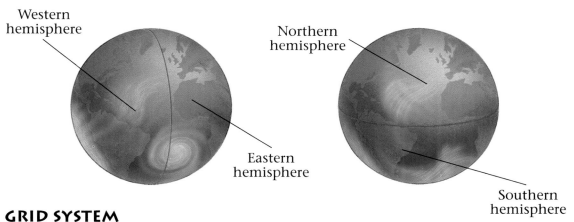

Western hemisphere

Northern hemisphere

Eastern hemisphere

Southern hemisphere

GRID SYSTEM

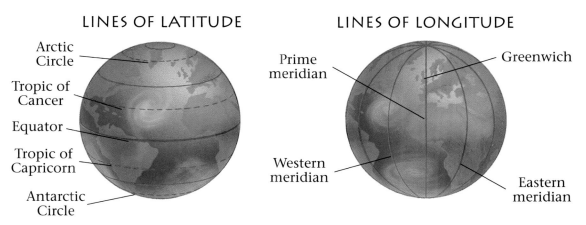

LINES OF LATITUDE

Arctic Circle

Tropic of Cancer

Equator

Tropic of Capricorn

Antarctic Circle

LINES OF LONGITUDE

Prime meridian

Greenwich

Western meridian

Eastern meridian

EARTH'S ATMOSPHERE

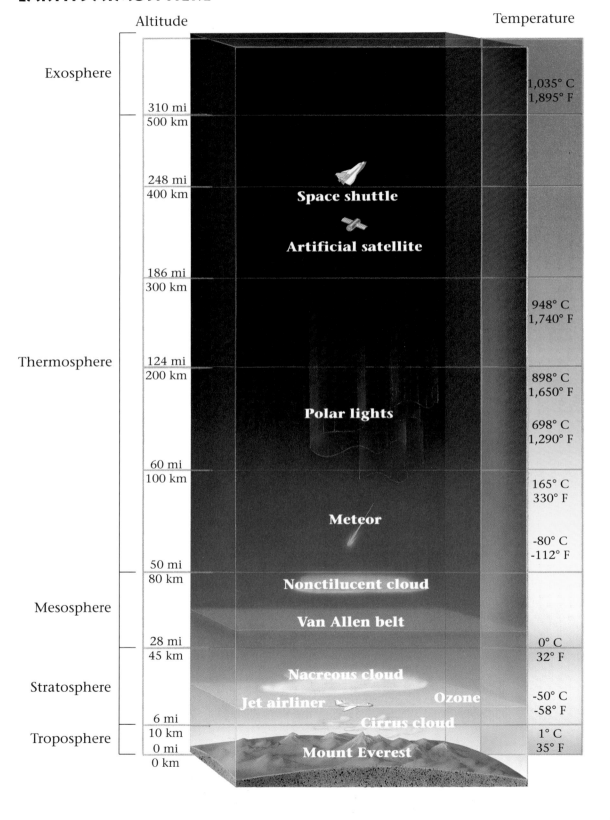

Altitude

Temperature

Exosphere

310 mi
500 km

1,035° C
1,895° F

248 mi
400 km

Space shuttle

Artificial satellite

186 mi
300 km

948° C
1,740° F

Thermosphere

124 mi
200 km

898° C
1,650° F

Polar lights

698° C
1,290° F

60 mi
100 km

165° C
330° F

Meteor

-80° C
-112° F

50 mi
80 km

Nonctilucent cloud

Mesosphere

Van Allen belt

28 mi
45 km

0° C
32° F

Nacreous cloud

Stratosphere

Jet airliner

Ozone

-50° C
-58° F

6 mi
10 km

Cirrus cloud

Troposphere

0 mi
0 km

Mount Everest

1° C
35° F

COMPOSITION OF DRY AIR
Average percent by volume

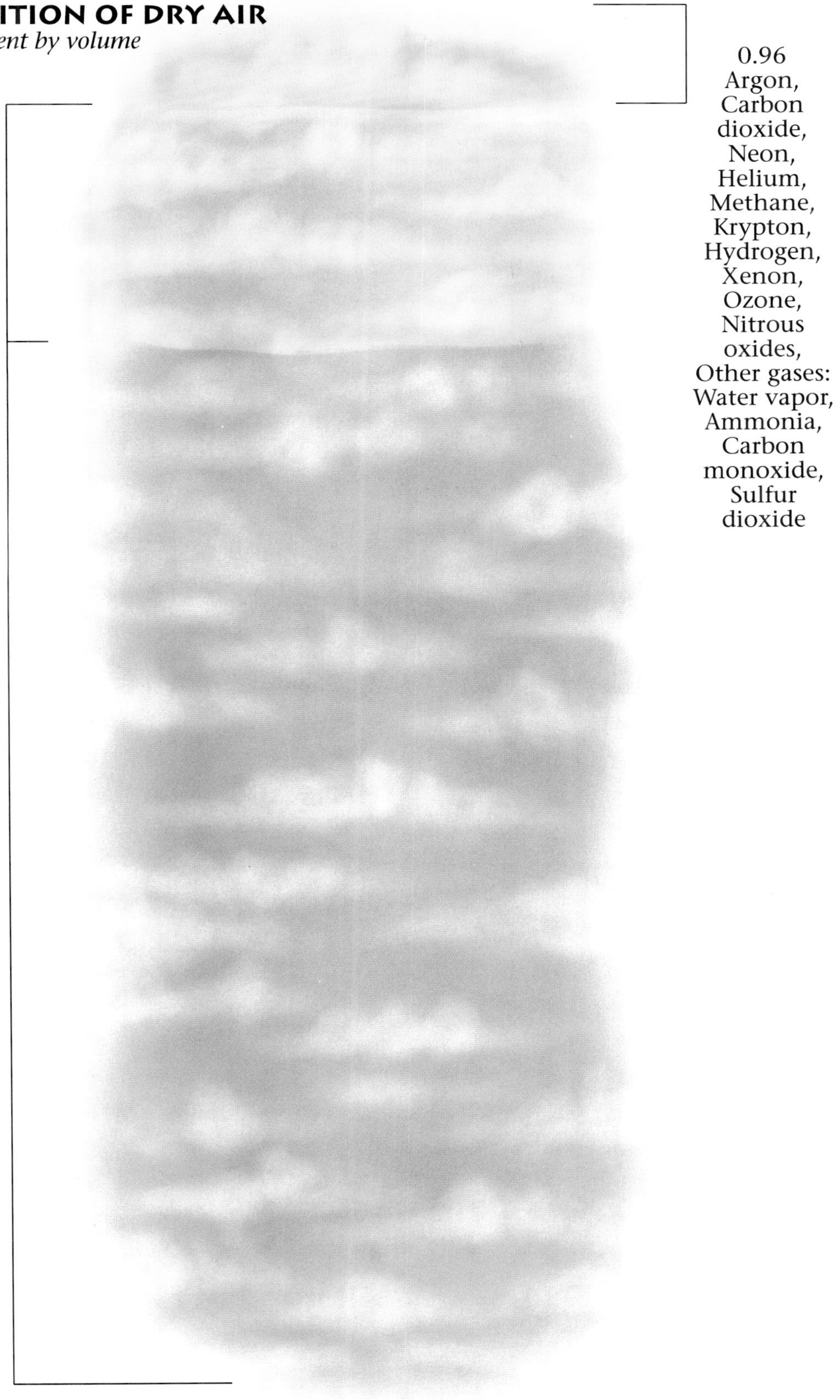

0.96
Argon,
Carbon
dioxide,
Neon,
Helium,
Methane,
Krypton,
Hydrogen,
Xenon,
Ozone,
Nitrous
oxides,
Other gases:
Water vapor,
Ammonia,
Carbon
monoxide,
Sulfur
dioxide

20.95
Oxygen

78.09
Nitrogen

THE WATER CYCLE

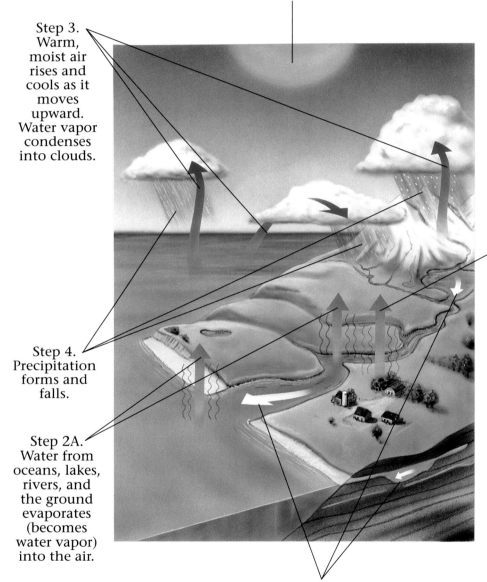

Step 1. Energy from the sun warms the Earth's surface and air above it.

Step 3. Warm, moist air rises and cools as it moves upward. Water vapor condenses into clouds.

Step 2B. Water from living things transpires (is released as water vapor) into the air.

Step 4. Precipitation forms and falls.

Step 2A. Water from oceans, lakes, rivers, and the ground evaporates (becomes water vapor) into the air.

Step 5. Runoff precipitation flows into rivers, lakes, and underground reservoirs and back to oceans.

CLOUD FORMATIONS

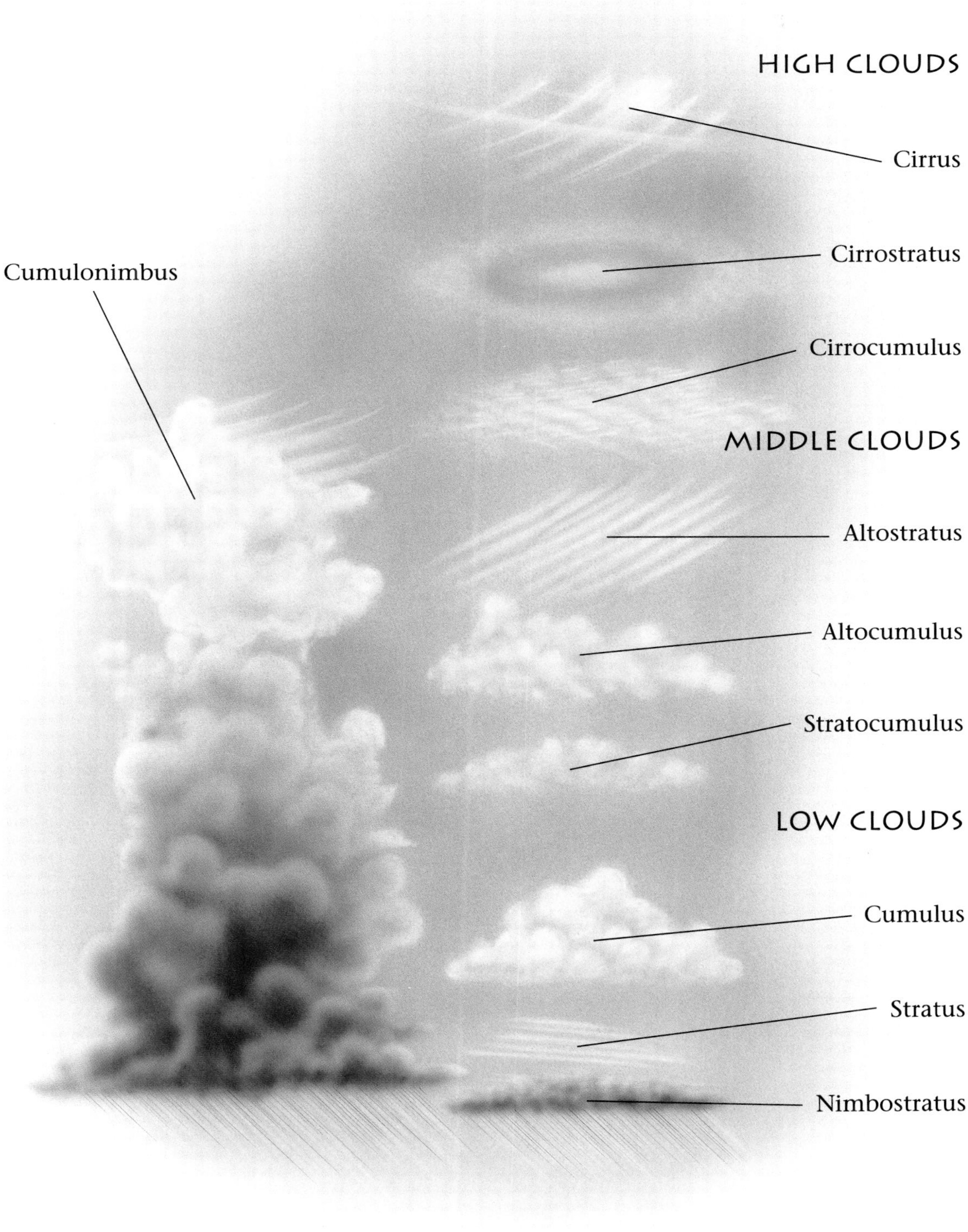

HIGH CLOUDS

Cirrus

Cirrostratus

Cirrocumulus

MIDDLE CLOUDS

Altostratus

Altocumulus

Stratocumulus

LOW CLOUDS

Cumulus

Stratus

Nimbostratus

Cumulonimbus

EARTH

TORNADO
Average land speed: 28 mph
Average distance traveled on land: 16 miles
Wind speed of funnel rotation: up to 250 to 300 mph

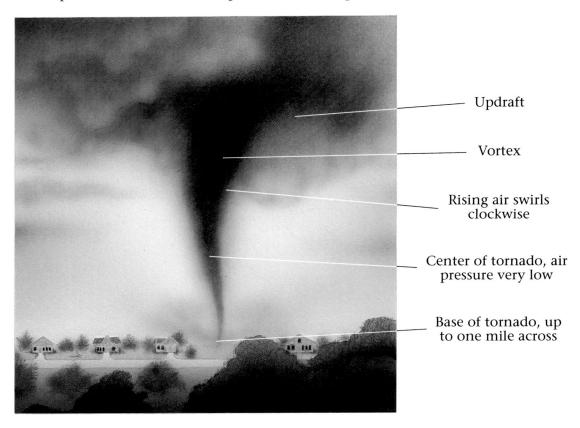

Updraft

Vortex

Rising air swirls
clockwise

Center of tornado, air
pressure very low

Base of tornado, up
to one mile across

HURRICANE
Wind speed of more than 190 mph

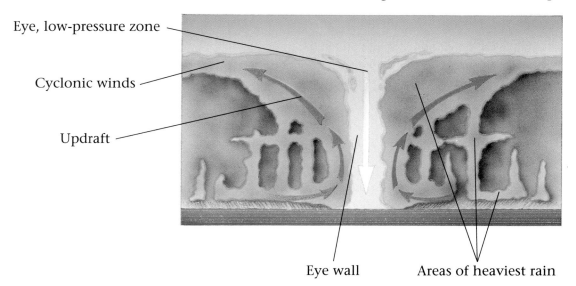

Eye, low-pressure zone

Cyclonic winds

Updraft

Eye wall

Areas of heaviest rain

CLASSIFICATION OF SNOW CRYSTALS

Column   Plate crystal   Needle   Irregular crystal   Sleet

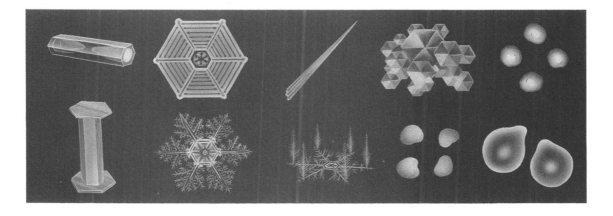

Capped column   Stellar crystal   Spatial dendrite   Snow pellet   Hail

WEATHER SATELLITE

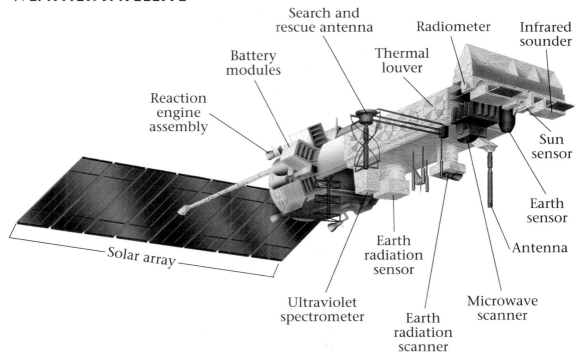

Search and rescue antenna

Radiometer

Infrared sounder

Battery modules

Thermal louver

Reaction engine assembly

Sun sensor

Earth sensor

Antenna

Solar array

Earth radiation sensor

Ultraviolet spectrometer

Earth radiation scanner

Microwave scanner

FORMATION OF RAIN

Step 1. Water vapor condenses into a cloud droplet.

Step 2. Cloud droplet grows as more water vapor condenses on it.

Step 3. Cloud droplets collide and water vapor condenses on them to form large cloud drop.

Step 4. Large cloud drops collide and water vapor condenses on them to form drizzle.

Step 5. Drizzle drops collide to form raindrop.

Step 6. Rain falls to ground.

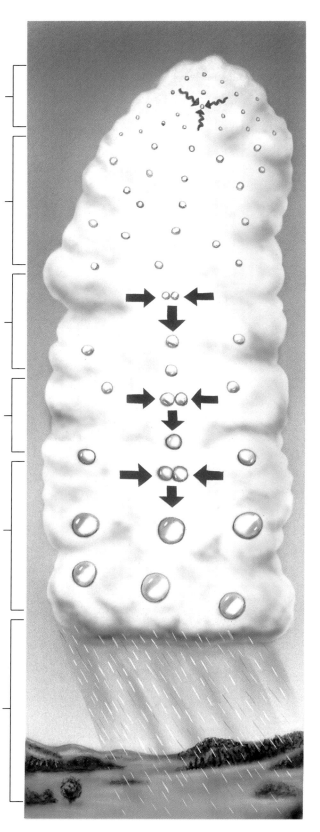

FORMATION OF SNOW

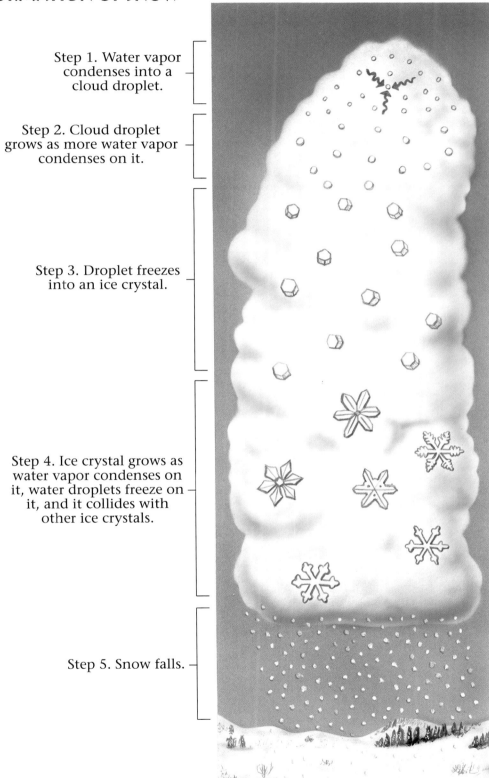

Step 1. Water vapor condenses into a cloud droplet.

Step 2. Cloud droplet grows as more water vapor condenses on it.

Step 3. Droplet freezes into an ice crystal.

Step 4. Ice crystal grows as water vapor condenses on it, water droplets freeze on it, and it collides with other ice crystals.

Step 5. Snow falls.

FORMATION OF HAIL

Step 1. Water vapor condenses into a cloud droplet.

Step 2. Cloud droplet grows as more water vapor condenses on it.

Step 3. Droplet freezes into an ice crystal.

Step 4. Air currents carry the crystal up, down, and horizontally through the cloud; droplets freeze around crystal in layers to form hail.

Step 5. Hail falls.

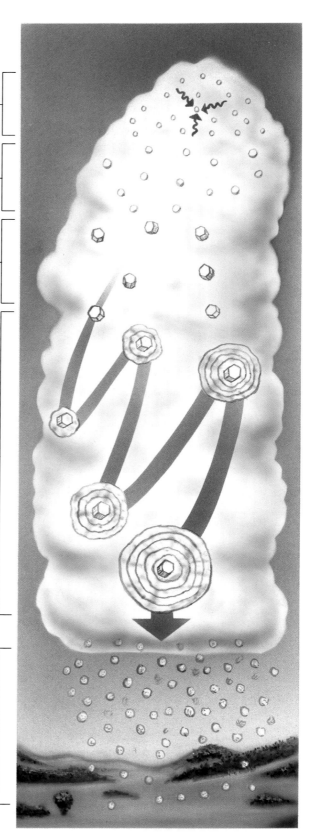

FORMATION OF LIGHTNING

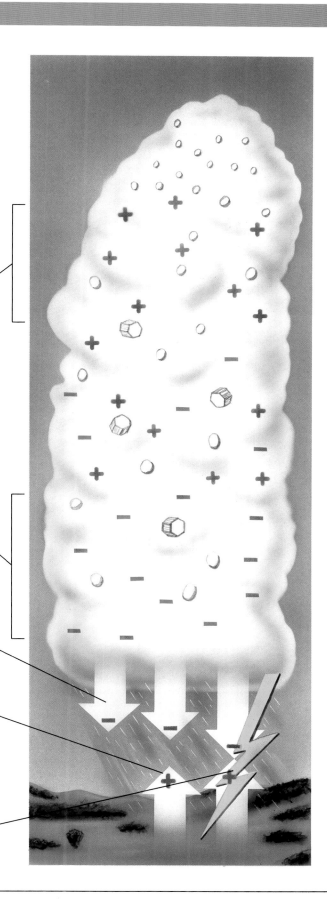

Step 1. Movement of water droplets and ice crystals creates areas of negative charge and positive charge.

Step 2. Negative charge moves from cloud toward ground.

Step 3. Negative charge draws positive charge upward from ground.

Step 4. Positive and negative charge meet and intense streams of charge travel between the cloud and the ground.

FORMATION OF A RAINBOW

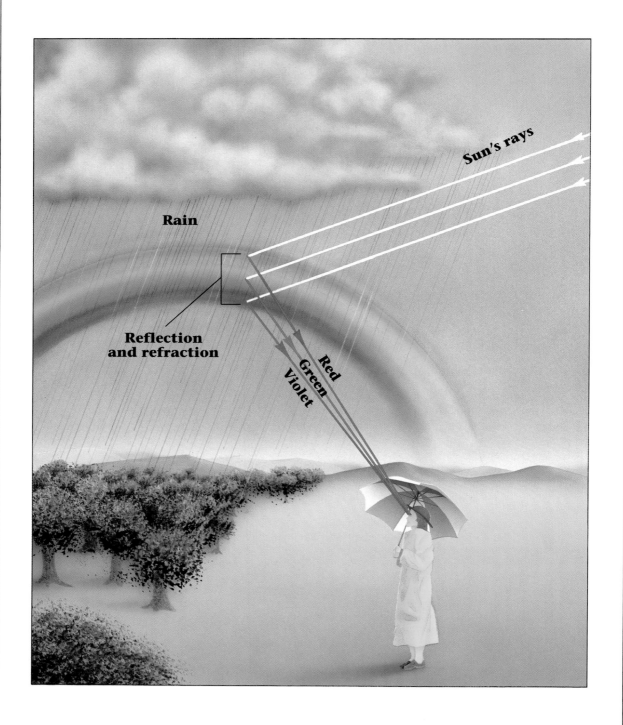

Sun's rays

Rain

Reflection
and refraction

Red
Green
Violet

ECOSYSTEMS OF THE WORLD

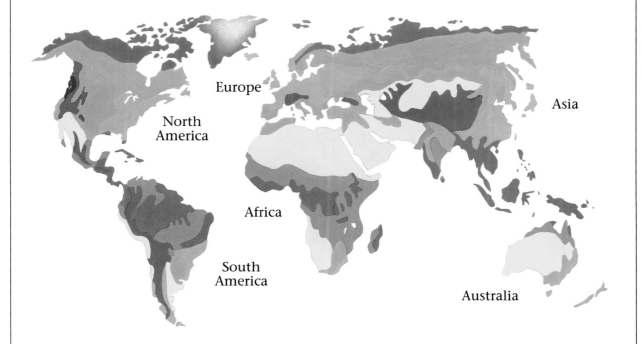

Europe

Asia

North
America

Africa

South
America

Australia

Desert/scrubland

Temperate rain forest

Temperate grassland

Savanna

Temperate forest

Tundra

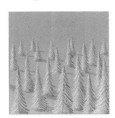

Tropical rain forest

Boreal forest

Mountains

GREENHOUSE EFFECT

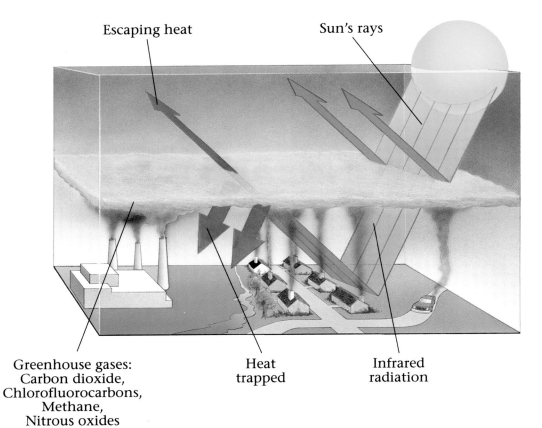

Escaping heat

Sun's rays

Greenhouse gases:
Carbon dioxide,
Chlorofluorocarbons,
Methane,
Nitrous oxides

Heat
trapped

Infrared
radiation

ATMOSPHERIC POLLUTION

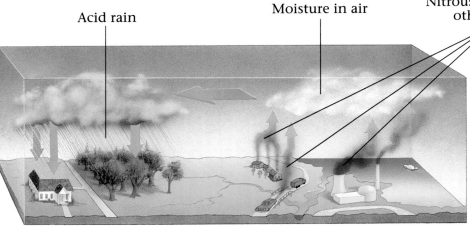

Acid rain

Moisture in air

Carbon dioxide,
Sulfur dioxide,
Carbon monoxide,
Nitrous oxides, and
other gases

Sources of pollution:
Burning fossil fuels:
motor vehicles,
industry, home

PLANTS

PLANTS ARE A SPECIAL GROUP of living organisms. Most plants cannot move around by themselves. They can, however, make their own food. Plants make sugars by using energy from the sun, water

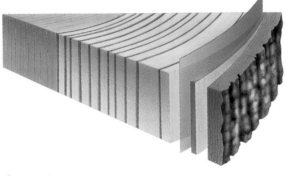

from the soil, and carbon dioxide from the air. Plants are a major food source for our planet. All animals depend on plants for food in one way or another. People use plants for food and for a great many other things. The next few pages will show you how we group plants to study them, and it will show you just a few of the ways we use plants.

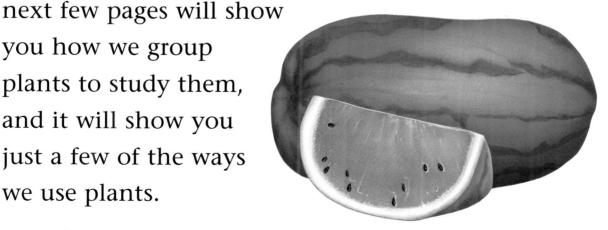

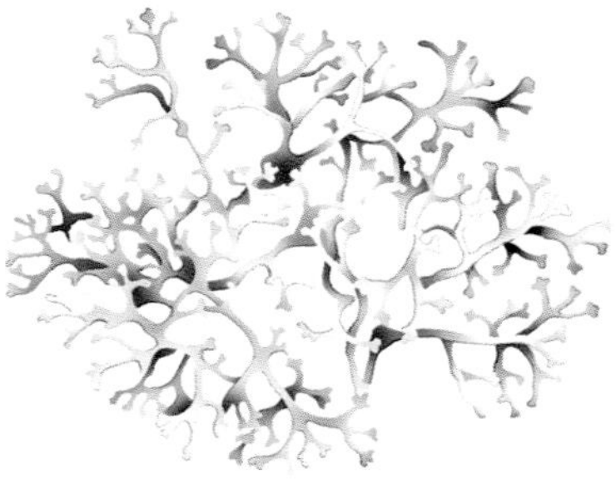

LICHEN

FUNGUS

MOSS

FERN

ALGA

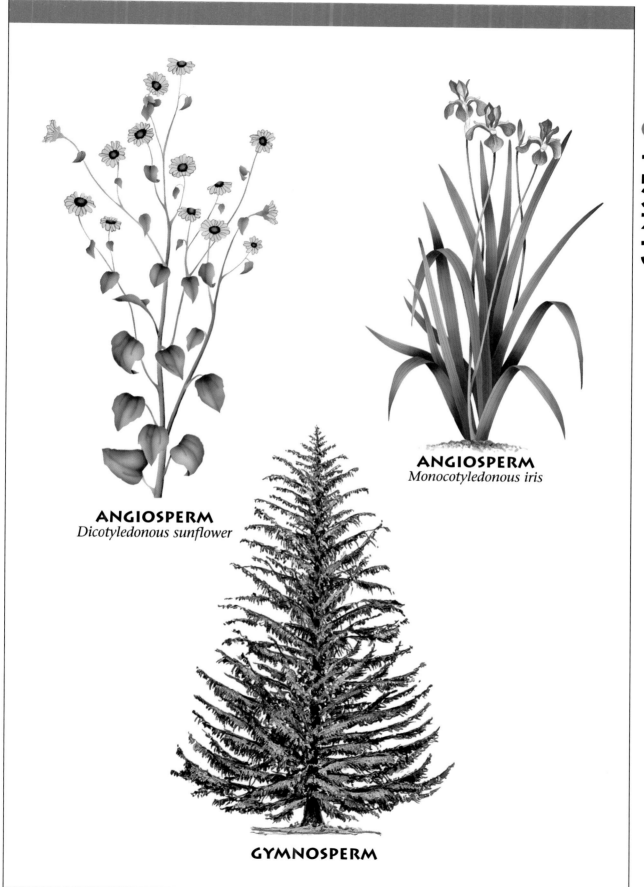

ANGIOSPERM
Dicotyledonous sunflower

ANGIOSPERM
Monocotyledonous iris

GYMNOSPERM

DECIDUOUS TREES

STRUCTURE OF A DECIDUOUS TREE

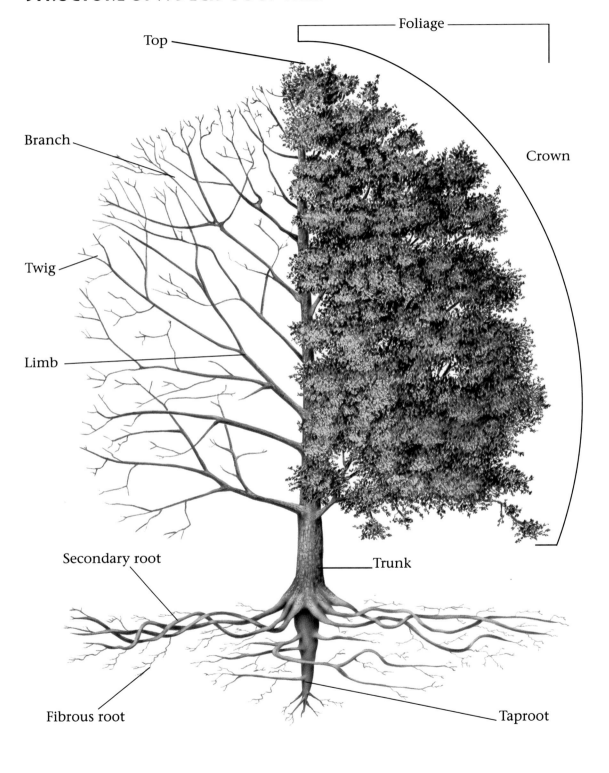

Foliage

Top

Branch

Crown

Twig

Limb

Secondary root

Trunk

Fibrous root

Taproot

LEAF TYPES

WILLOW

MAPLE

OAK

BEECH

WHITE ASH

HORSE CHESTNUT

CROSS SECTION OF A TRUNK

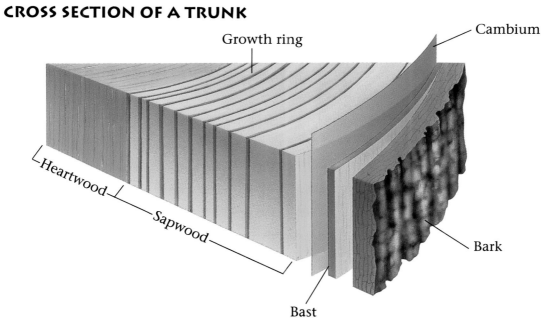

Growth ring

Cambium

Heartwood

Sapwood

Bast

Bark

TYPES OF CONIFERS

PLANTS

LAWSON CYPRESS

DOUGLAS FIR

SCOTCH PINE

COASTAL REDWOOD

LEAF TYPES

CYPRESS LEAVES

PINE NEEDLES

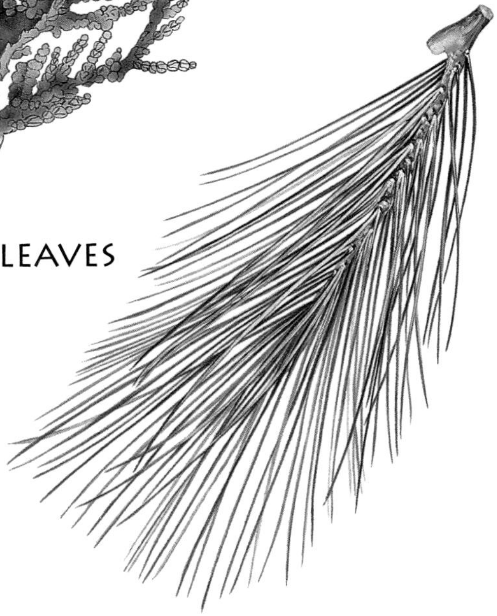

FIR NEEDLES

PINE CONES

MALE

FEMALE

AMERICAN
ARROWHEAD

WATER HYACINTH

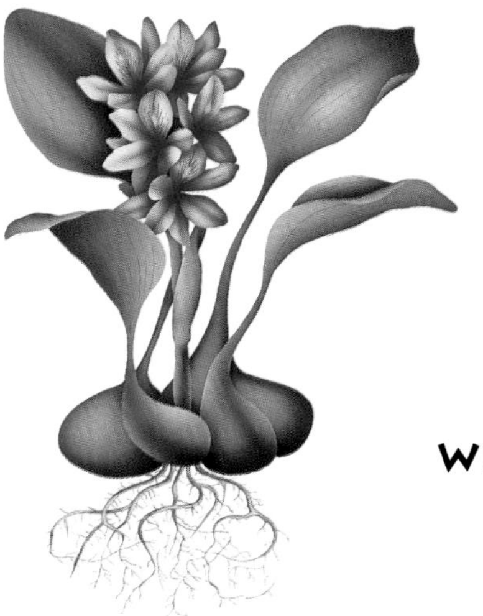

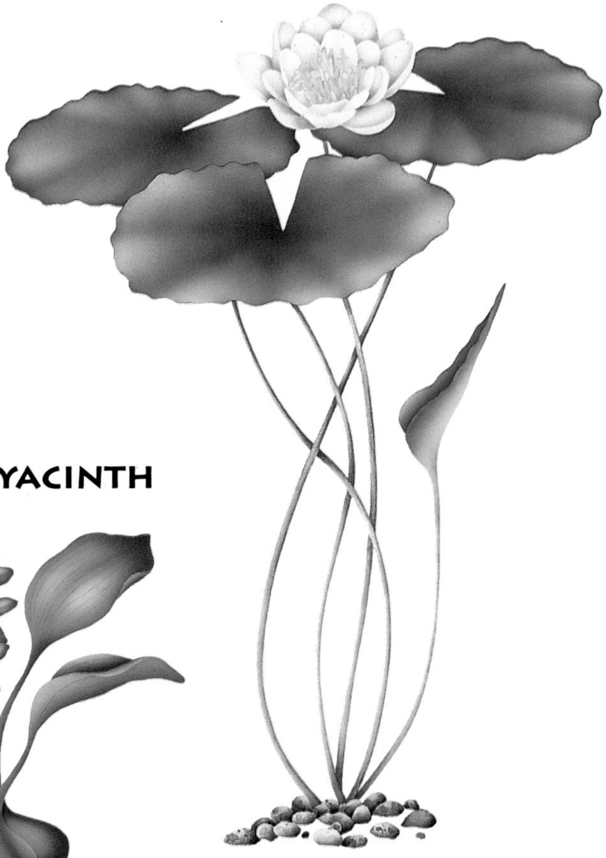

WHITE WATER LILY

YELLOW SKUNK CABBAGE

WATER LETTUCE

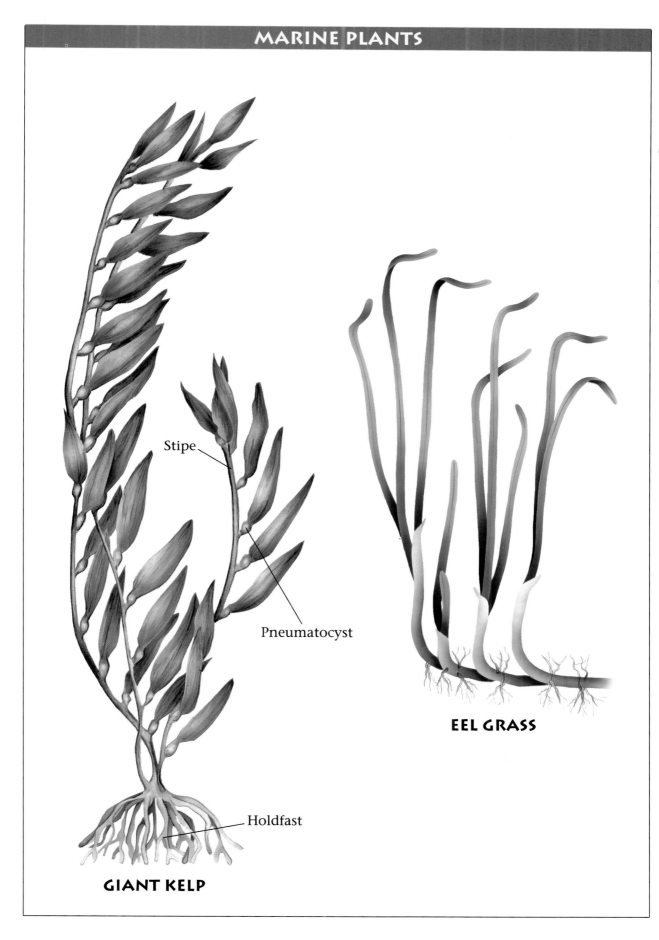

Stipe

Pneumatocyst

Holdfast

GIANT KELP

EEL GRASS

PLANTS

PLANT

Terminal bud

Flower

Axillary bud

Flower bud

Lateral branch

Leaf

Shoot

Leaf node

Internode

Anther

Stigma

Filament

Petal

Style

Stem

Sepal

Seed leaf

Ovary

Receptacle

Ovule

Primary root

Secondary root

Pedicel

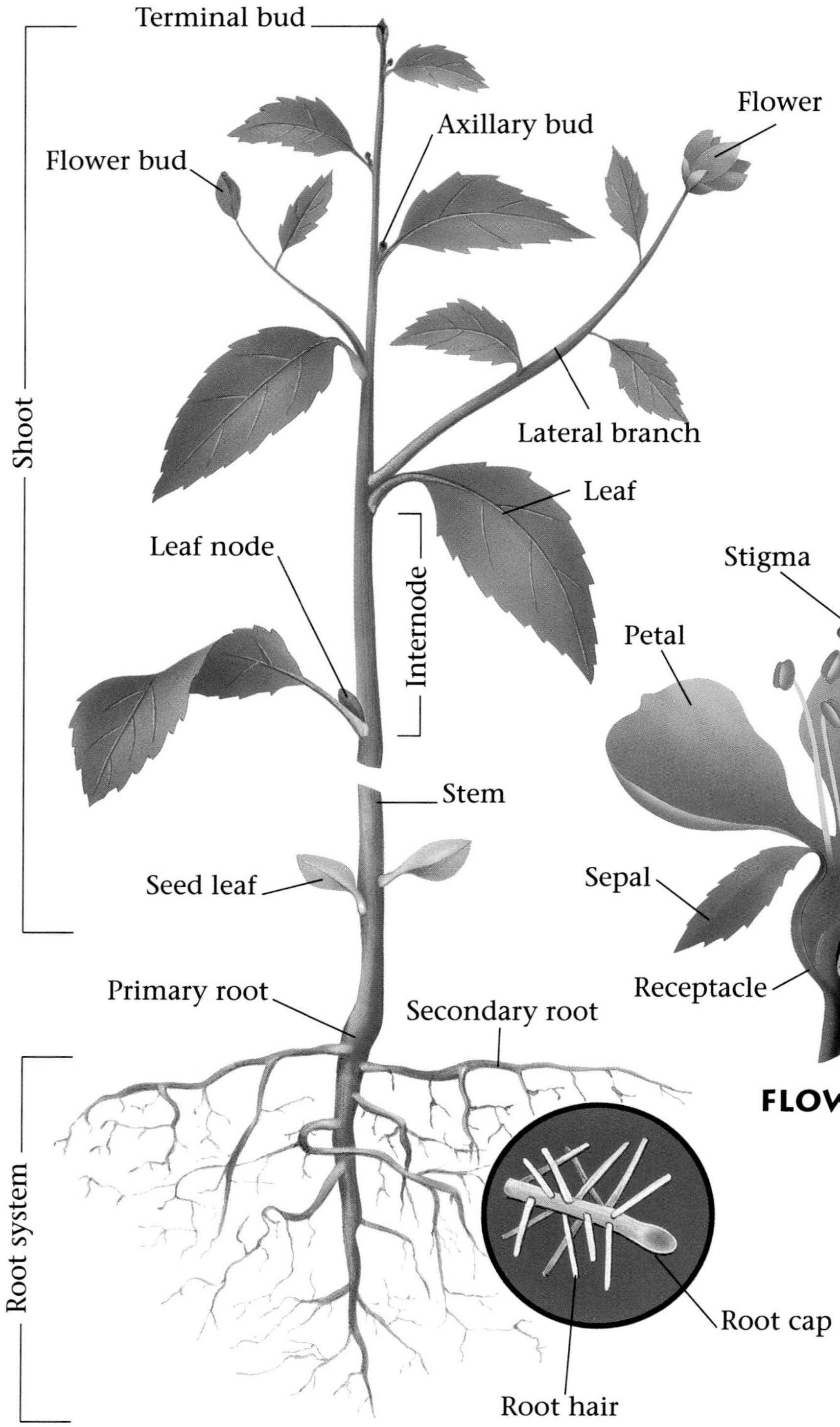

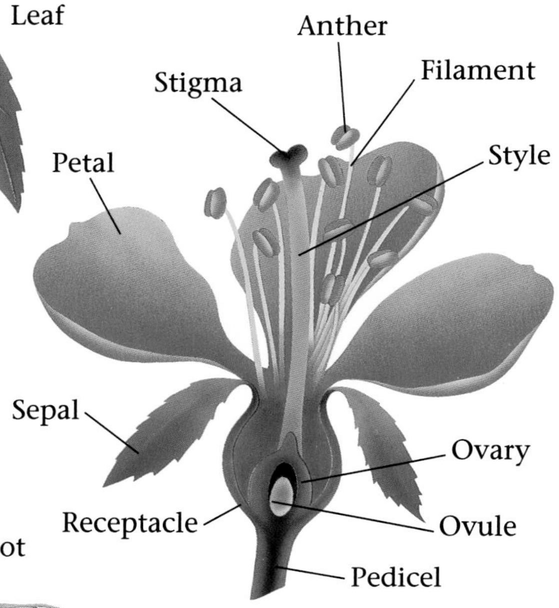

FLOWER

Root system

Root cap

Root hair

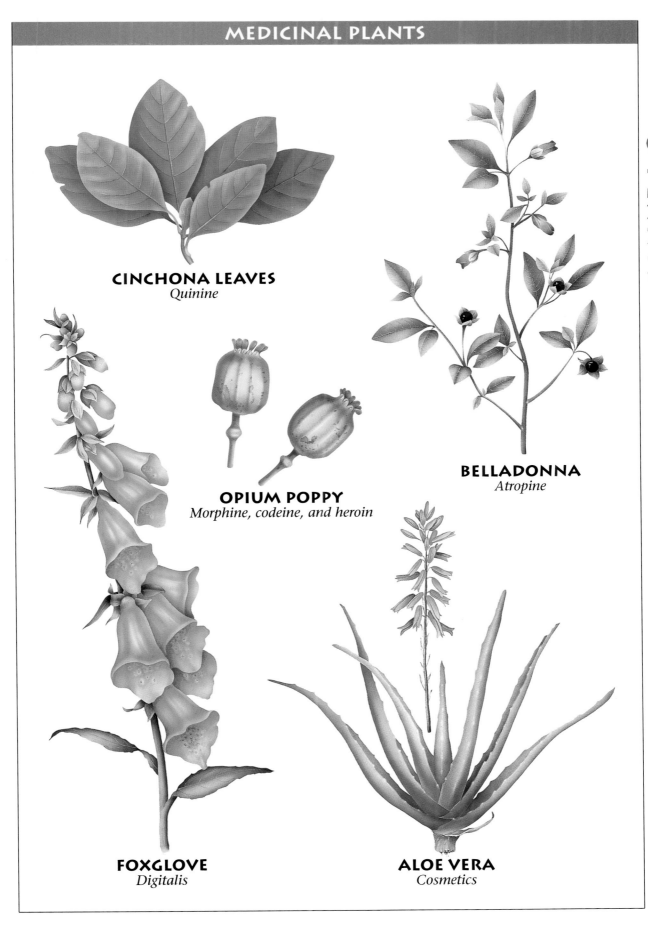

CINCHONA LEAVES
Quinine

BELLADONNA
Atropine

OPIUM POPPY
Morphine, codeine, and heroin

FOXGLOVE
Digitalis

ALOE VERA
Cosmetics

ROOT VEGETABLE
CARROT

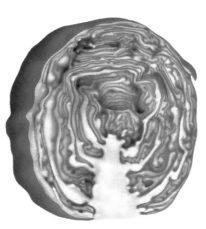

LEAF VEGETABLE
CABBAGE

SEED VEGETABLE
GREEN PEA

FLOWER VEGETABLE
ARTICHOKE

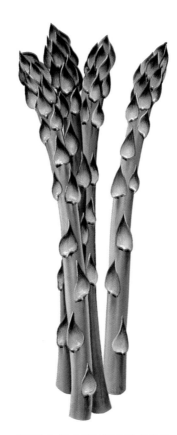

STALK VEGETABLE
ASPARAGUS

FRUIT VEGETABLE
TOMATO

TUBER VEGETABLE
POTATO

BULB VEGETABLE
ONION

POME
PEAR

DRUPE
CHERRIES

CITRUS BERRY
ORANGE

BERRY
GRAPES

GOURD BERRY
WATERMELON

NUT
ALMOND

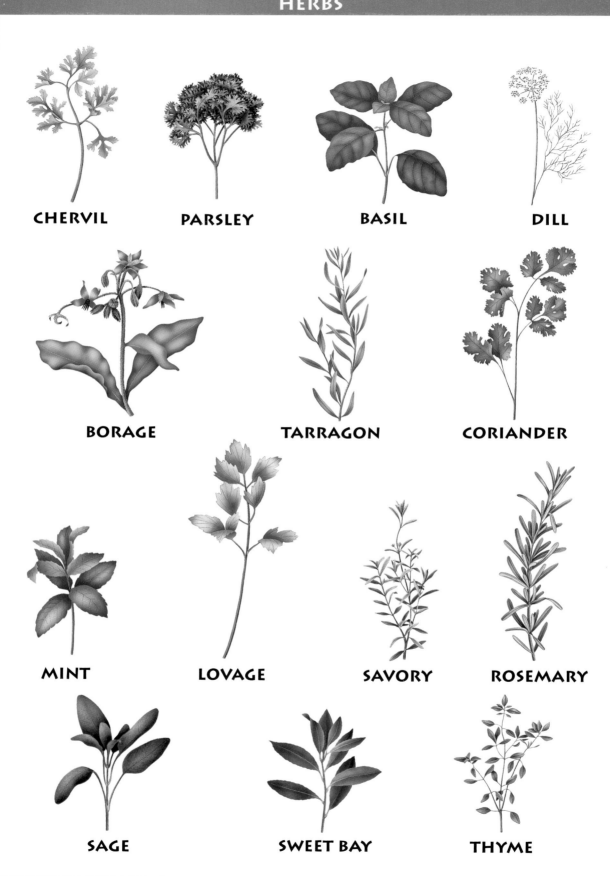

CHERVIL

PARSLEY

BASIL

DILL

BORAGE

TARRAGON

CORIANDER

MINT

LOVAGE

SAVORY

ROSEMARY

SAGE

SWEET BAY

THYME

ANIMALS

THE ANIMAL GROUP INCLUDES living organisms that are not able to make their own food. Most animals are able to move around, and they have sense organs that let them gather information about their environment. More than a million animal species are living on the Earth today, and many times that number lived in the past but have become extinct. On the following pages, you'll see some of the major groups of animals, and you'll learn what makes these groups special. You'll also find information about how some animals grow, how and where some live, and what special features or adaptations some have.

ANIMALS

YEARS AGO	ERA	PERIOD	EPOCH
10,000	CENOZOIC	QUATERNARY	HOLOCENE
2.5 MILLION			PLEISTOCENE
7 MILLION		TERTIARY	PLIOCENE
26 MILLION			MIOCENE
38 MILLION			OLIGOCENE
54 MILLION			EOCENE
65 MILLION			PALEOCENE
136 MILLION	MESOZOIC	CRETACEOUS	
190 MILLION		JURASSIC	
225 MILLION		TRIASSIC	
280 MILLION	UPPER PALEOZOIC	PERMIAN	
345 MILLION		CARBONIFEROUS	
395 MILLION		DEVONIAN	
430 MILLION	LOWER PALEOZOIC	SILURIAN	
500 MILLION		ORDOVICIAN	
570 MILLION		CAMBRIAN	
PRECAMBRIAN FROM 4.6 BILLION YEARS AGO			

Modern humans

Woolly mammoth

Early humans

Apes

Early horses

Mammals

Early birds

Dinosaurs

Turtles

Reptiles

Cockroach

Amphibians

Jawless fishes

Mollusks

Segmented worms

Trilobites

Bacteria

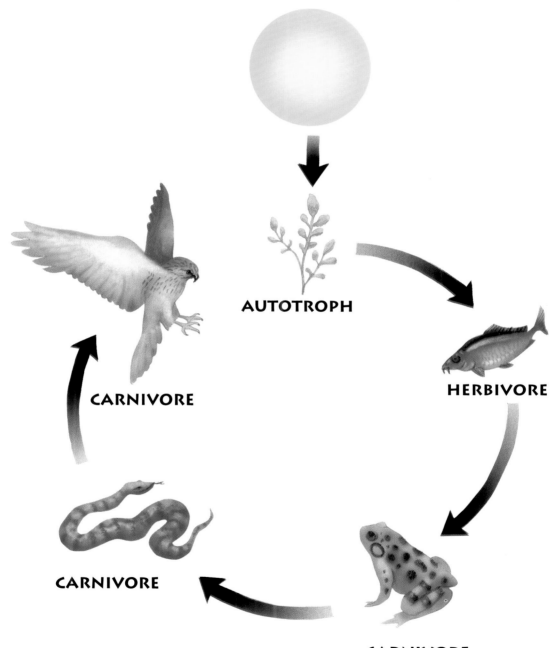

SUNLIGHT

AUTOTROPH

HERBIVORE

CARNIVORE

CARNIVORE

CARNIVORE

ANIMALS

SAURISCHIANS
Lizard-hipped dinosaurs

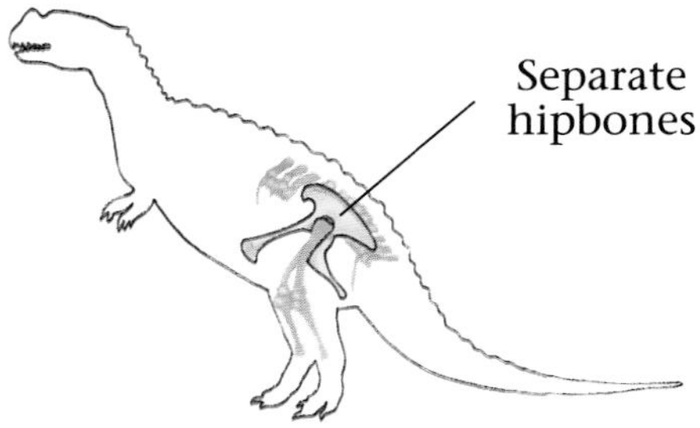

Separate
hipbones

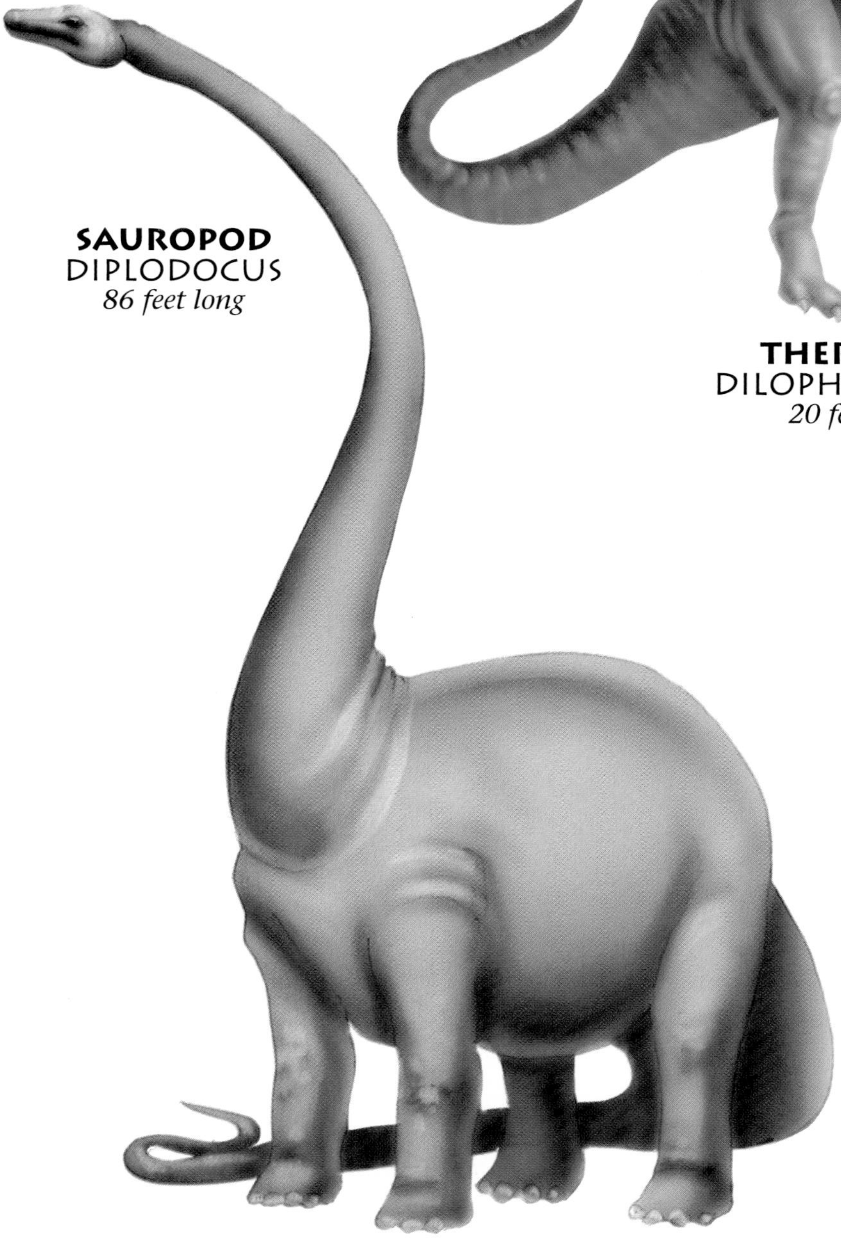

SAUROPOD
DIPLODOCUS
86 feet long

THEROPOD
DILOPHOSAURUS
20 feet long

THEROPOD
TYRANNOSAURUS REX
45 feet long

THEROPOD
COMPSOGNATHUS
3 feet long

SAUROPOD
APATOSAURUS
70 feet long

ORNITHISCHIANS
Bird-hipped dinosaurs

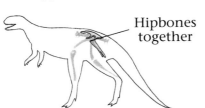

Hipbones
together

ANKYLOSAUR
SAUROPELTA
17 feet long

ORNITHOPOD
YANDUSAURUS
6 feet long

STEGOSAUR
TUOJIANGOSAURUS
20 feet long

CERATOPSIAN
TRICERATOPS
30 feet long

ANKYLOSAUR
EUOPLOCEPHALUS
20 feet long

PACHYCEPHALOSAUR
PRENOCEPHALE
6 feet long

ORNITHOPOD
LAMBEOSAURUS
50 feet long

ANIMALS WITHOUT BACKBONES

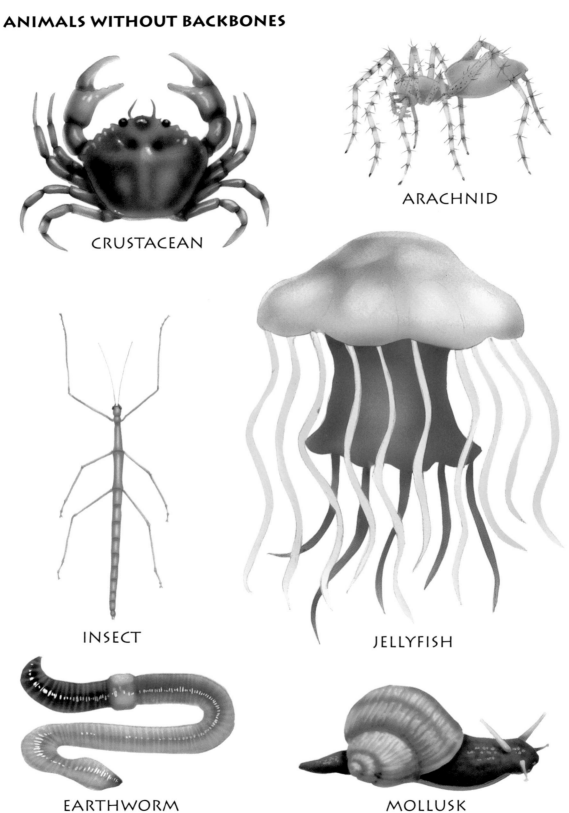

CRUSTACEAN

ARACHNID

INSECT

JELLYFISH

EARTHWORM

MOLLUSK

ANIMALS

68

ANIMALS WITH BACKBONES

MAMMAL

AMPHIBIAN

BIRD

REPTILE

FISH

SARCODINES
*Move using pseudopods
(false feet)*

DIFFLUGIA

Pseudopod

AMOEBA

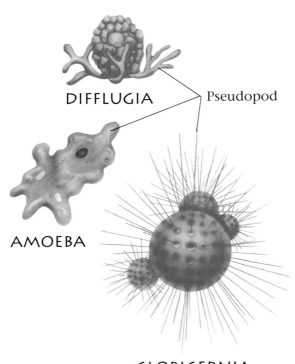

GLOBIGERNIA

FLAGELLATES
Move using flagella

VOLVOX

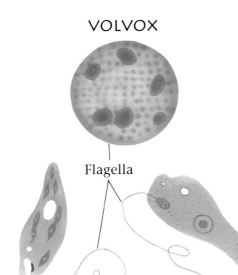

Flagella

EUGLENA

TRYPANOSOMA

CILIATES
Move using cilia

PARAMECIUM

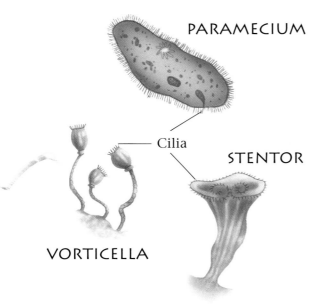

Cilia

STENTOR

VORTICELLA

SPOROZOANS
Immobile

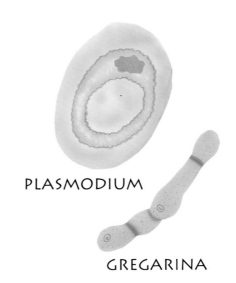

PLASMODIUM

GREGARINA

COMPOUND EYE

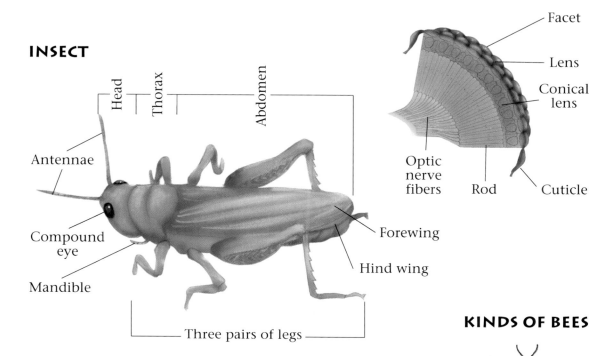

- Facet
- Lens
- Conical lens
- Cuticle
- Rod
- Optic nerve fibers

INSECT

- Head
- Thorax
- Abdomen
- Antennae
- Compound eye
- Mandible
- Forewing
- Hind wing
- Three pairs of legs

SPIDER

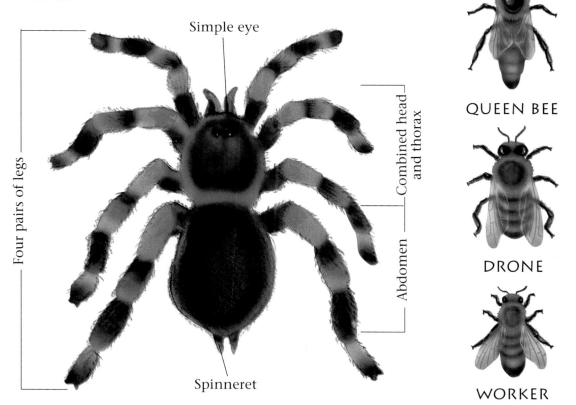

- Simple eye
- Four pairs of legs
- Combined head and thorax
- Abdomen
- Spinneret

KINDS OF BEES

QUEEN BEE

DRONE

WORKER

COLEOPTERA
STAG BEETLE

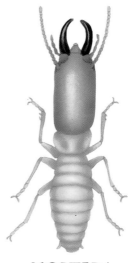

ISOPTERA
TERMITE

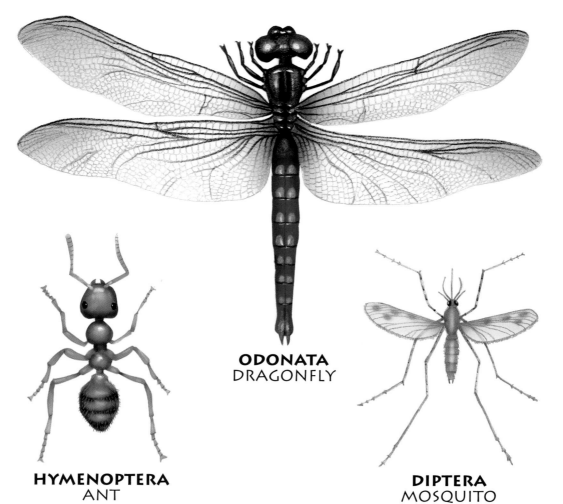

ODONATA
DRAGONFLY

HYMENOPTERA
ANT

DIPTERA
MOSQUITO

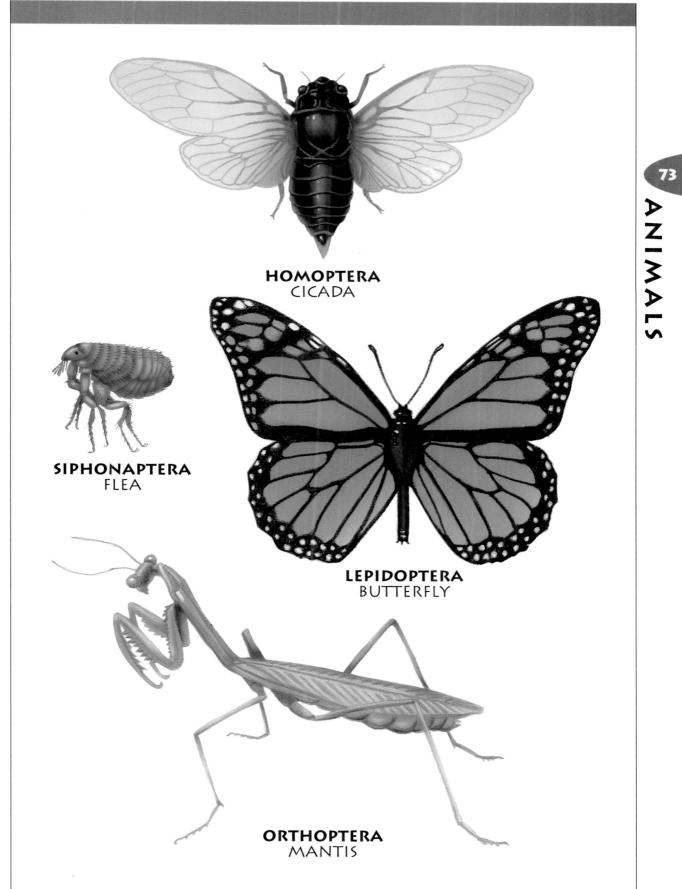

HOMOPTERA
CICADA

SIPHONAPTERA
FLEA

LEPIDOPTERA
BUTTERFLY

ORTHOPTERA
MANTIS

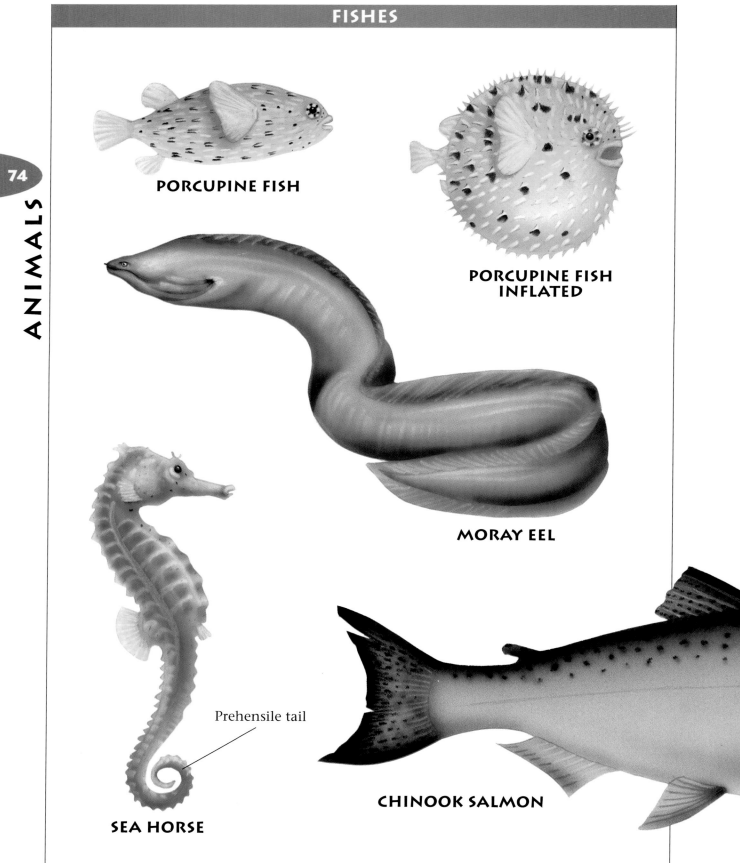

PORCUPINE FISH

**PORCUPINE FISH
INFLATED**

MORAY EEL

Prehensile tail

CHINOOK SALMON

SEA HORSE

LIONFISH

Poisonous barbs

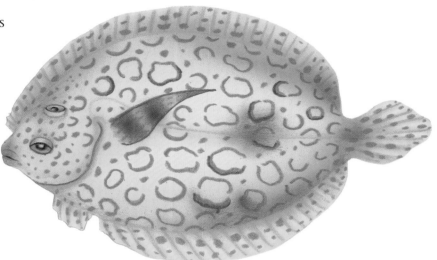

PIRANHA

FLOUNDER

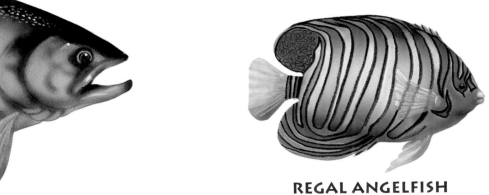

REGAL ANGELFISH

ANIMALS

JAWLESS FISH
LAMPREY

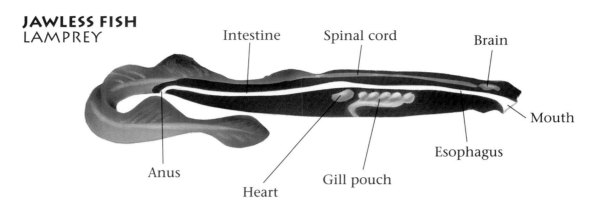

Intestine

Spinal cord

Brain

Mouth

Esophagus

Gill pouch

Heart

Anus

CARTILAGINOUS FISH
GREAT WHITE SHARK

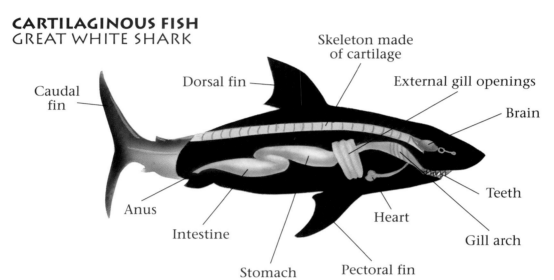

Skeleton made
of cartilage

External gill openings

Brain

Dorsal fin

Caudal
fin

Teeth

Anus

Heart

Gill arch

Intestine

Stomach

Pectoral fin

BONY FISH
PERCH

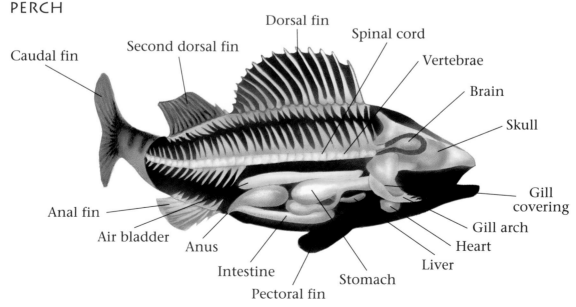

Dorsal fin

Spinal cord

Vertebrae

Second dorsal fin

Brain

Caudal fin

Skull

Gill
covering

Anal fin

Gill arch

Air bladder

Heart

Anus

Liver

Intestine

Stomach

Pectoral fin

LIFE CYCLE OF THE FROG

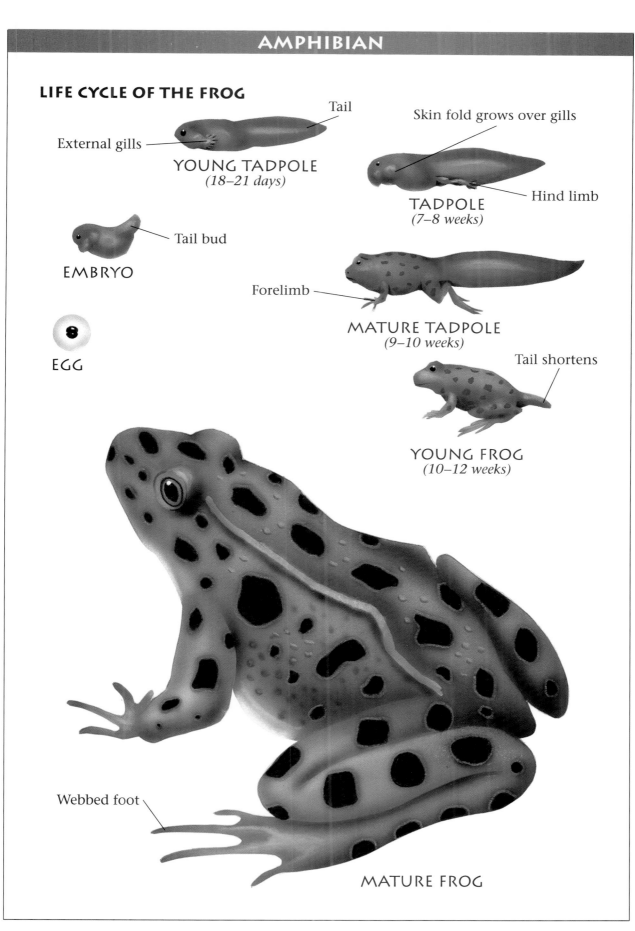

Tail

External gills

YOUNG TADPOLE
(18–21 days)

Skin fold grows over gills

Hind limb

TADPOLE
(7–8 weeks)

Tail bud

EMBRYO

Forelimb

MATURE TADPOLE
(9–10 weeks)

EGG

Tail shortens

YOUNG FROG
(10–12 weeks)

Webbed foot

MATURE FROG

77

ANIMALS

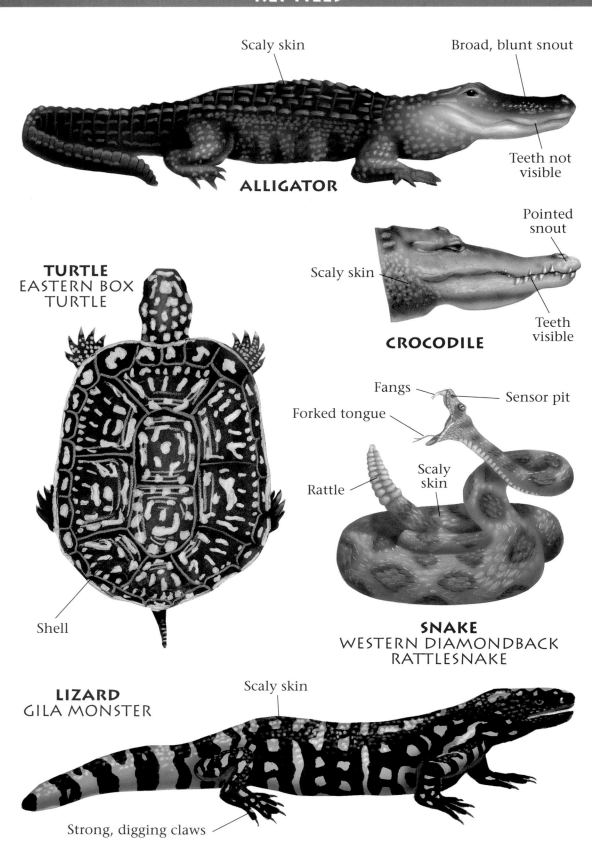

Scaly skin

Broad, blunt snout

ALLIGATOR

Teeth not visible

Pointed snout

Scaly skin

CROCODILE

Teeth visible

TURTLE
EASTERN BOX
TURTLE

Shell

Fangs

Sensor pit

Forked tongue

Scaly skin

Rattle

SNAKE
WESTERN DIAMONDBACK
RATTLESNAKE

LIZARD
GILA MONSTER

Scaly skin

Strong, digging claws

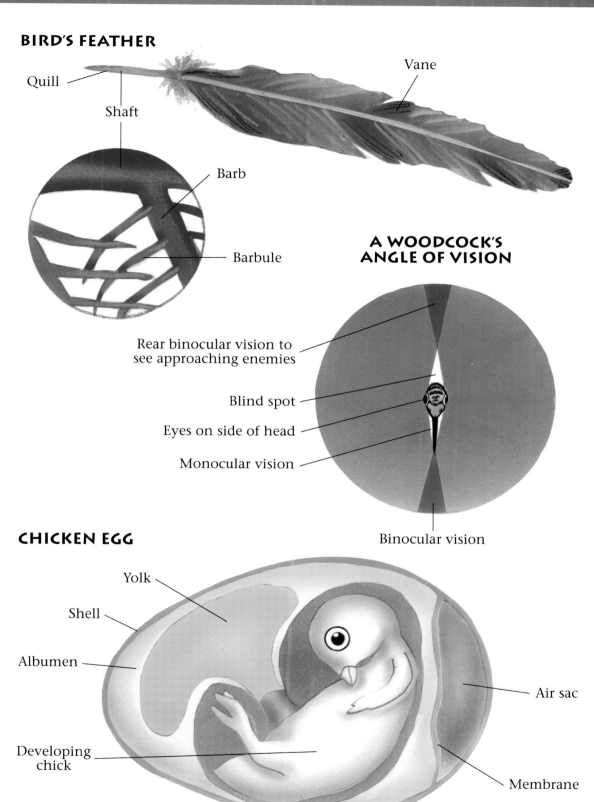

BIRD'S FEATHER

Quill

Vane

Shaft

Barb

Barbule

A WOODCOCK'S ANGLE OF VISION

Rear binocular vision to see approaching enemies

Blind spot

Eyes on side of head

Monocular vision

Binocular vision

CHICKEN EGG

Yolk

Shell

Albumen

Air sac

Developing chick

Membrane

SMALL WOODLAND BIRDS

RUBY-THROATED
HUMMINGBIRD

RED-HEADED
WOODPECKER

LARGE LAND BIRDS

RING-NECKED PHEASANT

WILD TURKEY

SMALL OPEN-COUNTRY BIRDS

WESTERN
BLUEBIRD

AMERICAN GOLDFINCH

BIRDS OF PREY

GREAT HORNED OWL

PEREGRINE FALCON

ANIMALS

LARGE WADING BIRDS

GREAT BLUE HERON

GREAT EGRET

SHOREBIRDS

AMERICAN WOODCOCK

PECTORAL SANDPIPER

Male

Female

DUCK FAMILY
WOOD DUCK

NORTHERN SEA BIRD
ATLANTIC PUFFIN

PELICAN FAMILY
AMERICAN WHITE PELICAN

CETACEAN
WHALE

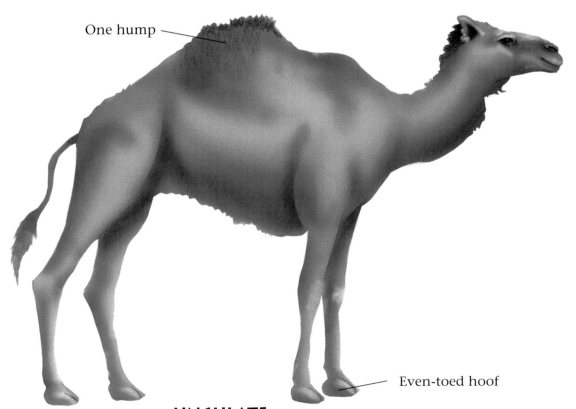

One hump

Even-toed hoof

UNGULATE
DROMEDARY CAMEL

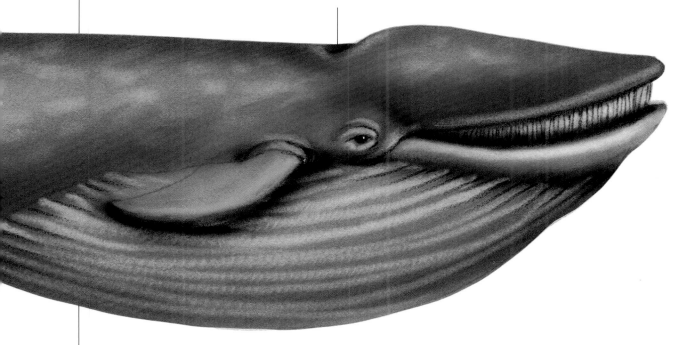

Blow hole

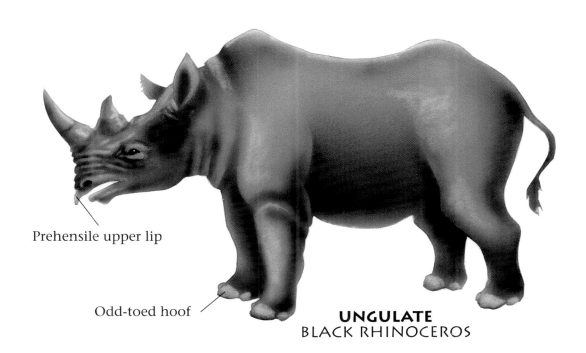

Prehensile upper lip

Odd-toed hoof

UNGULATE
BLACK RHINOCEROS

ANIMALS

CHIROPTERAN
BAT

RODENT
CHIPMUNK

Webbed
foot

MONOTREME
DUCK-BILLED PLATYPUS
Egg-laying mammal

Baby
kangaroo
(joey)

Pouch **MARSUPIAL**
KANGAROO

Prehensile tail

PRIMATE
SPIDER MONKEY

CARNIVORE
LION

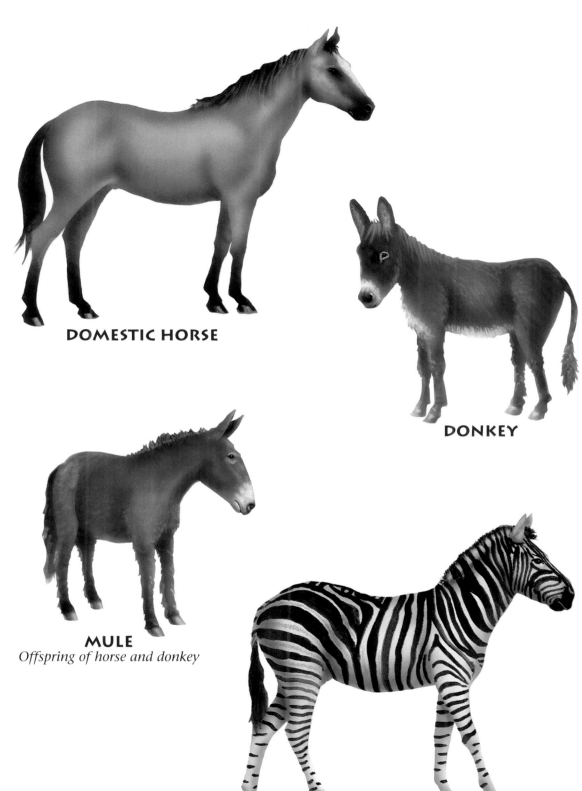

DOMESTIC HORSE

DONKEY

MULE
Offspring of horse and donkey

ZEBRA

CLYDESDALE

PALOMINO

THOROUGHBRED

SHETLAND PONY

ARABIAN

APPALOOSA

LIPPIZZANER

No tail

MANX

BURMESE

REX

MAINE COON

SIAMESE

PERSIAN

AMERICAN SHORTHAIR

CATS LAND ON THEIR FEET

Cat falls

Cat twists head around

Body follows

Legs stretch down

RETRACTED CLAW

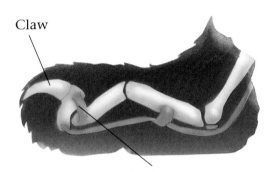

Claw

Elastic ligament

EXTENDED CLAW

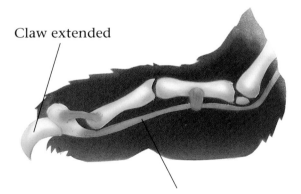

Claw extended

Lower tendon pulled

HOUND DOGS

BLOODHOUND

BEAGLE

SPORTING DOGS

IRISH SETTER

LABRADOR RETRIEVER

TOY BREEDS

PEKINGESE

CHIHUAHUA

WORKING DOGS

ST. BERNARD

COLLIE

TERRIERS

FOX TERRIER

MINIATURE SCHNAUZER

NONSPORTING BREEDS

DALMATIAN

BULLDOG

ANIMALS

96

BIRD'S WING

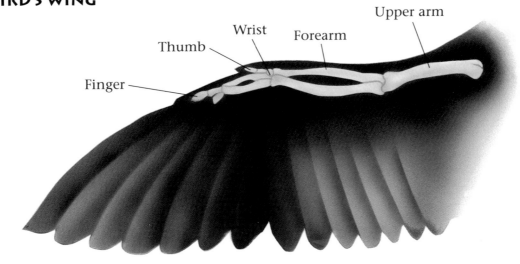

Thumb
Finger
Wrist
Forearm
Upper arm

BAT'S WING

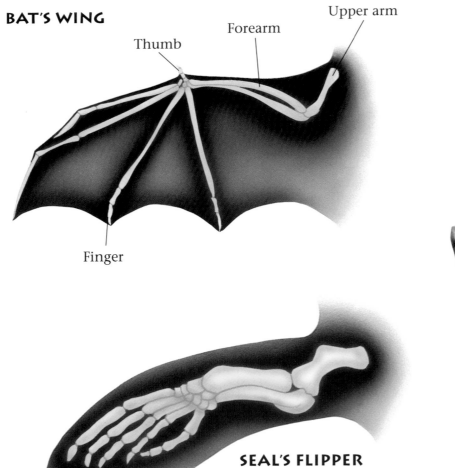

Thumb
Forearm
Upper arm

Finger

SEAL'S FLIPPER

GIBBON'S HAND

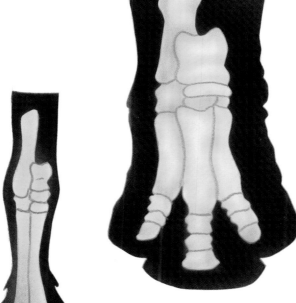

HORSE'S FOOT
One digit

CAMEL'S FOOT
Two digits

RHINOCEROS'S FOOT
Three digits

PIG'S FOOT
Four digits

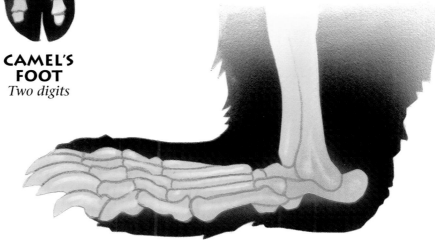

BEAR'S FOOT
Five digits

RODENT BEAVER

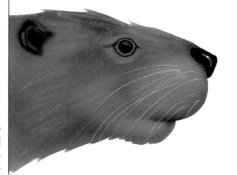

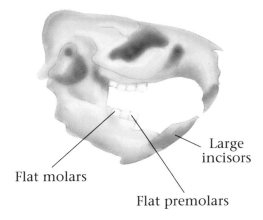

Large
incisors

Flat molars

Flat premolars

CARNIVORE LION

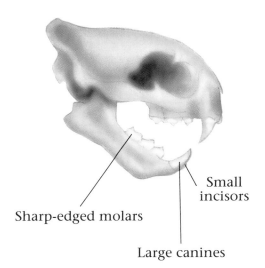

Small
incisors

Sharp-edged molars

Large canines

HERBIVORE RHINOCEROS

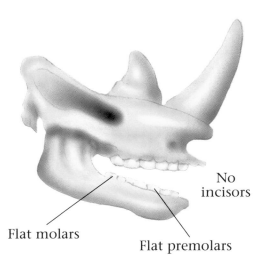

No
incisors

Flat molars

Flat premolars

GRAY SQUIRREL
Bounding

OPOSSUM
Walking

RACCOON
Running

TOAD

RABBIT
Leaping

SKUNK
Walking

MOUNTAIN GOAT
Walking

CANADA GOOSE

SIDEWINDER SNAKE

ANIMALS

GIANT PANDA

ORANGUTAN

AMERICAN CROCODILE

SUMATRAN RHINOCEROS

CALIFORNIA CONDOR

IVORY-BILLED
WOODPECKER

SNOW LEOPARD

EUROPEAN KINGFISHER
Europe

WATER DRAGON
Asia

RED SALAMANDER
North America

WATER SPIDER
Europe and Asia

RAINBOW TROUT
North America

RIVER OTTER
South America

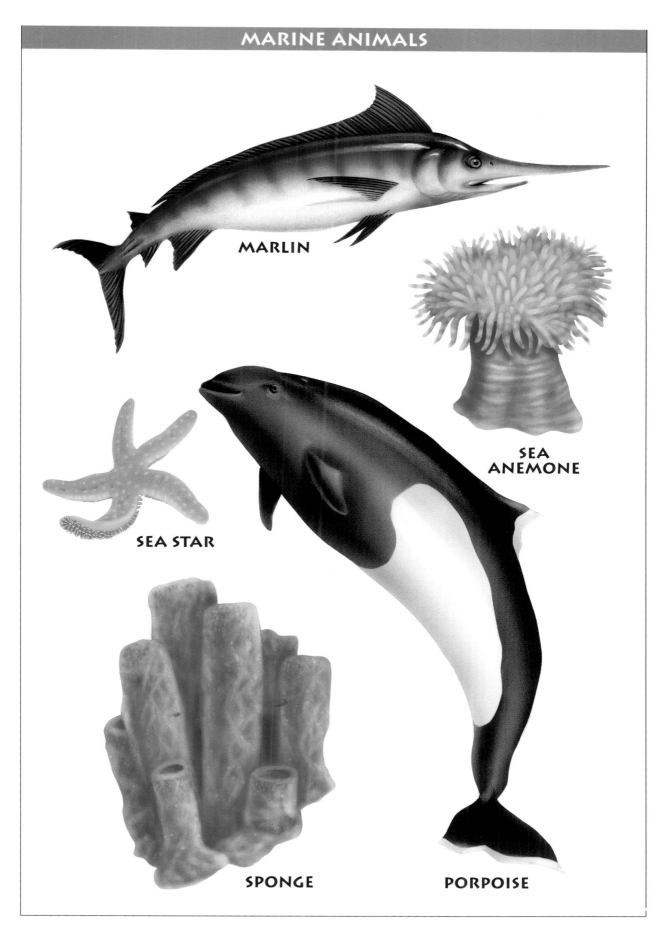

MARLIN

SEA ANEMONE

SEA STAR

SPONGE

PORPOISE

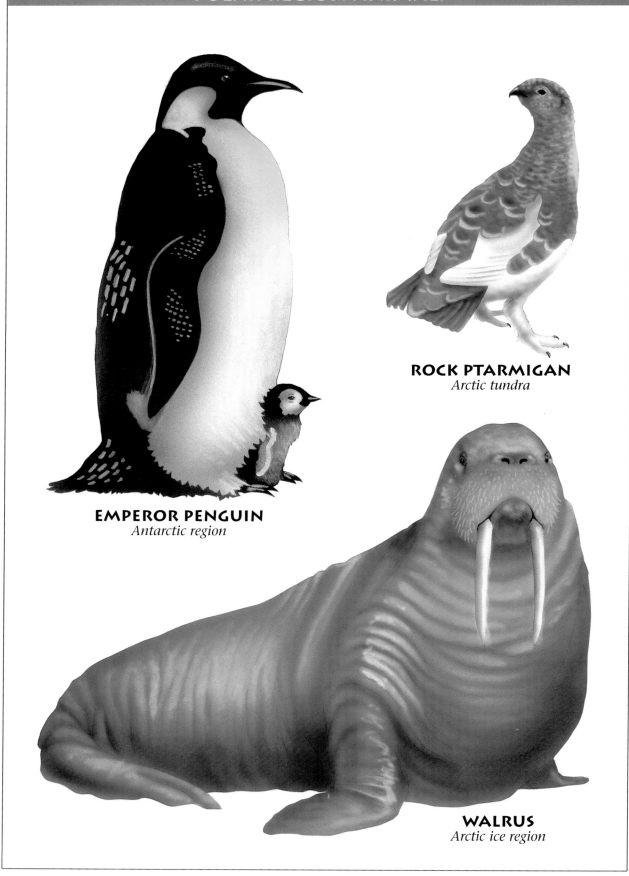

EMPEROR PENGUIN
Antarctic region

ROCK PTARMIGAN
Arctic tundra

WALRUS
Arctic ice region

POLAR BEAR
Arctic ice region

KRILL
Arctic Ocean and
Antarctic Ocean

SOUTHERN ELEPHANT SEAL
Antarctic region

JAGUAR
South America

RETICULATED PYTHON
Asia

HOWLER MONKEY
South America

GORILLA
Africa

**BIRD OF
PARADISE**
Papua New Guinea

ASIAN ELEPHANT
Asia

ROADRUNNER
North America

JACKRABBIT
North America

SCORPION
Africa

FENNEC FOX
Middle East

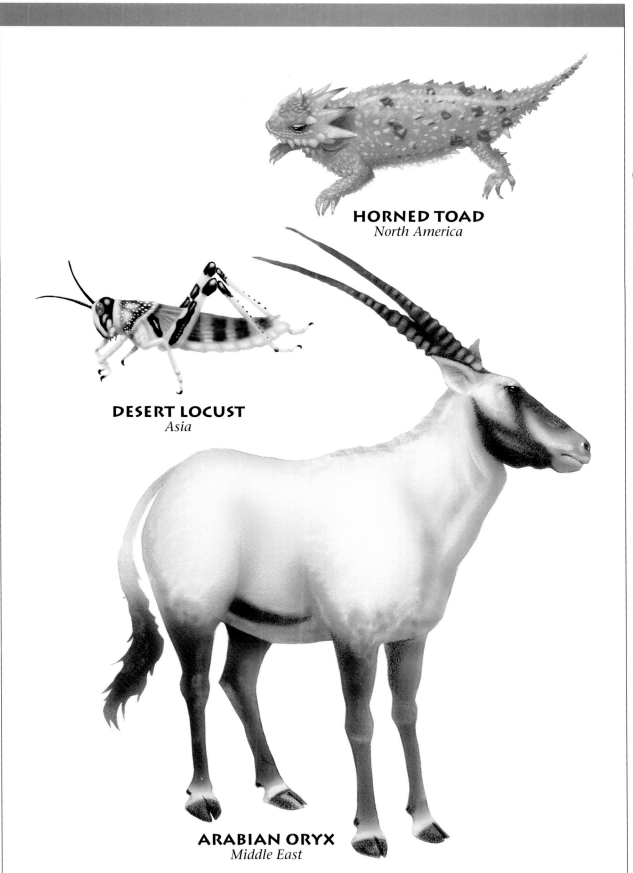

HORNED TOAD
North America

DESERT LOCUST
Asia

ARABIAN ORYX
Middle East

GIANT ANTEATER
South America

HINGED TORTOISE
Africa

EMU
Australia

CHEETAH
Africa

AMERICAN BISON
North America

SAIGA
Asia

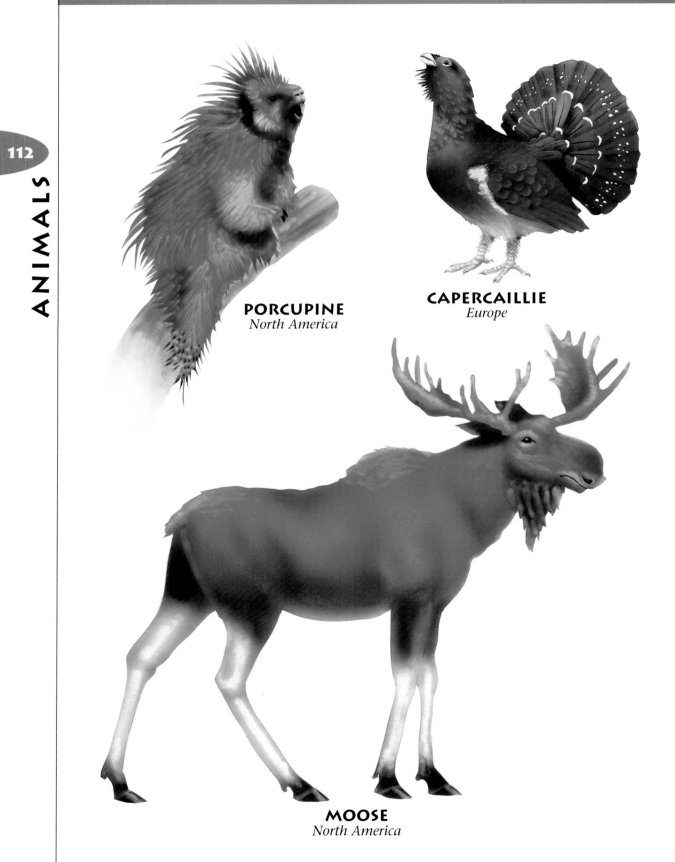

PORCUPINE
North America

CAPERCAILLIE
Europe

MOOSE
North America

BEAVER
North America

WOLVERINE
North America

BROWN BEAR
Europe

ANIMALS

EUROPEAN BADGER
Northern deciduous forest

TAWNY OWL
Northern deciduous forest

LESSER PANDA
Asian evergreen forest

KOALA
Australian evergreen forest

GRASS SNAKE
Northern deciduous forest

HUMAN BODY

THE HUMAN BODY WORKS in a beautifully complex way. Our bodies are made of trillions of tiny units, or *cells*. We have about 200 different kinds of cells, including skin cells, blood cells, and nerve cells. Similar cells group together to form what we call *tissue*, and tissue is grouped together to form different *organs* in our bodies. Your stomach, your lungs, your eyes, and your skin are all organs. Different organs work together as *systems* that perform certain functions. Your heart, your blood, and your veins and arteries work together as your circulatory system to move nutrients, waste, and other substances around in your body.

HUMAN BODY

MALE (FRONT)

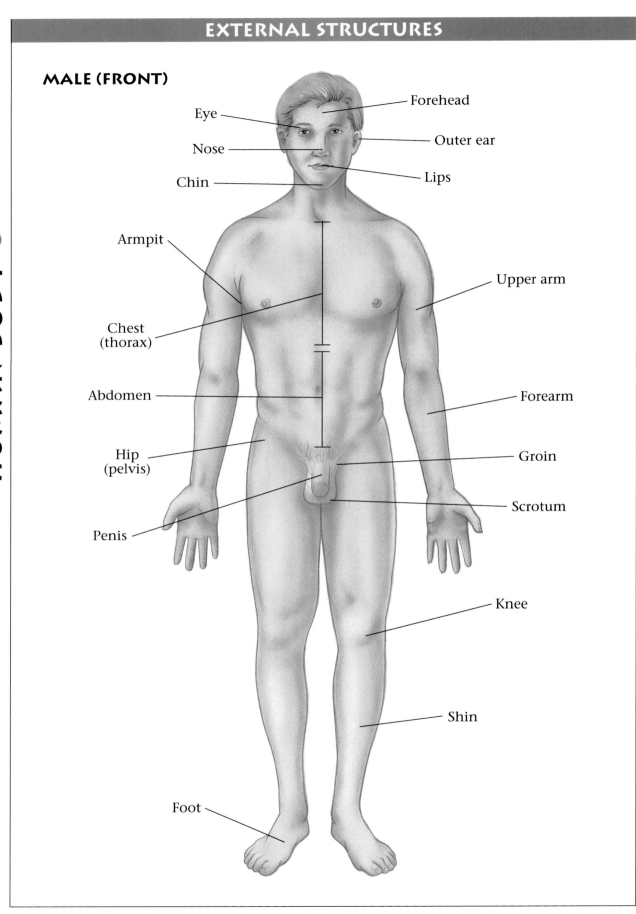

Forehead

Eye

Outer ear

Nose

Lips

Chin

Armpit

Upper arm

Chest
(thorax)

Abdomen

Forearm

Hip
(pelvis)

Groin

Scrotum

Penis

Knee

Shin

Foot

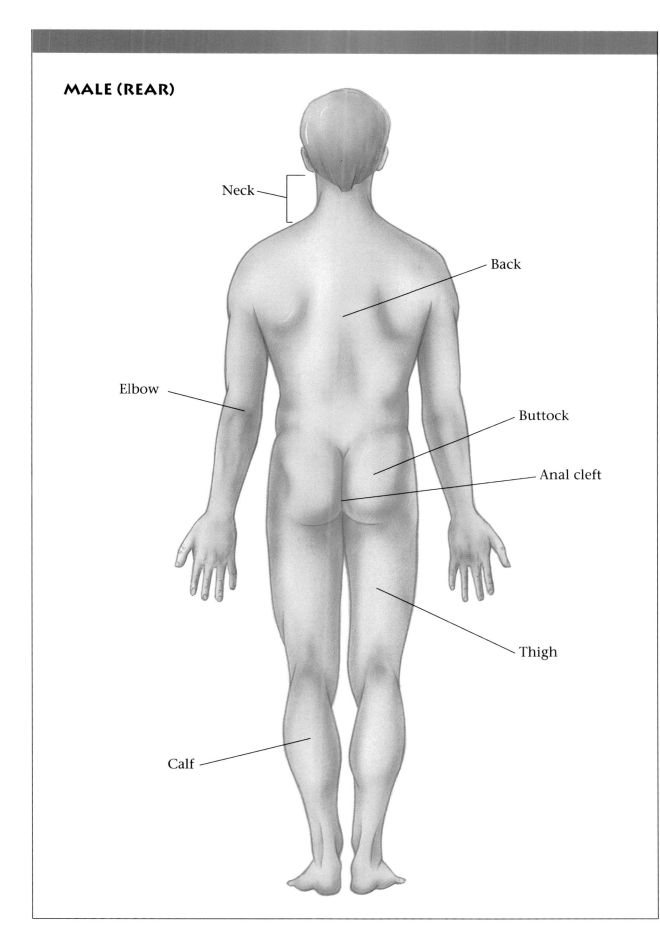

MALE (REAR)

Neck

Back

Elbow

Buttock

Anal cleft

Thigh

Calf

HUMAN BODY

FEMALE (FRONT)

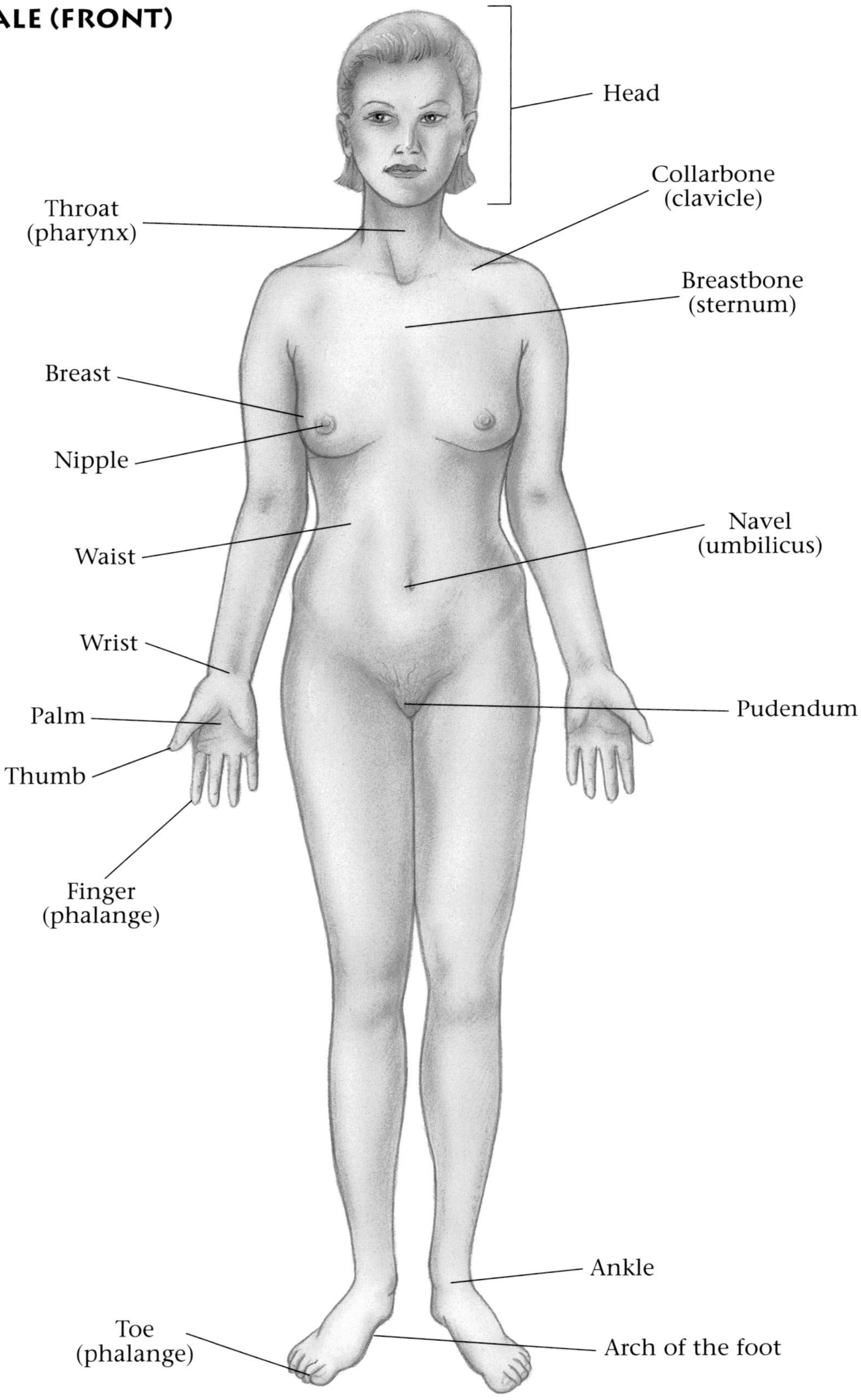

HUMAN BODY

Head

Collarbone
(clavicle)

Throat
(pharynx)

Breastbone
(sternum)

Breast

Nipple

Navel
(umbilicus)

Waist

Wrist

Palm

Pudendum

Thumb

Finger
(phalange)

Ankle

Toe
(phalange)

Arch of the foot

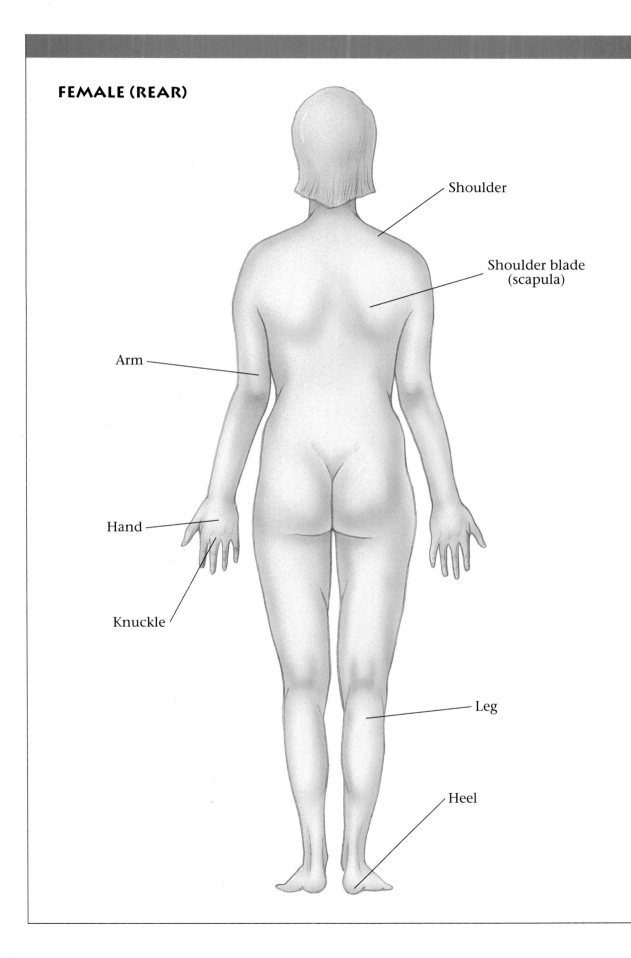

FEMALE (REAR)

Shoulder

Shoulder blade
(scapula)

Arm

Hand

Knuckle

Leg

Heel

HUMAN BODY

MAJOR BONES

Cranium

Cheekbone
(zygomatic bone and arch)

Ulna

Radius

Maxilla

Opening for auditory nerve
(external auditory meatus)

Humerus

Jawbone
(mandible)

Collarbone
(clavicle)

Hyoid bone

Wrist bones
(carpals)

Hand bones
(metacarpals)

Shoulder blade
(scapula)

Breastbone
(sternum)

Ribs
(costae)

Finger bones
(phalanges)

Backbone
(vertebrae)

Ilium

Hipbone
(pelvis)

Pubis

Sacrum

Ischium

Tailbone
(coccyx)

Thighbone
(femur)

Kneecap
(patella)

Shinbone
(tibia)

Fibula

Foot bones
(metatarsals)

Anklebones
(tarsals)

Toe bones
(phalanges)

JOINT STRUCTURE (KNEE)

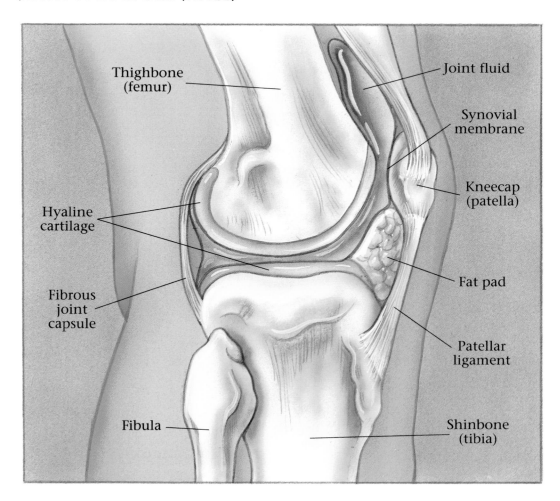

Thighbone (femur)

Joint fluid

Synovial membrane

Hyaline cartilage

Kneecap (patella)

Fibrous joint capsule

Fat pad

Patellar ligament

Fibula

Shinbone (tibia)

TYPES OF MOVABLE HUMAN JOINTS (UPPER LIMB)

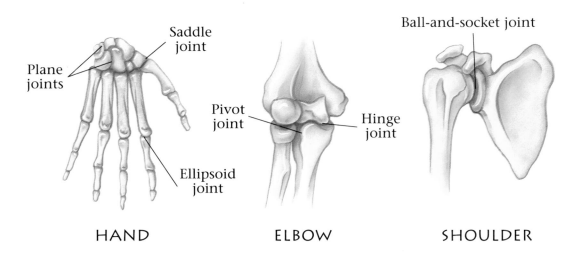

Saddle joint

Ball-and-socket joint

Plane joints

Pivot joint

Hinge joint

Ellipsoid joint

HAND

ELBOW

SHOULDER

MAJOR MUSCLES (FRONT)

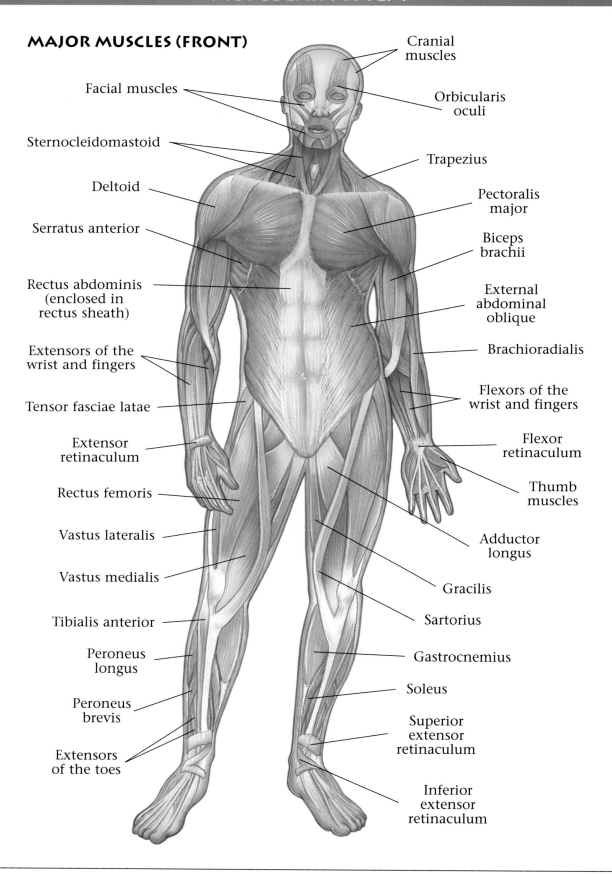

Cranial muscles

Facial muscles

Orbicularis oculi

Sternocleidomastoid

Trapezius

Deltoid

Pectoralis major

Serratus anterior

Biceps brachii

Rectus abdominis (enclosed in rectus sheath)

External abdominal oblique

Brachioradialis

Extensors of the wrist and fingers

Flexors of the wrist and fingers

Tensor fasciae latae

Extensor retinaculum

Flexor retinaculum

Rectus femoris

Thumb muscles

Vastus lateralis

Adductor longus

Vastus medialis

Gracilis

Tibialis anterior

Sartorius

Peroneus longus

Gastrocnemius

Soleus

Peroneus brevis

Superior extensor retinaculum

Extensors of the toes

Inferior extensor retinaculum

MAJOR MUSCLES (BACK)

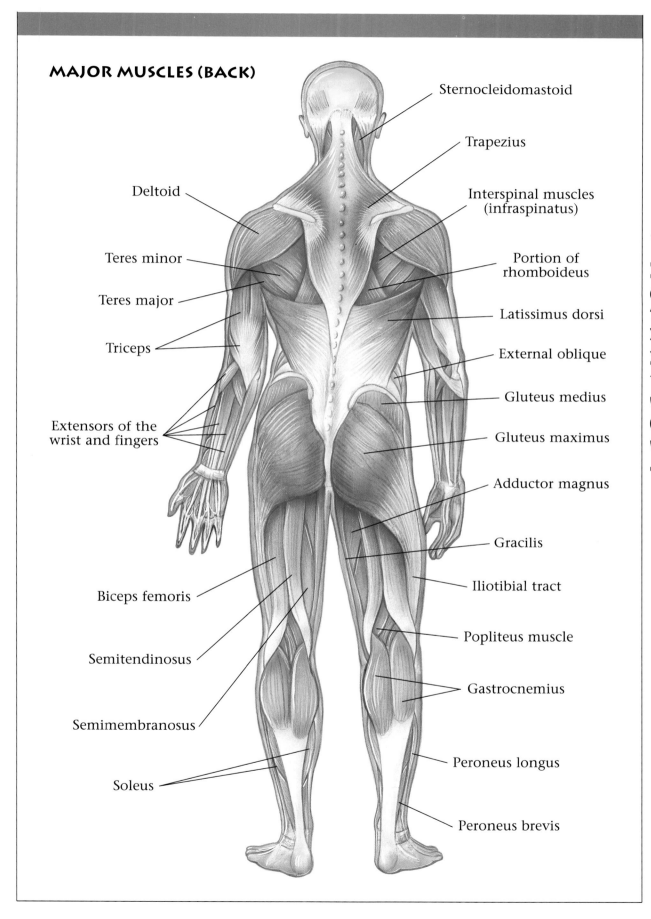

Sternocleidomastoid

Trapezius

Interspinal muscles
(infraspinatus)

Deltoid

Portion of
rhomboideus

Teres minor

Latissimus dorsi

Teres major

External oblique

Triceps

Gluteus medius

Extensors of the
wrist and fingers

Gluteus maximus

Adductor magnus

Gracilis

Iliotibial tract

Biceps femoris

Popliteus muscle

Semitendinosus

Gastrocnemius

Semimembranosus

Peroneus longus

Soleus

Peroneus brevis

HUMAN BODY

HUMAN BODY

124

CENTRAL AND PERIPHERAL NERVOUS SYSTEMS

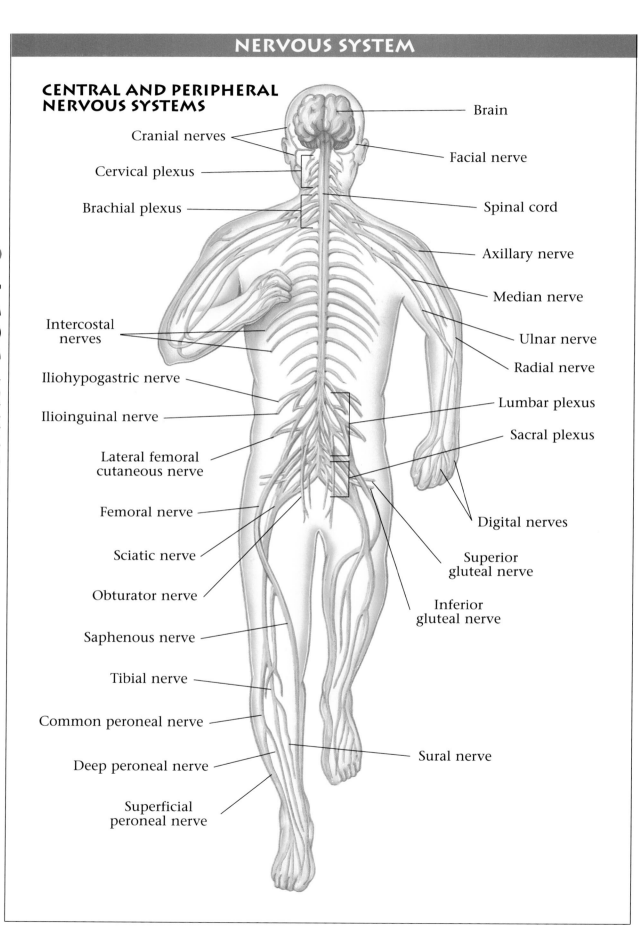

Cranial nerves

Cervical plexus

Brachial plexus

Intercostal nerves

Iliohypogastric nerve

Ilioinguinal nerve

Lateral femoral cutaneous nerve

Femoral nerve

Sciatic nerve

Obturator nerve

Saphenous nerve

Tibial nerve

Common peroneal nerve

Deep peroneal nerve

Superficial peroneal nerve

Brain

Facial nerve

Spinal cord

Axillary nerve

Median nerve

Ulnar nerve

Radial nerve

Lumbar plexus

Sacral plexus

Digital nerves

Superior gluteal nerve

Inferior gluteal nerve

Sural nerve

BRAIN ANATOMY

Corpus callosum

Septum pellucidum

Body of fornix

Skull (cranium)

Diencephalon

Optic chiasma

Pituitary gland

Medulla oblongata

Cerebrum

Pineal gland

Midbrain

Cerebellum

Pons

SPINAL COLUMN

Vertebral column

Spinal cord

Medullary cone

Terminal filament

Dura mater

NERVE CELL (NEURON)

Nucleus

Dendrites

Cell body

Nissl bodies (granules)

Node of Ranvier

Schwann cell nucleus

Neurolemma

Neurofibril

Axon

Myelin sheath

Nerve fiber

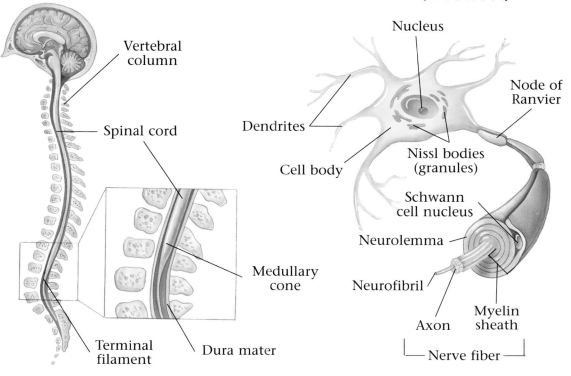

MAPPING OF THE CEREBRAL CORTEX

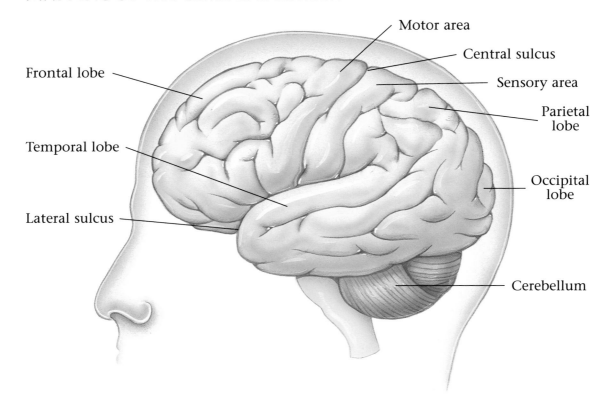

Motor area

Central sulcus

Sensory area

Parietal lobe

Frontal lobe

Occipital lobe

Temporal lobe

Lateral sulcus

Cerebellum

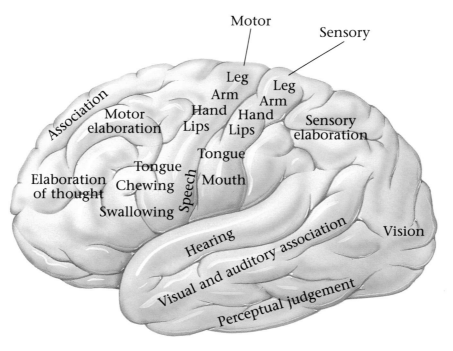

Motor

Sensory

Leg
Arm
Hand
Lips

Leg
Arm
Hand
Lips

Association

Motor elaboration

Tongue

Sensory elaboration

Elaboration of thought

Tongue
Chewing

Speech

Mouth

Swallowing

Hearing

Visual and auditory association

Vision

Perceptual judgement

Soft palate

Nasal cavity

Tongue

Throat
(pharynx)

Voice box
(larynx)

Windpipe
(trachea)

Left lung
(two lobes)

Principal
bronchus

Apex

Right lung
(three lobes)

Upper lobe

Middle lobe

Lower lobe

Base

Lobar
bronchi

Segmental
bronchi

Diaphragm

Capillaries

Terminal
bronchiole

Alveolus

PRINCIPAL VEINS AND ARTERIES

Ulnar veins

Median cubital vein

Basilic vein

Palmar venous arches

Brachial vein

Radial vein

Cephalic vein

Axillary vein

External carotid artery

External jugular vein

Internal carotid artery

Internal jugular vein

Subclavian vein

Common carotid artery

Left brachiocephalic vein

Superior vena cava

Arch of aorta

Pulmonary trunk

Axillary artery

Splenic artery

Inferior vena cava

Renal artery

Renal vein

Brachial artery

Superior mesenteric artery

Radial artery

Aorta

Ulnar artery

Inferior mesenteric artery

Common iliac artery

Common iliac vein

External iliac artery

Femoral vein

Deep femoral artery

Internal iliac artery

Great saphenous vein

Femoral artery

Popliteal vein

Popliteal artery

Posterior tibial artery

Peroneal vein

Anterior tibial artery

Posterior tibial vein

Anterior tibial veins

Peroneal artery

Dorsal pedis artery

Dorsal venous arch

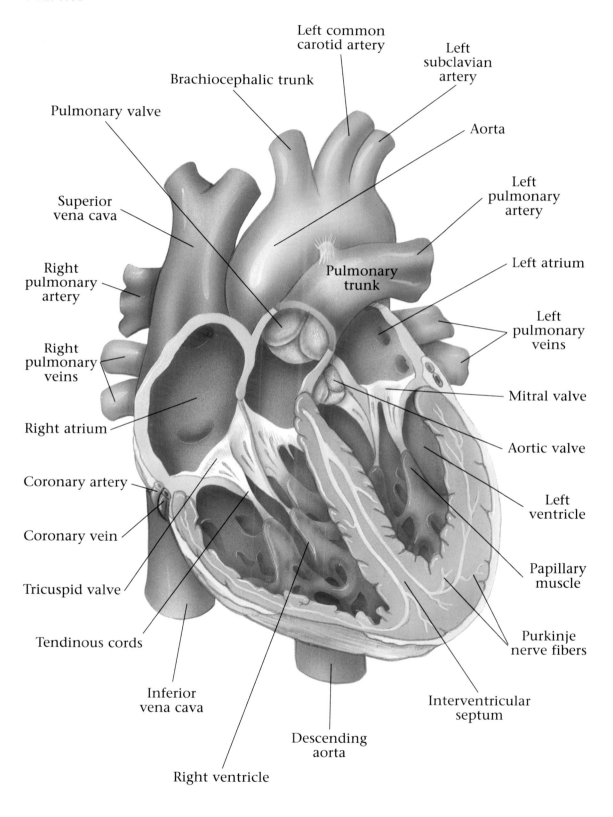

Left common
carotid artery

Left
subclavian
artery

Brachiocephalic trunk

Aorta

Pulmonary valve

Left
pulmonary
artery

Superior
vena cava

Pulmonary
trunk

Left atrium

Right
pulmonary
artery

Left
pulmonary
veins

Right
pulmonary
veins

Mitral valve

Right atrium

Aortic valve

Coronary artery

Left
ventricle

Coronary vein

Papillary
muscle

Tricuspid valve

Purkinje
nerve fibers

Tendinous cords

Inferior
vena cava

Interventricular
septum

Descending
aorta

Right ventricle

MAJOR DIGESTIVE STRUCTURES

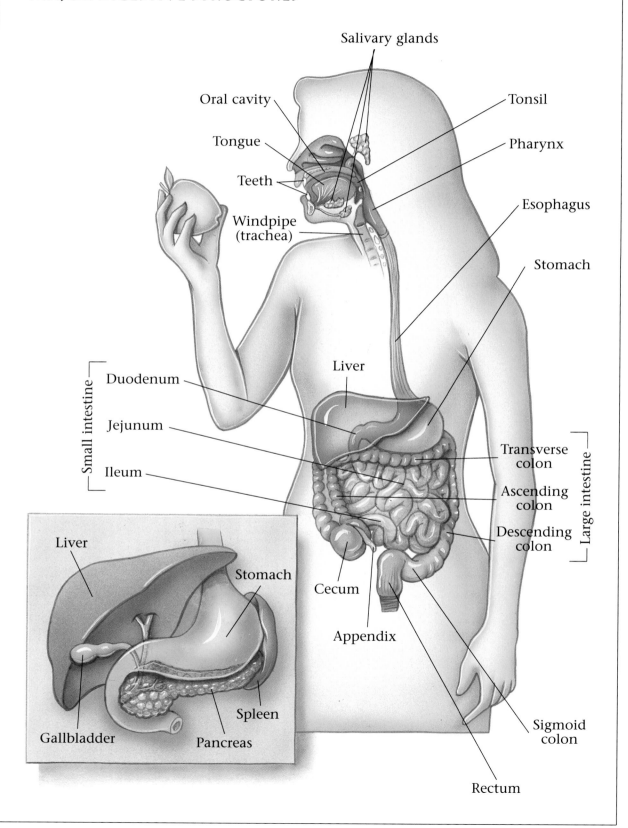

Salivary glands

Oral cavity

Tongue

Teeth

Windpipe (trachea)

Tonsil

Pharynx

Esophagus

Stomach

Liver

Small intestine
Duodenum

Jejunum

Ileum

Transverse colon

Ascending colon

Descending colon

Large intestine

Cecum

Appendix

Sigmoid colon

Rectum

Liver

Stomach

Gallbladder

Pancreas

Spleen

TOOTH STRUCTURE

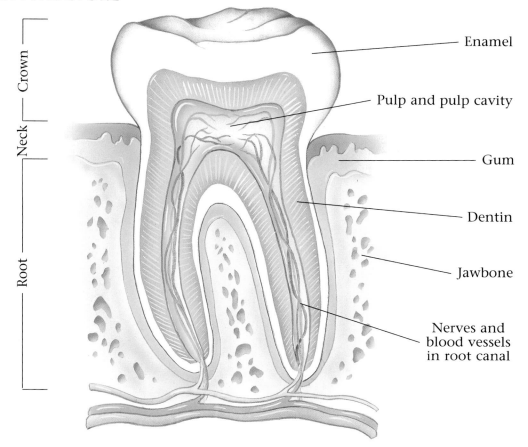

Crown

Neck

Root

Enamel

Pulp and pulp cavity

Gum

Dentin

Jawbone

Nerves and blood vessels in root canal

PERMANENT TEETH

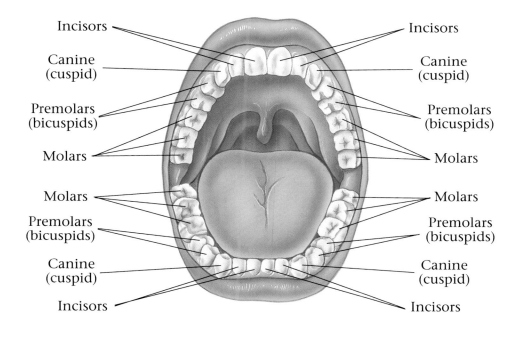

Incisors

Canine (cuspid)

Premolars (bicuspids)

Molars

Molars

Premolars (bicuspids)

Canine (cuspid)

Incisors

Incisors

Canine (cuspid)

Premolars (bicuspids)

Molars

Molars

Premolars (bicuspids)

Canine (cuspid)

Incisors

Sebaceous
gland

Arrector
pili muscle

Meissner's corpuscle
(touch receptor)

Skin surface

Hair

Hair shaft

Pore

Stratum
corneum

Stratum
lucidum

Stratum
granulosum

Stratum
spinosum

Stratum
basale

Ruffini's
corpuscle
(heat receptor)

Connective
tissue

Sudoriferous
duct

Eccrine
sweat gland

Nerve fiber

Nerve

Artery

Vein

Hair follicle

Hair bulb

Capillary
blood vessel

Papilla

Apocrine
sweat gland

Pacinian corpuscle
(pressure receptor)

Adipose
tissue

Epidermis

Dermis

Subcutaneous
tissue

INTERNAL STRUCTURES

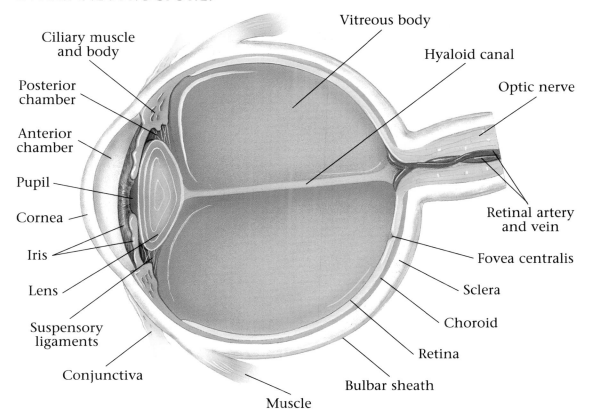

Ciliary muscle and body

Posterior chamber

Anterior chamber

Pupil

Cornea

Iris

Lens

Suspensory ligaments

Conjunctiva

Muscle

Vitreous body

Hyaloid canal

Optic nerve

Retinal artery and vein

Fovea centralis

Sclera

Choroid

Retina

Bulbar sheath

EXTERNAL STRUCTURES

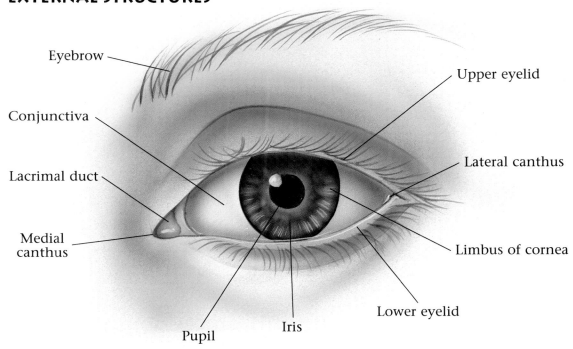

Eyebrow

Conjunctiva

Lacrimal duct

Medial canthus

Pupil

Iris

Upper eyelid

Lateral canthus

Limbus of cornea

Lower eyelid

HUMAN BODY

134

EAR

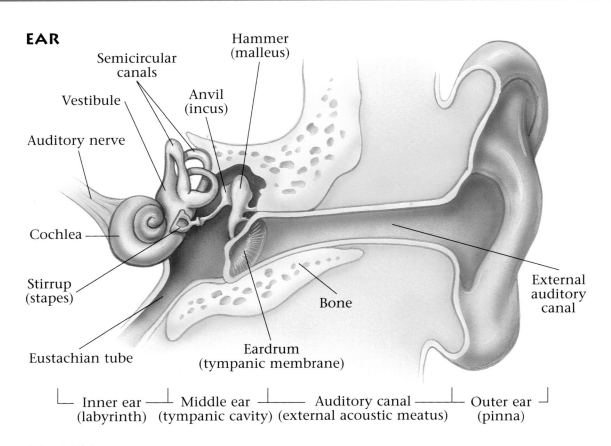

Hammer (malleus)

Semicircular canals

Vestibule

Anvil (incus)

Auditory nerve

Cochlea

Stirrup (stapes)

Eustachian tube

Eardrum (tympanic membrane)

Bone

External auditory canal

Inner ear (labyrinth) — Middle ear (tympanic cavity) — Auditory canal (external acoustic meatus) — Outer ear (pinna)

SINUSES

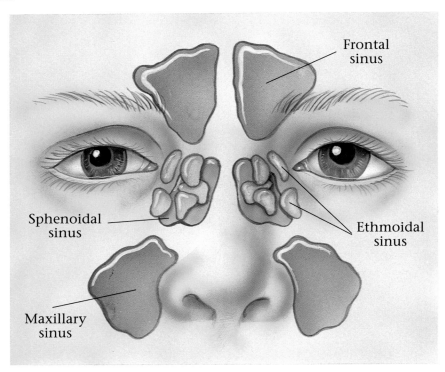

Frontal sinus

Sphenoidal sinus

Ethmoidal sinus

Maxillary sinus

WORLD CULTURES

PEOPLE SHARE A CULTURE WHEN THEY HAVE the same arts, beliefs, and customs. Culture can include music, painting, religion, clothing, poetry, government, and technology. Sometimes different countries share the same culture. Sometimes one country can have several different cultures. Very often, one culture will grow and change by borrowing parts of another culture. This section will show you a few examples that represent culture. There are many more cultures than are shown here, and the section does not show everything about any one culture. Some of the examples you'll see are parts of modern cultures, and some are from older cultures. What kinds of characteristics make up your culture? What kinds of art, religion, and clothing are in your life? Do you know of any other cultures that are a part of your community?

STAR OF DAVID
Judaism

CRESCENT
Islam

CRUCIFIX
Christianity

YIN-YANG
Taoism

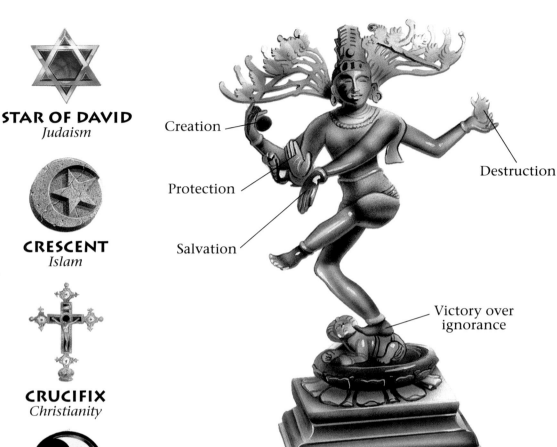

Creation

Protection

Salvation

Destruction

Victory over ignorance

STATUE OF SHIVA
Hinduism

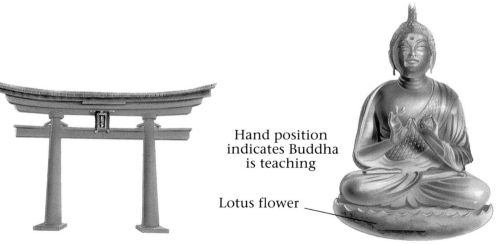

TORI
Shintoism

Hand position indicates Buddha is teaching

Lotus flower

STATUE OF BUDDHA
Buddhism

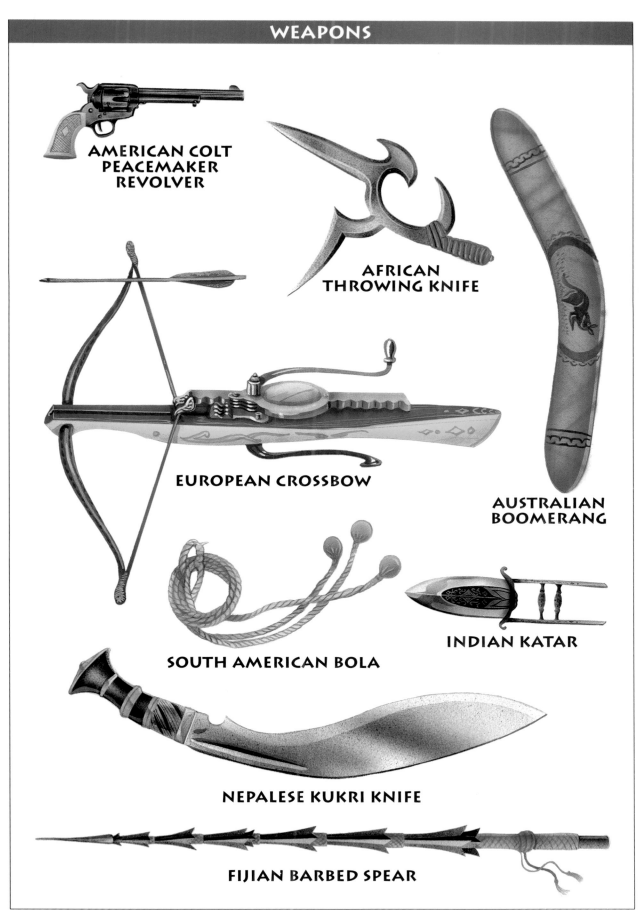

AMERICAN COLT PEACEMAKER REVOLVER

AFRICAN THROWING KNIFE

EUROPEAN CROSSBOW

AUSTRALIAN BOOMERANG

SOUTH AMERICAN BOLA

INDIAN KATAR

NEPALESE KUKRI KNIFE

FIJIAN BARBED SPEAR

137

WORLD CULTURES

FLUTES

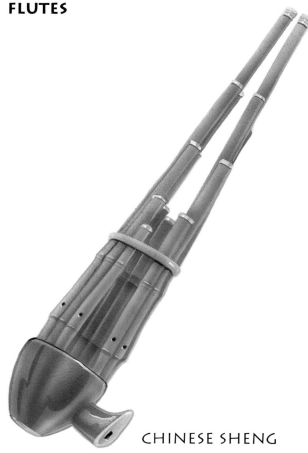

CHINESE SHENG

EUROPEAN
DOUBLE
FLAGEOLET

SOUTH
PACIFIC
NOSE FLUTE

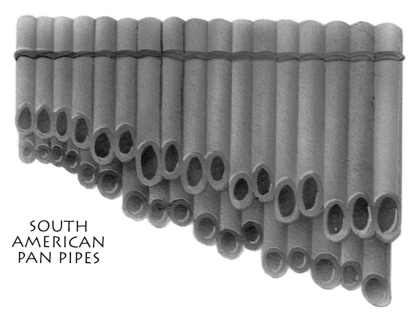

SOUTH
AMERICAN
PAN PIPES

PERCUSSION

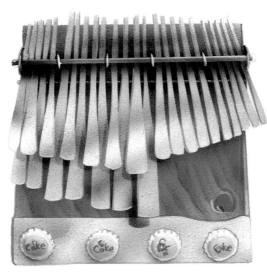

AFRICAN MBIRA

JAPANESE TSUZUMI

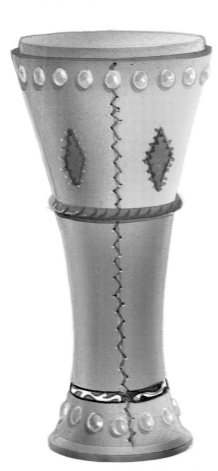

ARAB GOBLET DRUM

SOUTH AMERICAN MARACAS

WORLD CULTURES

140

STRINGS

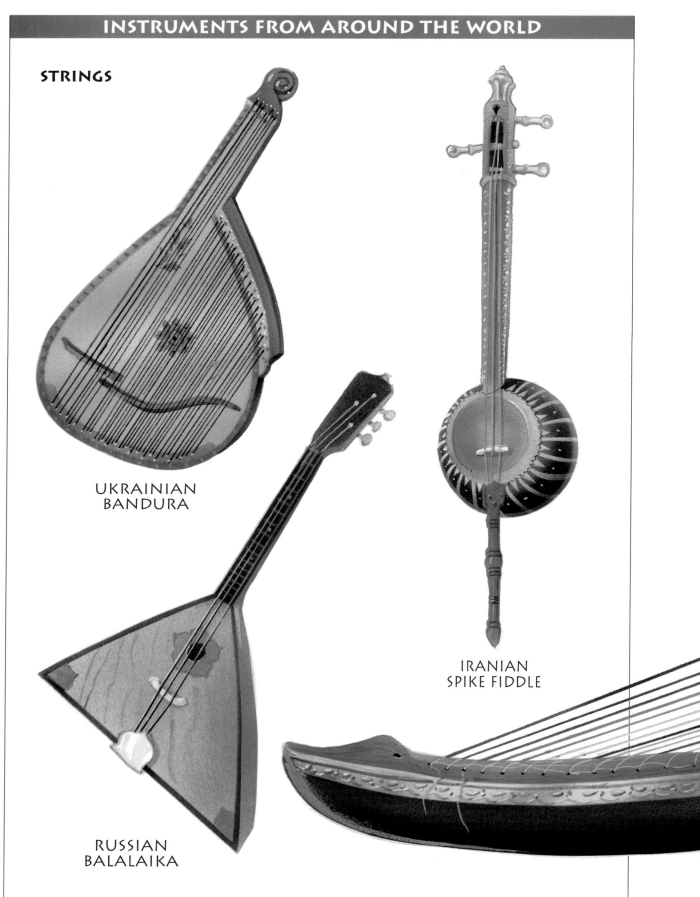

UKRAINIAN
BANDURA

IRANIAN
SPIKE FIDDLE

RUSSIAN
BALALAIKA

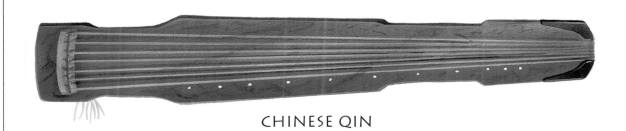

CHINESE QIN

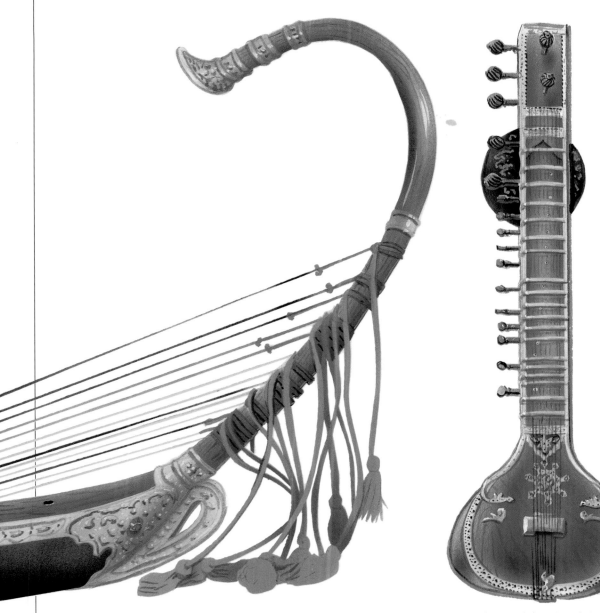

BURMESE SAUNG-GAUK

INDIAN SITAR

SCULPTURE

WORLD CULTURES

WOOD FIGURE
Japan

TUSK CARVING
Native American (Eskimo)

JADE FIGURE
China

WOOD FIGURE
New Zealand (Maori)

WOOD FIGURE
West Africa (Yoruba)

WORLD CULTURES

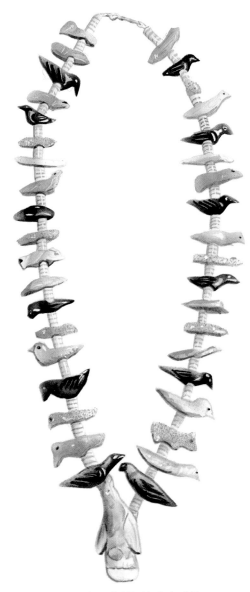

FETISH NECKLACE
Native American (Zuni)

WOOD FIGURE
New Ireland (Melanesian)

CERAMICS

PORCELAIN VASE
China

POTTERY VASE
England (Wedgwood)

DEVIL DANCER FIGURE
Bolivia

STORYTELLER FIGURE
Native American (Pueblo)

CLAY PITCHER
Mexico

BIDRI PITCHER
India

METAL AND GLASS

WORLD CULTURES

GOLD FIGURE
Mexico (Mayan)

SILVER PENDANT
Morocco

BRONZE SCULPTURE
China

CRYSTAL DECANTER
AND GLASS
Ireland

GLASS VASE
Italy

GOLD PITCHER
Persia

FABRIC

WORLD CULTURES

IKAT FABRIC
Sumba (Indonesia)

RAFFIA FABRIC
Zaire

WOVEN CARPET
Turkey

TAPA (BARK CLOTH)
Samoa

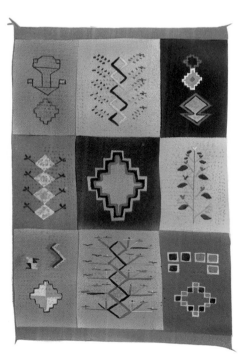

WOVEN RUG
Native American (Navajo)

AMERICAN AMISH

AMERICAN AMISH

AMERICAN WEST

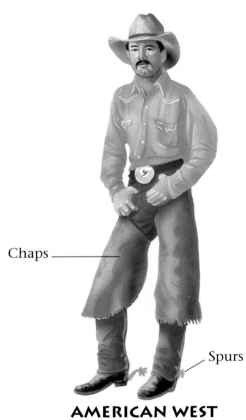

Chaps

Spurs

AMERICAN WEST

Poncho

ARGENTINA
Gaucho

BALI
Dancer

Kabaya

Sarong

BALI

BOLIVIA

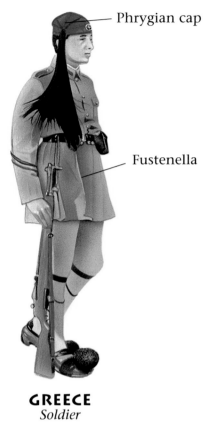

Phrygian cap

Fustenella

GREECE
Soldier

GREECE

HUNGARY

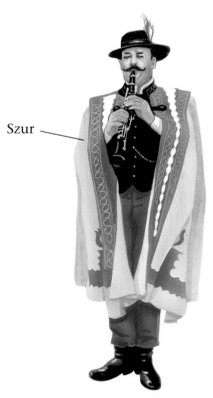

Szur

HUNGARY

WORLD CULTURES

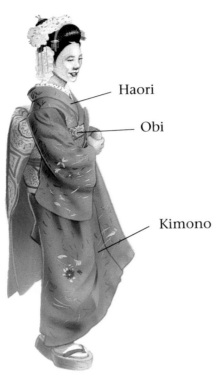

Haori

Obi

Kimono

JAPAN

Kimona

JAPAN

KENYA

LAPLAND

153

WORLD CULTURES

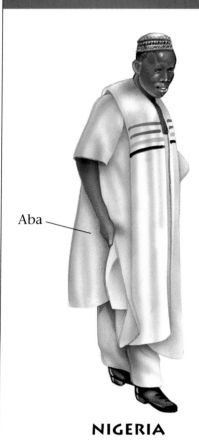

Aba

NIGERIA

PERU
Festival dress

POLAND
Bride

Agal

Kaffiyeh

SAUDI ARABIA
Royal family member

Kilt

Sporran

SCOTLAND
Highland piper

SPAIN
Toreador

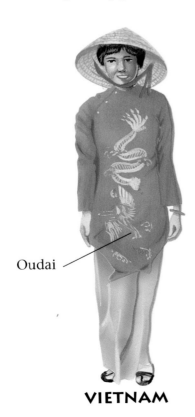

Oudai

VIETNAM

WALES

WORLD CULTURES

JAPANESE GASSHO HOUSE

SUMATRAN HUT

MUSIC

WHEN SOUNDS ARE combined in a way that people find pleasing, we call it *music*. Musical instruments create sounds by causing air to vibrate. A steady vibration is called a *note*. When the vibration is faster, we say the note is higher. By combining notes in different orders and by controlling their timing or rhythm, we create music. This section will show you the system that people use for writing down music, and it will show you some of the instruments we use to make music. Most of these instruments are used as part of a symphony orchestra, which is one kind of musical group.

MUSIC

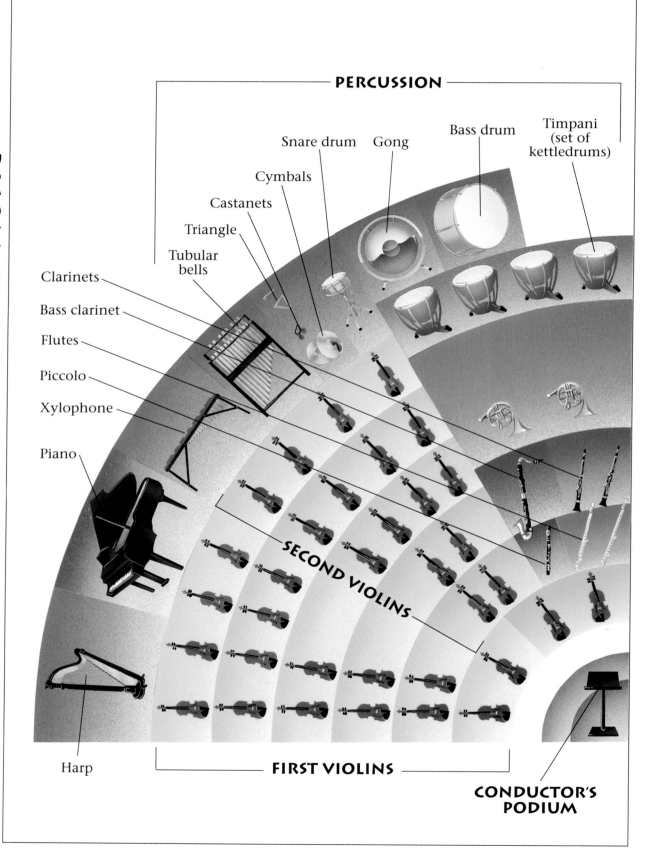

PERCUSSION

Snare drum   Gong

Bass drum

Timpani
(set of
kettledrums)

Cymbals

Castanets

Triangle

Tubular
bells

Clarinets

Bass clarinet

Flutes

Piccolo

Xylophone

Piano

SECOND VIOLINS

Harp

FIRST VIOLINS

CONDUCTOR'S
PODIUM

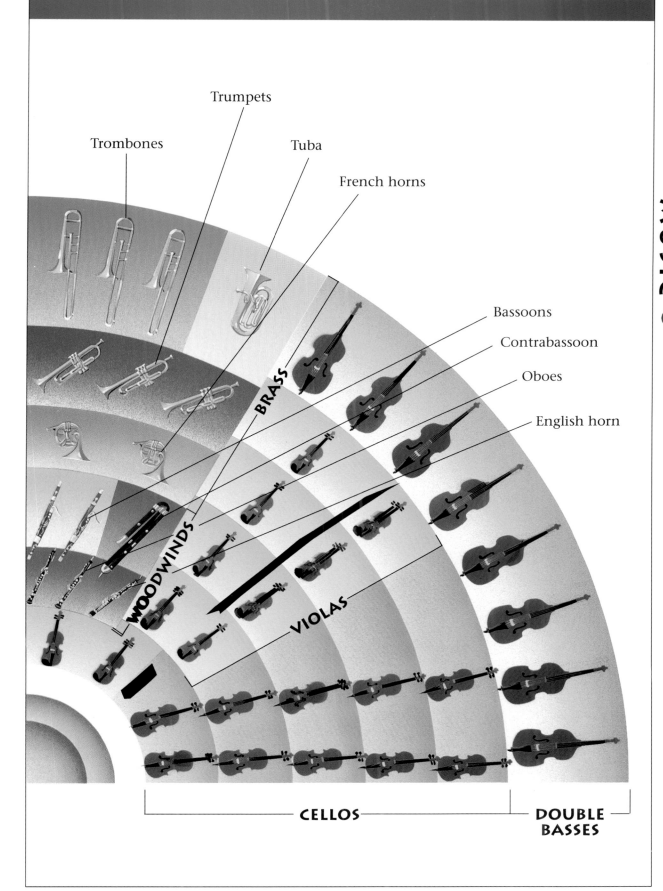

Trombones

Trumpets

Tuba

French horns

Bassoons

Contrabassoon

Oboes

English horn

BRASS

WOODWINDS

VIOLAS

CELLOS

DOUBLE BASSES

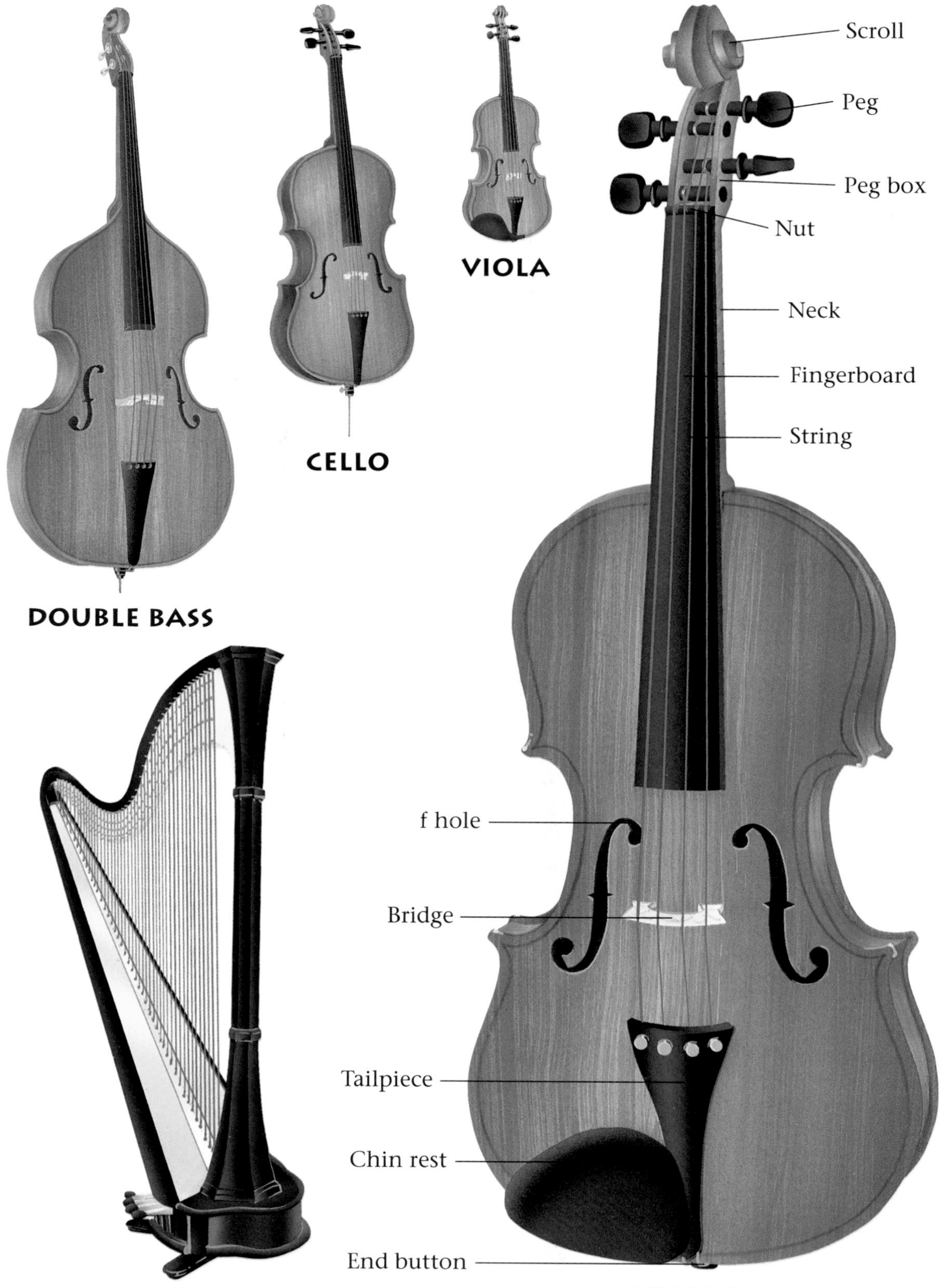

DOUBLE BASS

CELLO

VIOLA

Scroll

Peg

Peg box

Nut

Neck

Fingerboard

String

f hole

Bridge

Tailpiece

Chin rest

End button

HARP

VIOLIN

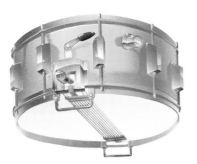

SNARE DRUM

XYLOPHONE

CYMBALS

CASTANETS

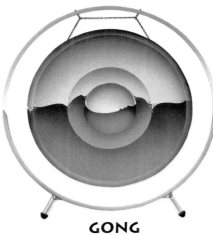

GONG

TUBULAR BELLS

KETTLEDRUM

MUSIC

SAXOPHONE

Octave key

Mouthpiece

Key

Bell

SINGLE REEDS

BASS SAXOPHONE

CLARINET

DOUBLE REEDS

OBOE

BASSOON

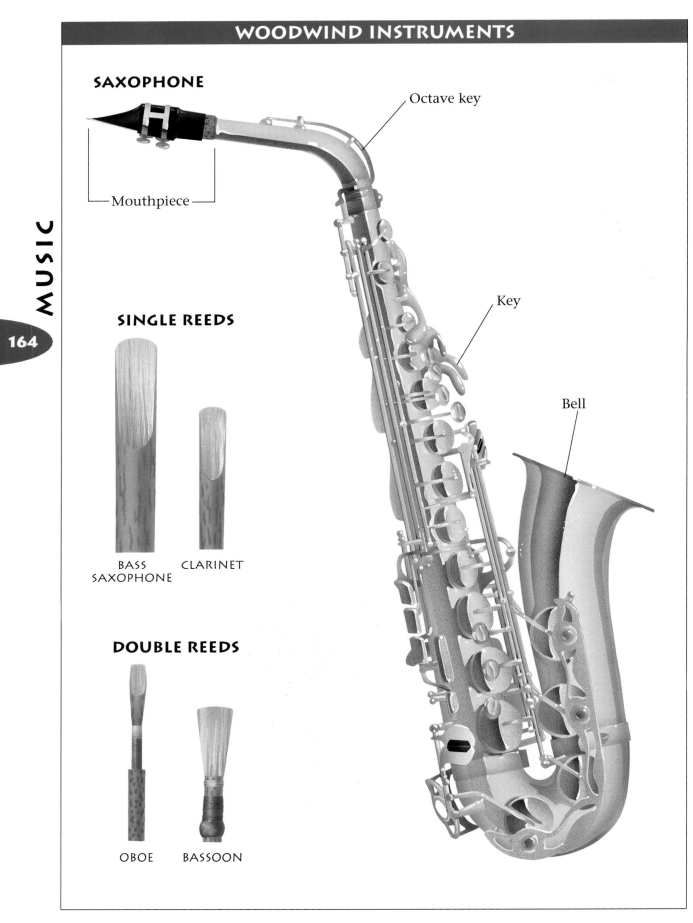

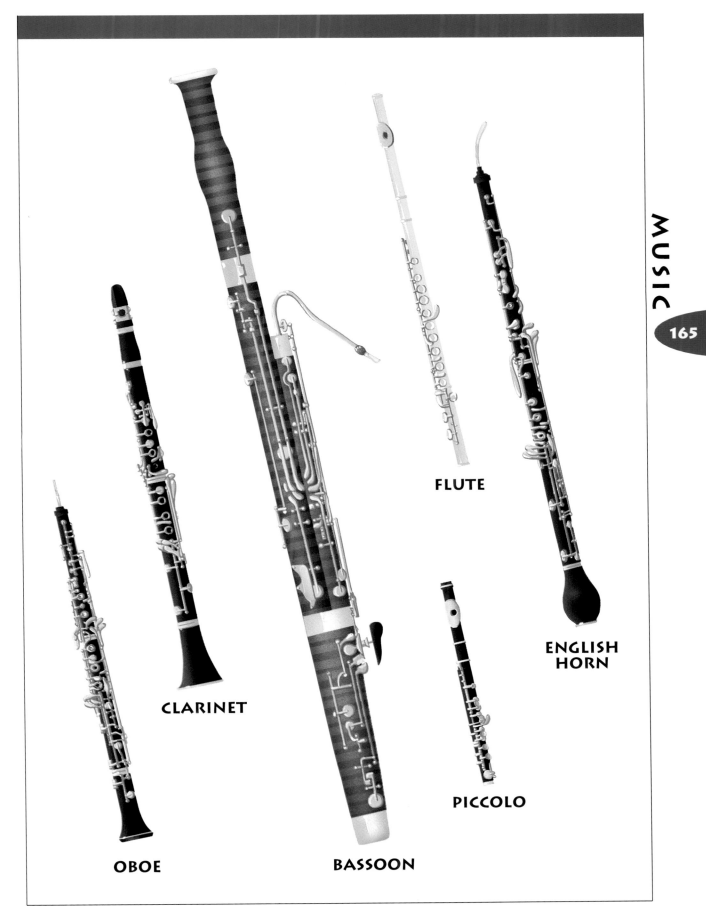

CLARINET

FLUTE

OBOE

BASSOON

PICCOLO

ENGLISH
HORN

MUSIC

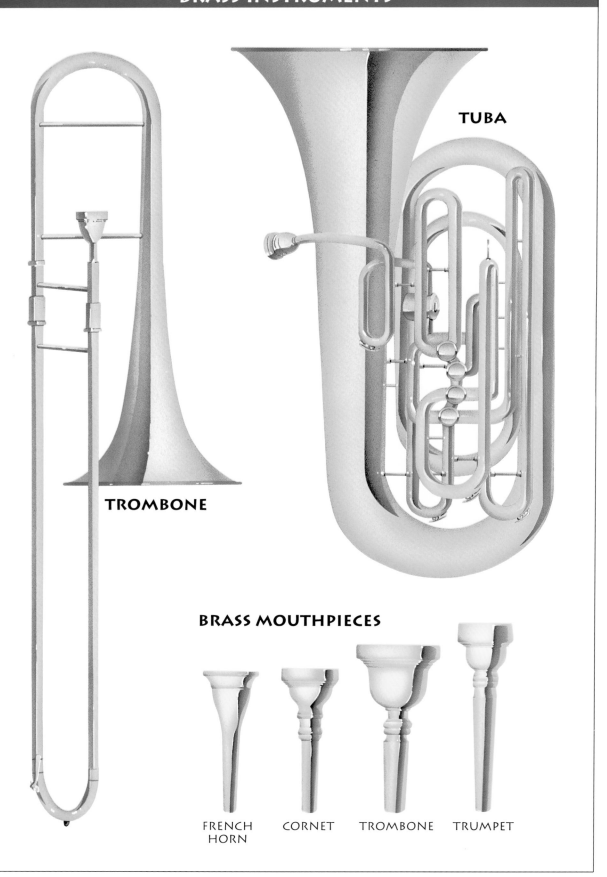

TUBA

TROMBONE

BRASS MOUTHPIECES

FRENCH
HORN

CORNET

TROMBONE

TRUMPET

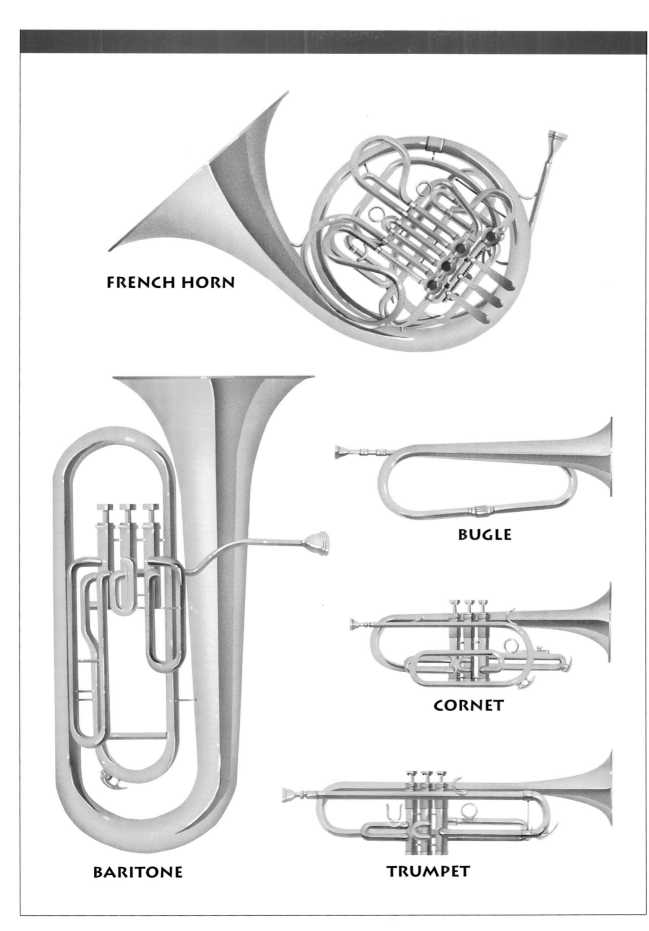

FRENCH HORN

BUGLE

CORNET

BARITONE

TRUMPET

MUSIC

UPRIGHT PIANO

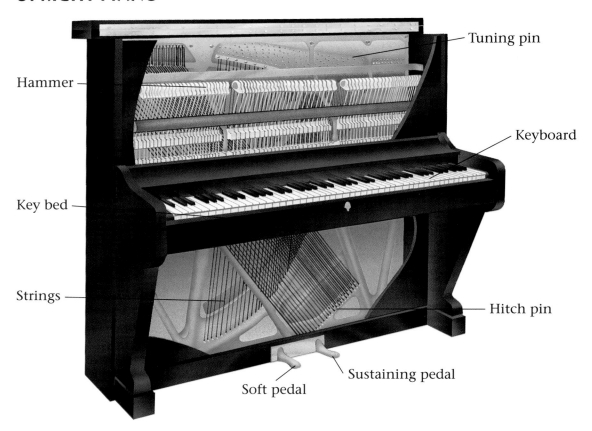

Tuning pin

Hammer

Keyboard

Key bed

Strings

Hitch pin

Soft pedal

Sustaining pedal

COMPARATIVE PITCH RANGE OF COMMON ORCHESTRAL INSTRUMENTS

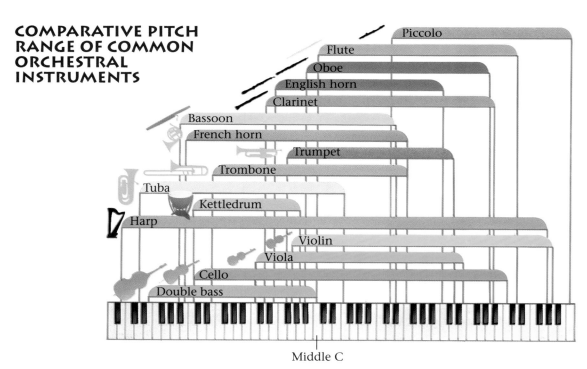

Piccolo

Flute

Oboe

English horn

Clarinet

Bassoon

French horn

Trumpet

Trombone

Tuba

Kettledrum

Harp

Violin

Viola

Cello

Double bass

Middle C

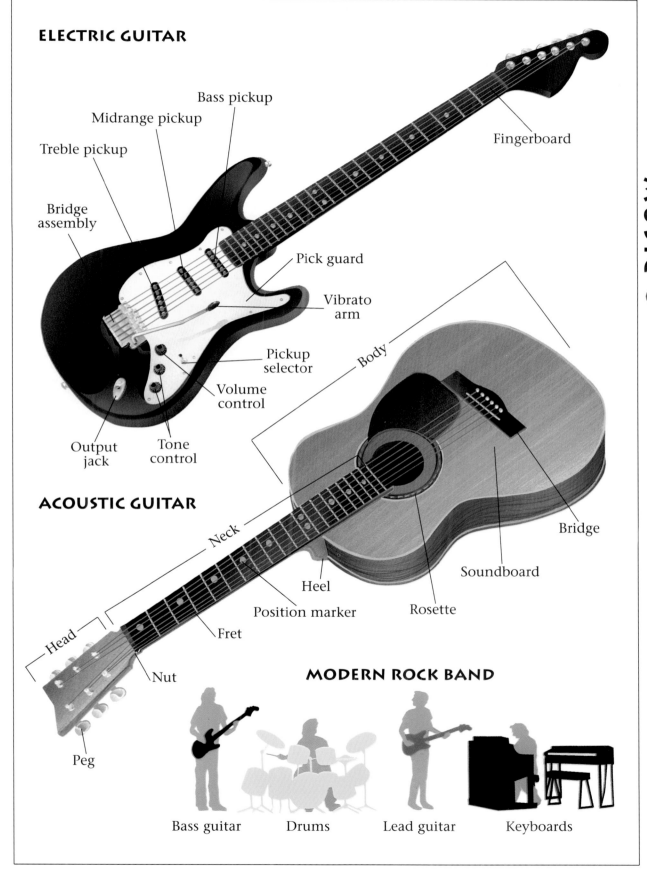

ELECTRIC GUITAR

Bass pickup

Midrange pickup

Treble pickup

Bridge assembly

Fingerboard

Pick guard

Vibrato arm

Pickup selector

Volume control

Output jack

Tone control

ACOUSTIC GUITAR

Body

Neck

Head

Nut

Peg

Heel

Position marker

Fret

Rosette

Soundboard

Bridge

MUSIC

169

MODERN ROCK BAND

Bass guitar

Drums

Lead guitar

Keyboards

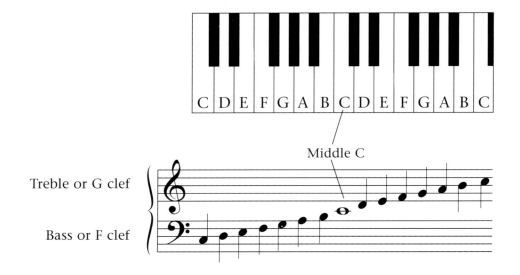

MUSIC

Middle C

Treble or G clef

Bass or F clef

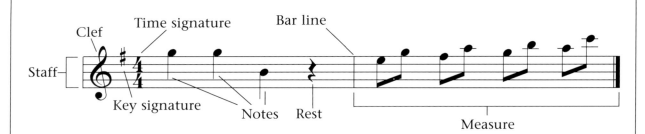

Clef

Time signature

Bar line

Staff

Key signature

Notes

Rest

Measure

TIME VALUES

NOTES

Whole   ½   ¼   ⅛

RESTS

Whole   ½   ¼   ⅛

¾ TIME

Down in the val - ley

¼ TIME

Row, row, row your boat   gent - ly down the stream

ARCHITECTURE

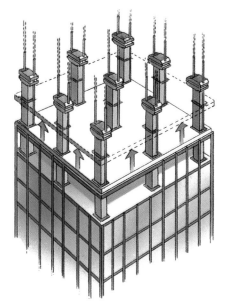

ARCHITECTS DESIGN HOW a building will look and plan how it will be built. They use science and technology to choose building materials, to test the safety of their designs, and to find new ways to make buildings. They also use their artistic skills to create beautiful designs and to make sure their buildings match their surroundings. In this section, you'll see styles of Western architecture that have been used throughout history. Some designs are based mostly on how the building will be used,

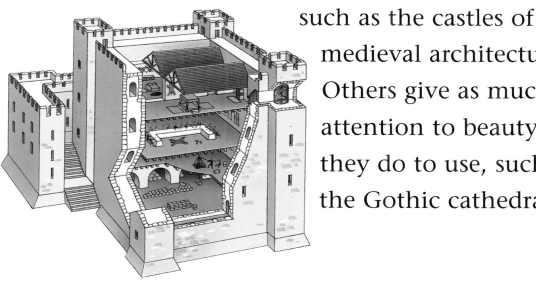

such as the castles of medieval architecture. Others give as much attention to beauty as they do to use, such as the Gothic cathedrals.

CONTRIBUTIONS OF THE ANCIENTS

NEOLITHIC CULTURE (STONEHENGE)

Lintel

Post

POST AND LINTEL SYSTEM

ANCIENT GREEK ARCHITECTURAL ORDERS

CORINTHIAN

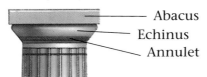

Abacus

Acanthus

DORIC

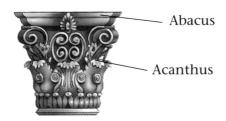

Abacus

Echinus

Annulet

IONIC

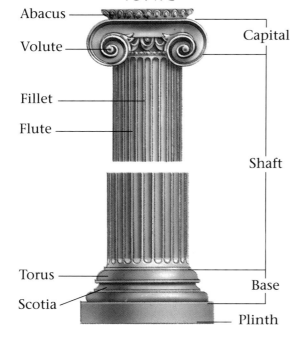

Abacus

Volute

Fillet

Flute

Capital

Shaft

Torus

Scotia

Base

Plinth

ANCIENT ROMAN ARCHES

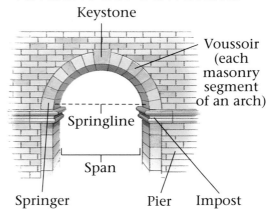

Keystone

Voussoir (each masonry segment of an arch)

Springline

Span

Springer

Pier

Impost

EARLY CHRISTIAN DOMES

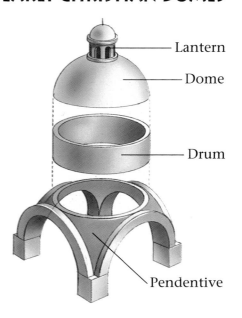

Lantern

Dome

Drum

Pendentive

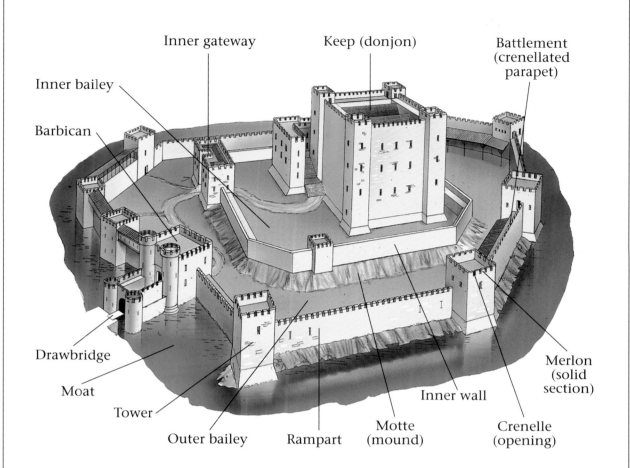

Inner gateway

Keep (donjon)

Battlement (crenellated parapet)

Inner bailey

Barbican

Drawbridge

Moat

Tower

Outer bailey

Rampart

Motte (mound)

Inner wall

Merlon (solid section)

Crenelle (opening)

INTERIOR OF KEEP

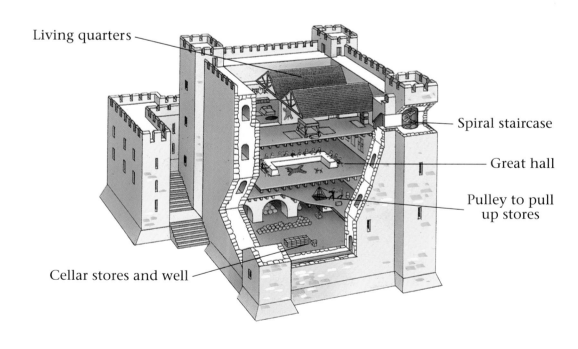

Living quarters

Spiral staircase

Great hall

Pulley to pull up stores

Cellar stores and well

ARCHITECTURE

174

Spire

Tower

Clerestory

Gallery

Aisle

Tympanum

Portals

Narthex

Arcade

Transept

Rose window

Tracery

Flying buttress

Apse (semicircular or polygonal termination)

Nave

Pointed arch

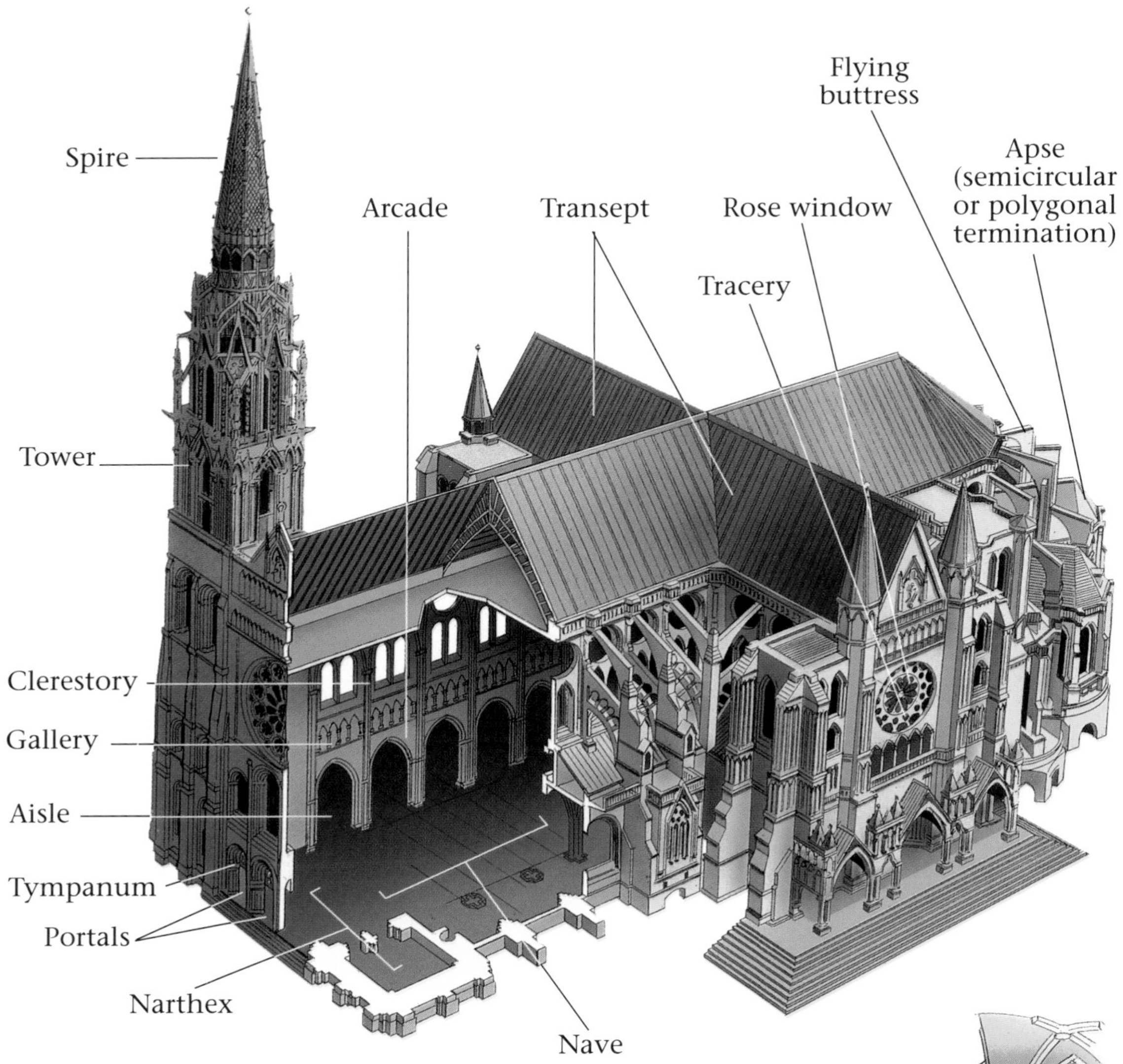

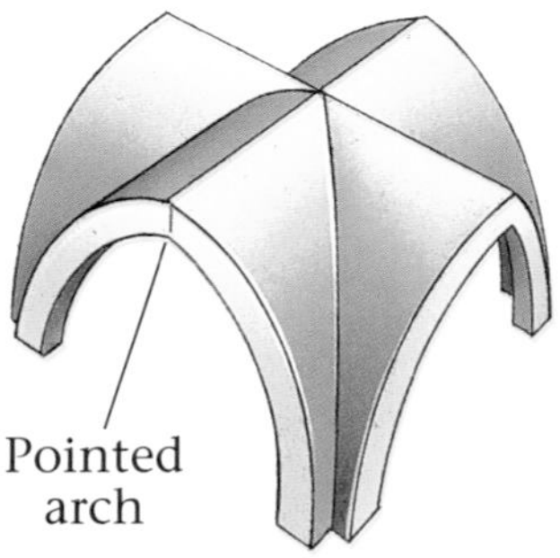

VAULT

GARGOYLE

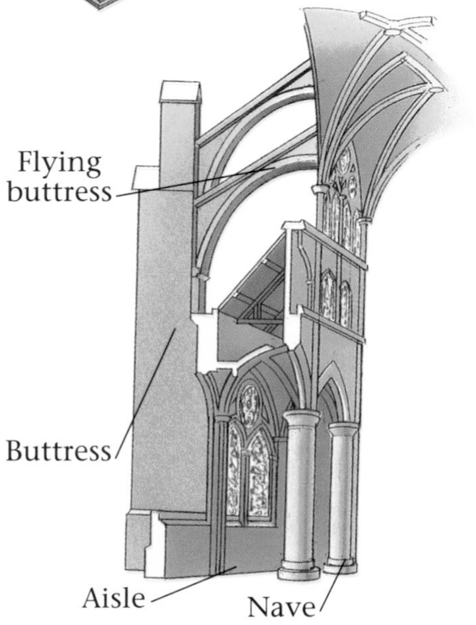

Flying buttress

Buttress

Aisle

Nave

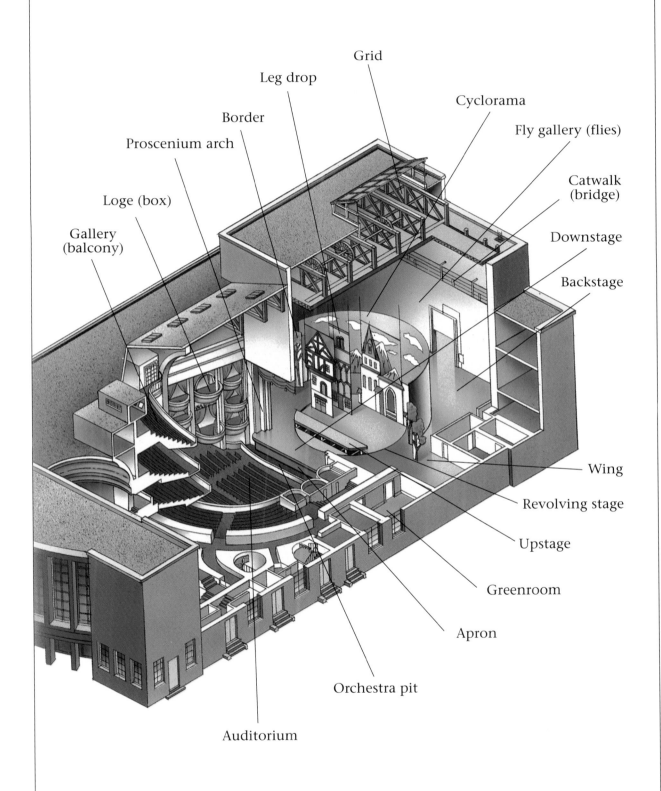

Grid

Leg drop

Cyclorama

Border

Fly gallery (flies)

Proscenium arch

Catwalk
(bridge)

Loge (box)

Downstage

Gallery
(balcony)

Backstage

Wing

Revolving stage

Upstage

Greenroom

Apron

Orchestra pit

Auditorium

STRUCTURAL SYSTEMS FOR SKYSCRAPERS

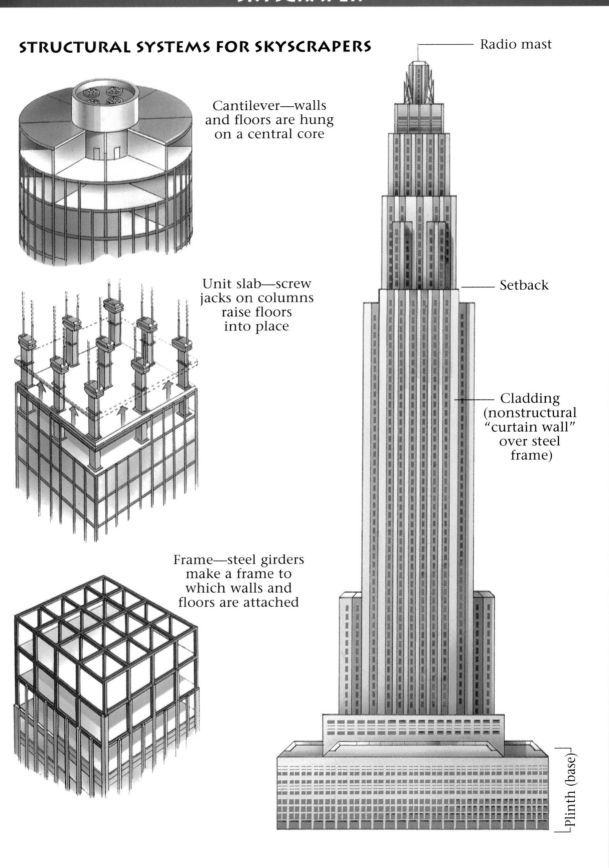

Cantilever—walls and floors are hung on a central core

Unit slab—screw jacks on columns raise floors into place

Frame—steel girders make a frame to which walls and floors are attached

Radio mast

Setback

Cladding (nonstructural "curtain wall" over steel frame)

Plinth (base)

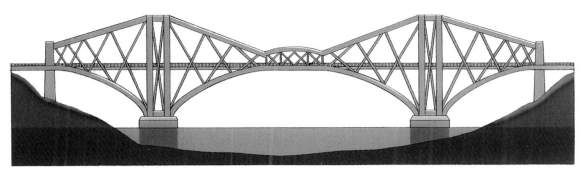

CANTILEVER BRIDGE

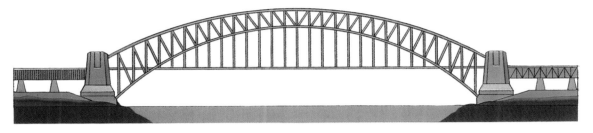

TRUSSED ARCH BRIDGE

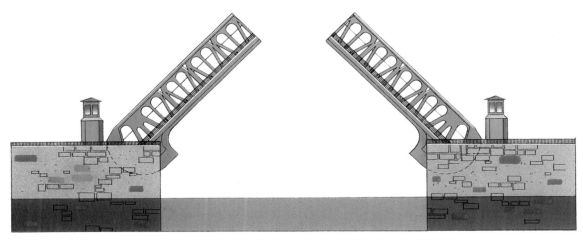

MOVABLE BRIDGE: DOUBLE BASCULE

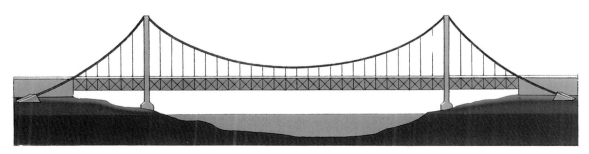

SUSPENSION BRIDGE

TYPES OF ROOFS

DOME

LEAN-TO

FLAT

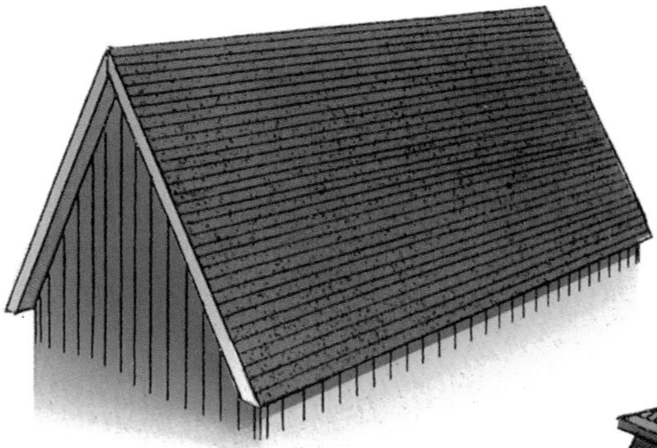

PITCHED

MANSARD

WINDOW

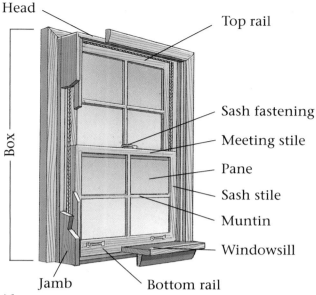

Head

Top rail

Sash fastening

Meeting stile

Pane

Sash stile

Muntin

Windowsill

Box

Jamb

Bottom rail

TYPES OF WINDOWS

PIVOTING

CASEMENT

DOUBLE HUNG

SLIDING

JALOUSIE

DOOR

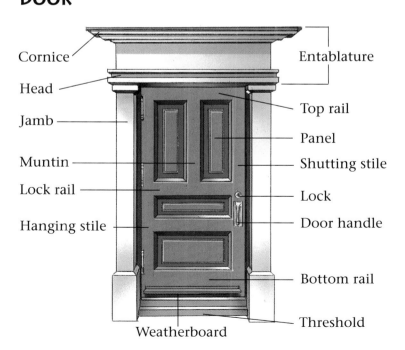

Cornice

Head

Jamb

Muntin

Lock rail

Hanging stile

Weatherboard

Entablature

Top rail

Panel

Shutting stile

Lock

Door handle

Bottom rail

Threshold

TYPES OF DOORS

SWINGING

SLIDING

FOLDING

STRUCTURE OF A HOUSE

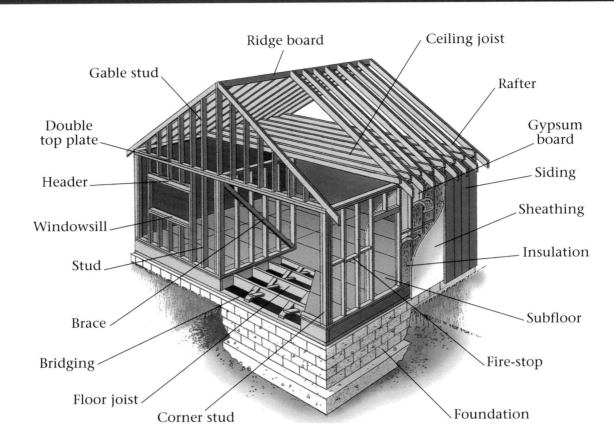

Ridge board

Ceiling joist

Gable stud

Rafter

Double top plate

Gypsum board

Header

Siding

Windowsill

Sheathing

Stud

Insulation

Brace

Subfloor

Bridging

Fire-stop

Floor joist

Corner stud

Foundation

PERIMETER WALL FOUNDATION

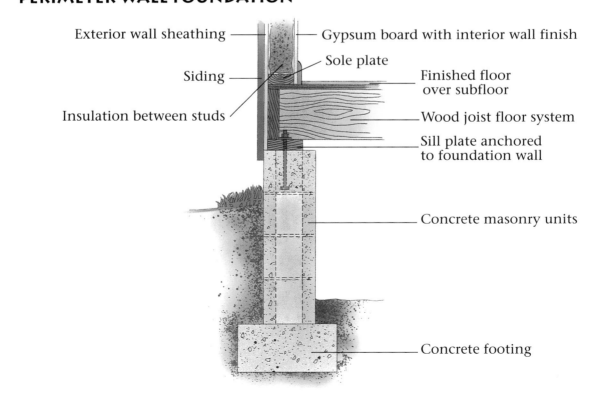

Exterior wall sheathing

Gypsum board with interior wall finish

Sole plate

Siding

Finished floor over subfloor

Insulation between studs

Wood joist floor system

Sill plate anchored to foundation wall

Concrete masonry units

Concrete footing

SPORTS

SPORTS ARE GAMES OR CONTESTS that usually involve physical activity. A sport has a set of rules that say what players are and aren't allowed to do, what kinds of equipment can be used, and what the playing field should be like. The rules make the sport safe and fair for all players. Sometimes sports are played for fun or recreation, and other times the players are very serious and competitive. In sports like soccer and baseball, whole teams play against each other. In sports like weight lifting and diving, individuals compete against each other or against themselves. Often, people get as much enjoyment from watching sports as they do from playing sports.

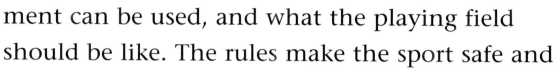

BASEBALL FIELD

Center fielder

Second baseman

Warning track

Right fielder

Left fielder

Fence

Foul line

Shortstop

Third baseman

Outfield

First baseman

Second base

Umpire

Third base

First base

Coach's box

Coach

Pitcher

Infield

On-deck circle

Dugout

Pitcher's mound

HOME-PLATE AREA

Home plate

Batter's box

Batter

Catcher

Home-plate umpire

BASEBALL

Yarn

Cork

Rubber

Stitches

Cowhide cover

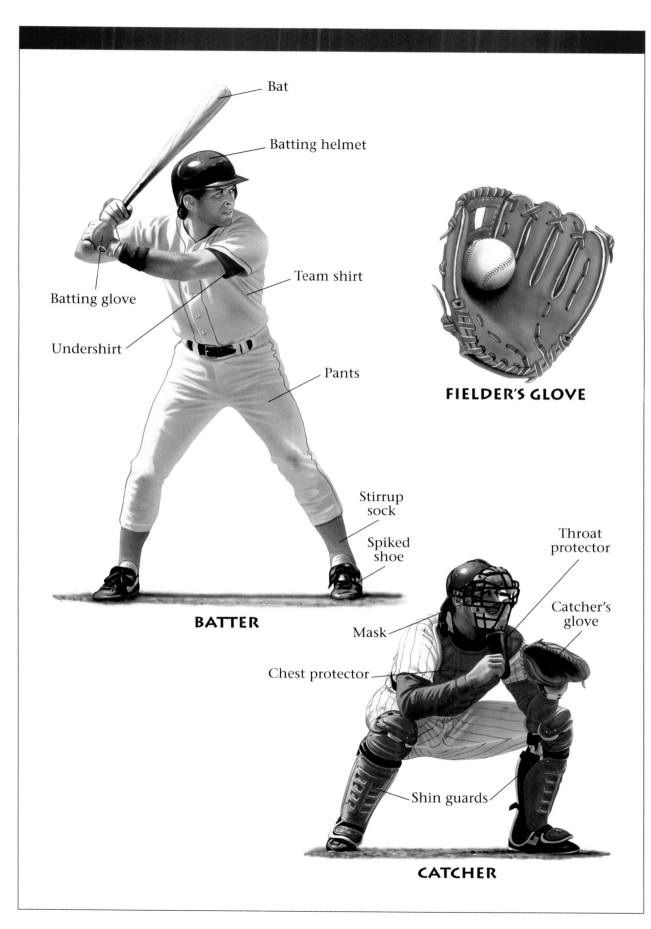

Bat

Batting helmet

Batting glove

Undershirt

Team shirt

Pants

Stirrup sock

Spiked shoe

BATTER

FIELDER'S GLOVE

Throat protector

Catcher's glove

Mask

Chest protector

Shin guards

CATCHER

FOOTBALL FIELD

Goal line

Coaches' box

50-yard line

Sideline

Goal posts

160 feet

End line

End zone

10 yards

Hash marks

100 yards

FOOTBALL FIELD: CLOSE-UP

Head linesman

Line of scrimmage

Left cornerback

Outside linebacker

Left defensive end

Back judge

Safety

Left tackle

Umpire

Middle linebacker

Safety

Right tackle

Right cornerback

Outside linebacker

Right defensive end

Split end

Right tackle

Right guard

Center

Fullback

Halfback

Quarterback

Left guard

Referee

Left tackle

Flanker

Tight end

Line judge

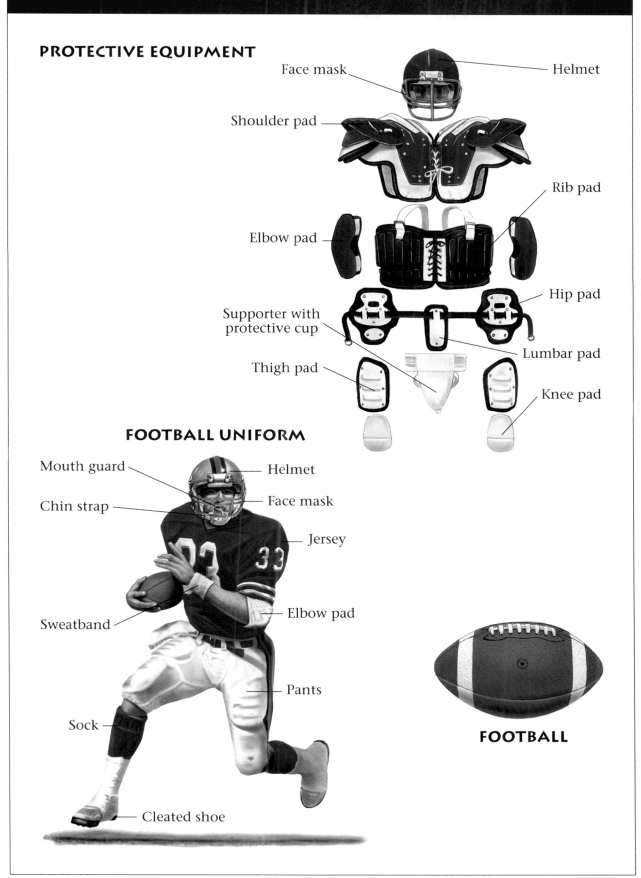

PROTECTIVE EQUIPMENT

Face mask

Helmet

Shoulder pad

Rib pad

Elbow pad

Supporter with protective cup

Hip pad

Lumbar pad

Thigh pad

Knee pad

FOOTBALL UNIFORM

Mouth guard

Helmet

Chin strap

Face mask

Jersey

Sweatband

Elbow pad

Pants

Sock

Cleated shoe

FOOTBALL

SOCCER FIELD

SPORTS

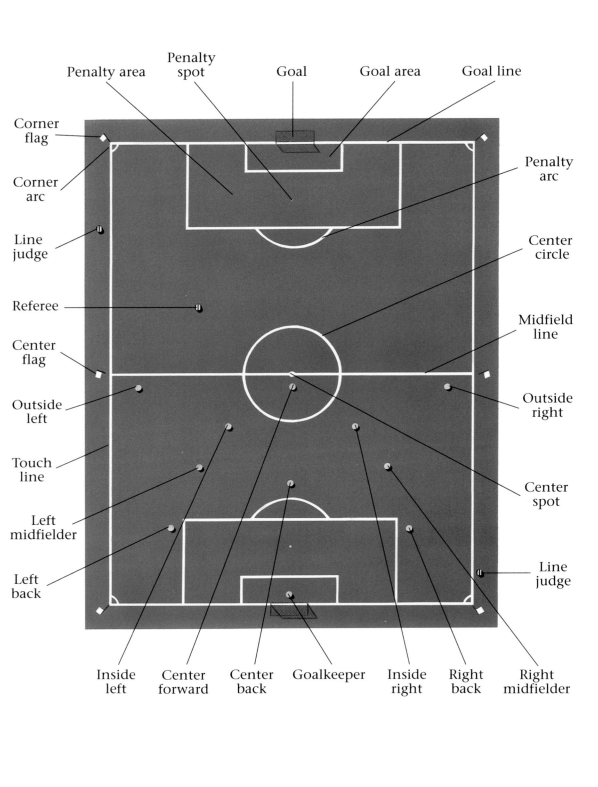

Penalty area • Penalty spot • Goal • Goal area • Goal line • Corner flag • Corner arc • Penalty arc • Line judge • Center circle • Referee • Midfield line • Center flag • Outside right • Outside left • Touch line • Center spot • Left midfielder • Left back • Inside left • Center forward • Center back • Goalkeeper • Inside right • Right back • Right midfielder • Line judge

SOCCER EQUIPMENT

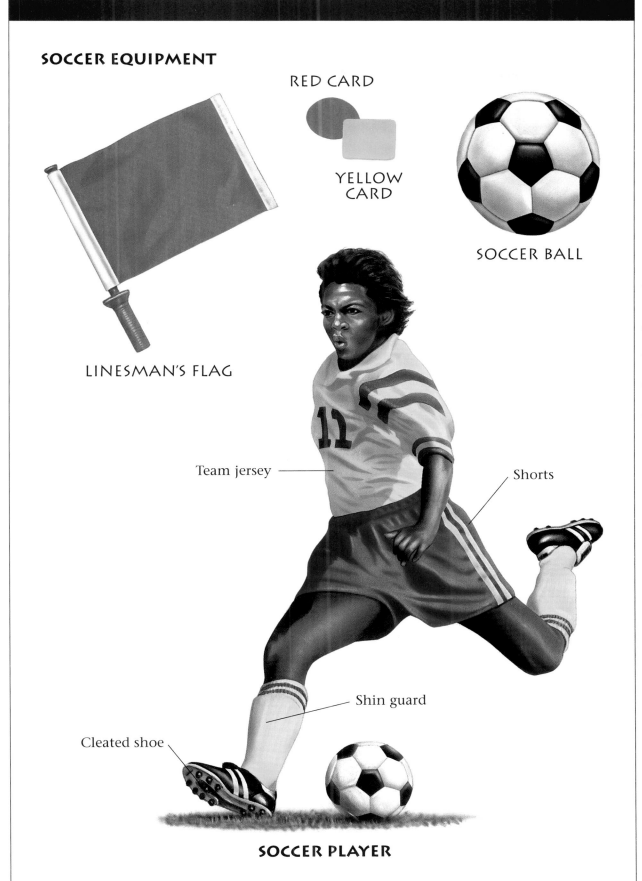

RED CARD

YELLOW CARD

SOCCER BALL

LINESMAN'S FLAG

Team jersey

Shorts

Shin guard

Cleated shoe

SOCCER PLAYER

TENNIS COURT

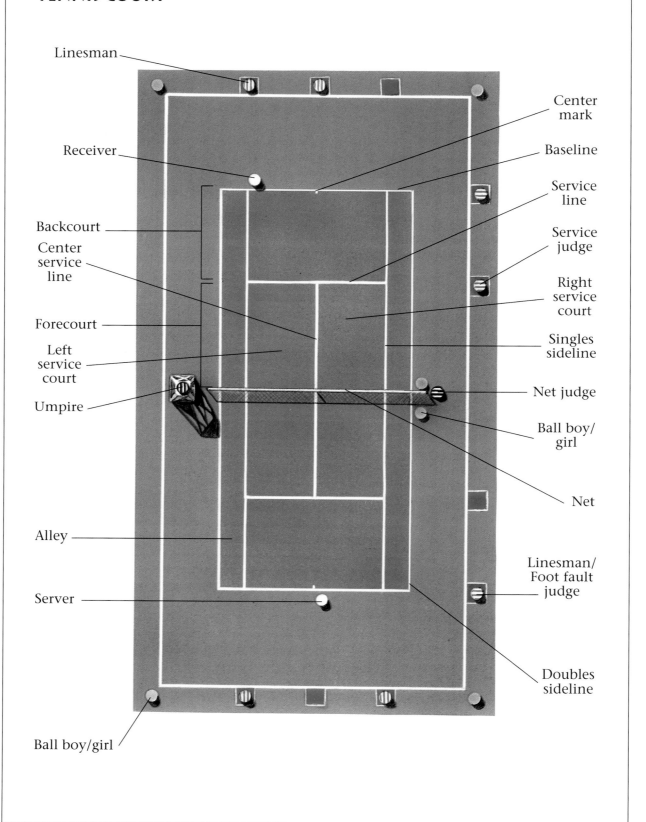

Linesman

Center mark

Receiver

Baseline

Service line

Backcourt

Service judge

Center service line

Right service court

Forecourt

Singles sideline

Left service court

Umpire

Net judge

Ball boy/ girl

Net

Alley

Linesman/ Foot fault judge

Server

Doubles sideline

Ball boy/girl

BASIC SERVE

| Ready position | Arm drop | Toss | Backswing | Start of racket drop | Racket drop | Start of hit |

| Contact | └─── Follow through ───┘ | Finish position |

FOREHAND

| Take back | Contact | Follow through |

BACKHAND

| Initial take back | Full take back | Contact | Follow through |

TYPES OF GRIP

Eastern forehand

Western forehand

Continental

GOLF COURSE

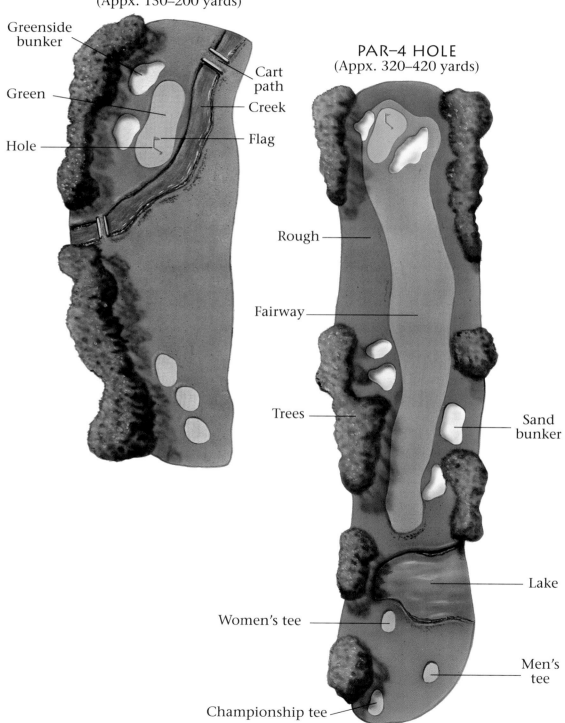

PAR–3 HOLE
(Appx. 150–200 yards)

Greenside bunker

Green

Hole

Cart path

Creek

Flag

PAR–4 HOLE
(Appx. 320–420 yards)

Rough

Fairway

Trees

Sand bunker

Lake

Women's tee

Men's tee

Championship tee

SPORTS

GOLF CLUBS

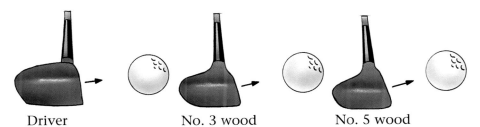

Driver   No. 3 wood   No. 5 wood

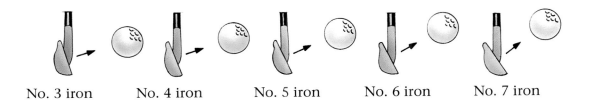

No. 3 iron   No. 4 iron   No. 5 iron   No. 6 iron   No. 7 iron

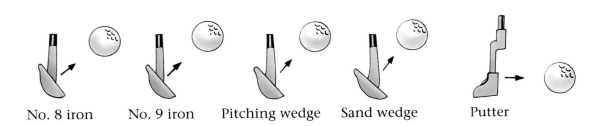

No. 8 iron   No. 9 iron   Pitching wedge   Sand wedge   Putter

FULL SWING

AUSTRALIAN CRAWL

1 Kick

2

3

4

5

6

BREASTSTROKE

1

2

3

4 Kick

5

6

BUTTERFLY STROKE

1 Butterfly kick

2

3

4

5

6

GOLF CLUBS

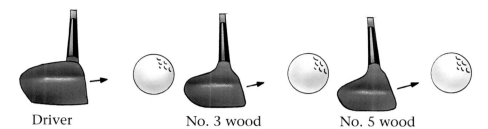

Driver   No. 3 wood   No. 5 wood

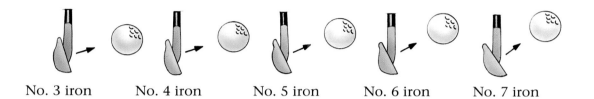

No. 3 iron   No. 4 iron   No. 5 iron   No. 6 iron   No. 7 iron

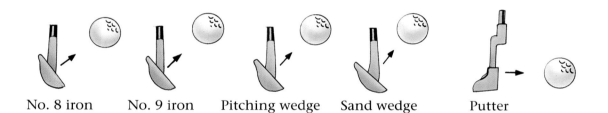

No. 8 iron   No. 9 iron   Pitching wedge   Sand wedge   Putter

FULL SWING

WEIGHT TRAINING

FREE WEIGHT BENCH PRESS EXERCISE

Preparation phase · Execution phase 1 · Execution phase 2 · Racking the bar

BACK SQUAT EXERCISE

Side view Front view

└ Preparation phase ┘ └ Downward phase ┘ Bottom position └ Upward phase ┘

BENT-OVER-ROW EXERCISE

Preparation phase · Execution phase 1 · Execution phase 2

SEATED BEHIND-THE-NECK PRESS EXERCISE

Preparation phase └ Upward phase ┘ └ Downward phase ┘

FREE WEIGHT BICEP CURL EXERCISE

Preparation phase · Execution phase 1 · Execution phase 2

SPORTS

192

FRONT PUNCH (BARO-JIREUGI)

Neutral stance

SIDE KICK (YEOP-CHAGI)

Neutral stance

ROUND KICK (DOLLYO-CHAGI)

Neutral
stance

Kick

COLORS OF BELTS

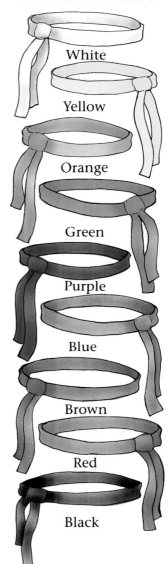

White

Yellow

Orange

Green

Purple

Blue

Brown

Red

Black

SPORTS

193

AUSTRALIAN CRAWL

1 Kick

2

3

4

5

6

BREASTSTROKE

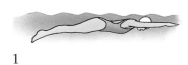

1

2

3

4 Kick

5

6

BUTTERFLY STROKE

1 Butterfly kick

2

3

4

5

6

FORWARD DIVE—LAYOUT

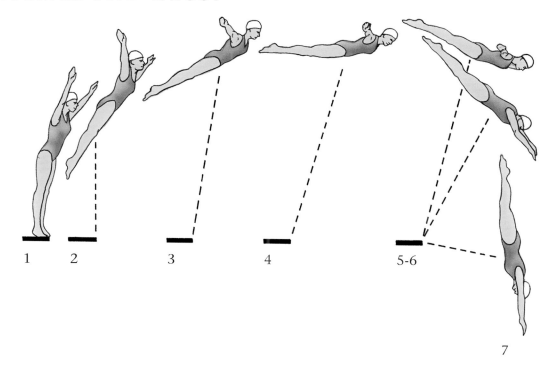

1   2   3   4   5-6

7

REVERSE 1½ SOMERSAULTS—TUCK

BACK DIVE—PIKE

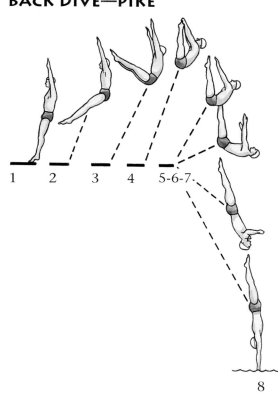

1   2   3   4   5-6-7

8

1   2   3   4   5   6-7   8

9

SIT SPIN

FORWARD LAYBACK SPIN

LUTZ JUMP

AXEL JUMP

TRANSPORTATION

THOUSANDS OF YEARS AGO, walking was the only way people had to get from one place to another, and they had to carry whatever they brought with them. In time, people used animals, such as oxen, to carry goods and later to pull carts and wagons.

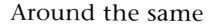

Around the same time, sailing ships allowed travel by water. In the 1700s, steam engines were invented. First they were used to power ships and then to power trains. Air travel also started at this time with the invention of the hot-air balloon. Today, we use electric motors, internal combustion engines, and jet engines to drive many kinds of vehicles.

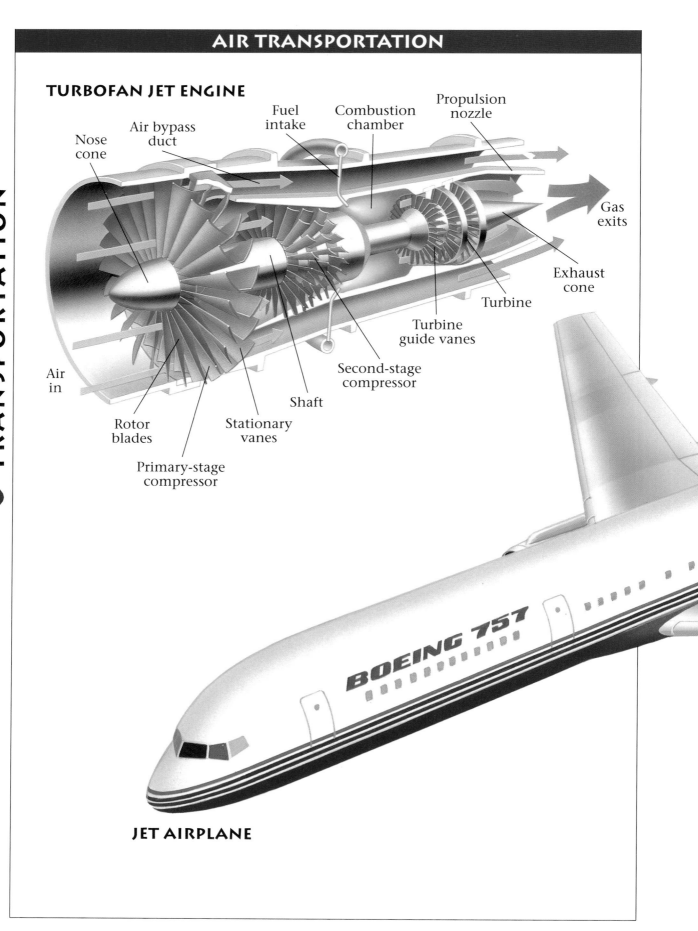

TURBOFAN JET ENGINE

Nose cone

Air bypass duct

Fuel intake

Combustion chamber

Propulsion nozzle

Gas exits

Exhaust cone

Turbine

Turbine guide vanes

Second-stage compressor

Shaft

Air in

Rotor blades

Stationary vanes

Primary-stage compressor

JET AIRPLANE

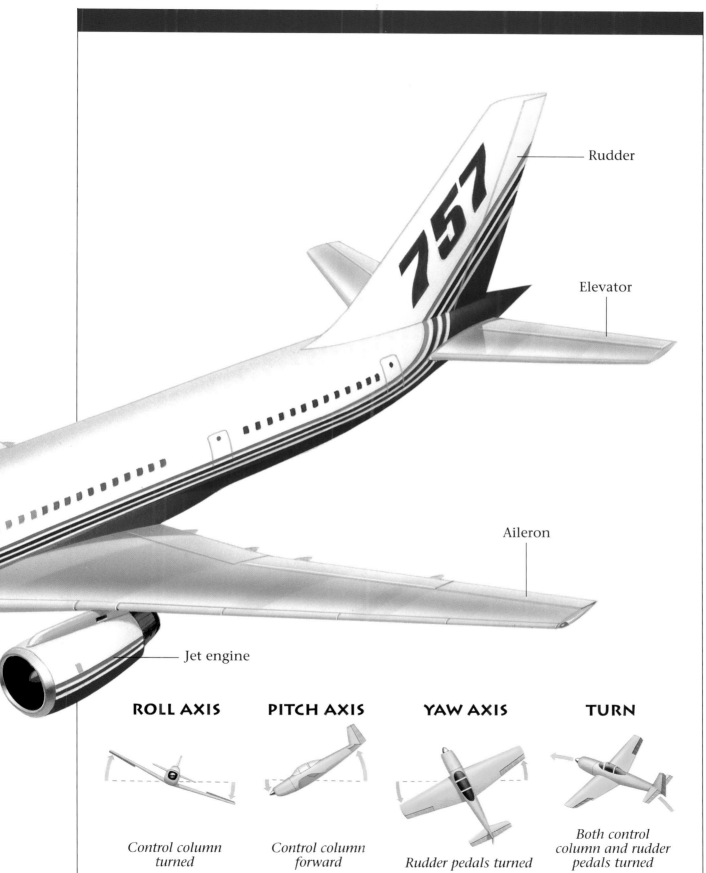

Rudder

Elevator

Aileron

Jet engine

ROLL AXIS

*Control column
turned*

PITCH AXIS

*Control column
forward*

YAW AXIS

Rudder pedals turned

TURN

*Both control
column and rudder
pedals turned*

SUPERSONIC PLANE

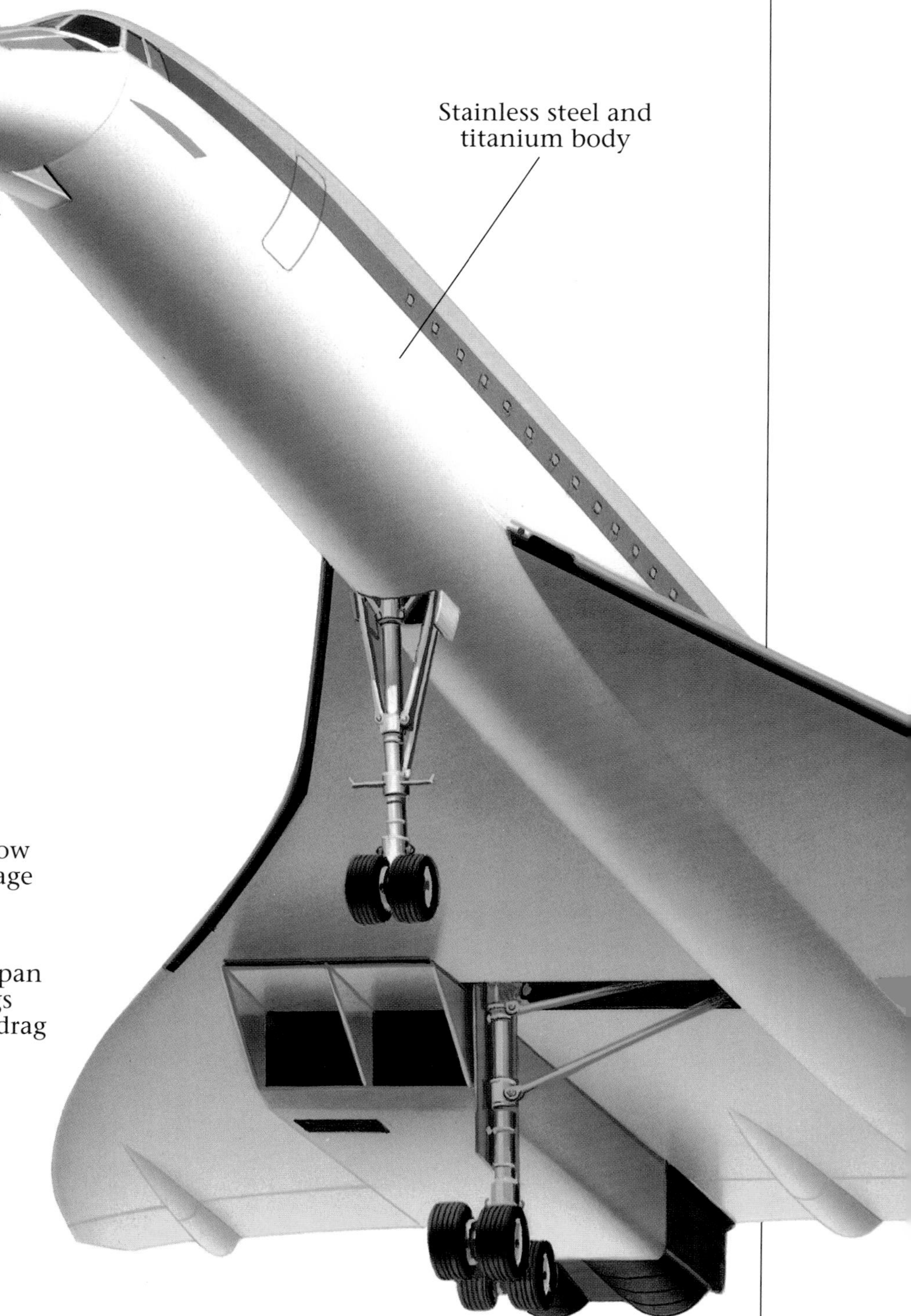

Nose lowers at takeoff and
landing so pilot can see

Stainless steel and
titanium body

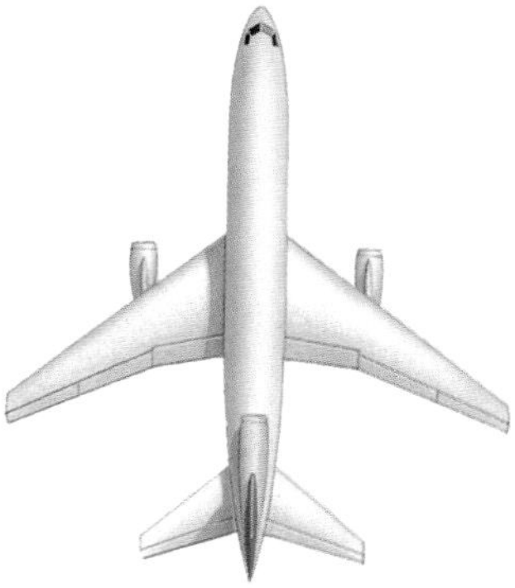

**SUBSONIC
PLANE SHAPE**

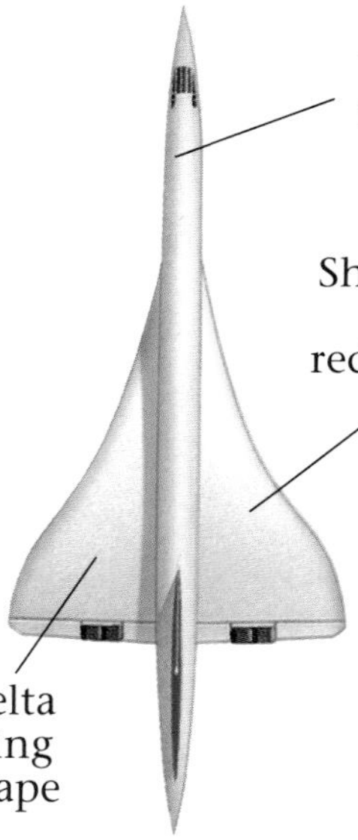

Narrow
fuselage

Short-span
wings
reduce drag

Delta
wing
shape

**SUPERSONIC
PLANE SHAPE**

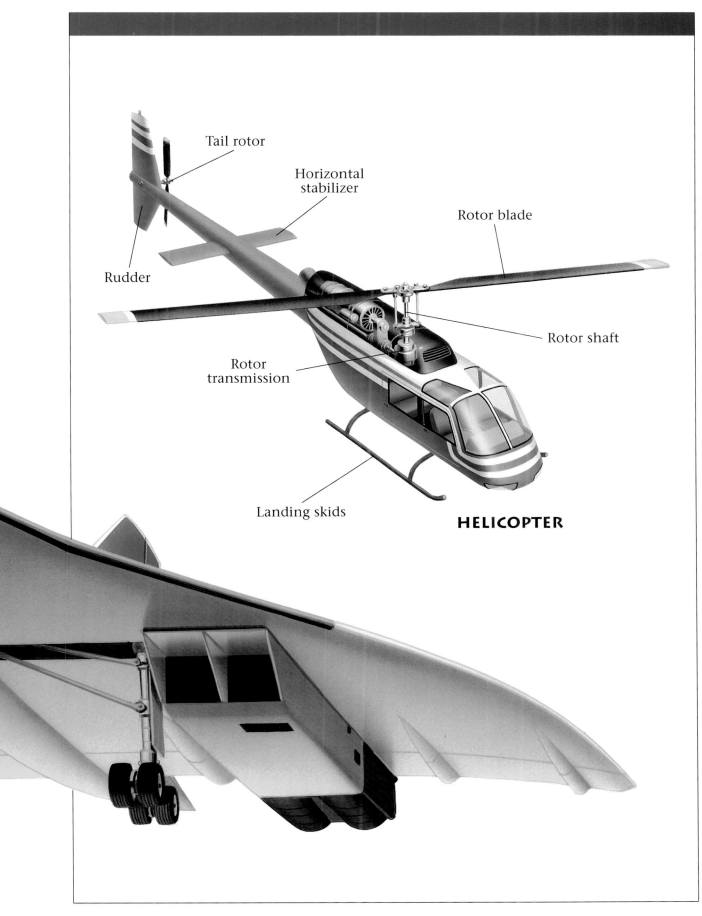

Tail rotor

Horizontal
stabilizer

Rotor blade

Rudder

Rotor shaft

Rotor
transmission

Landing skids

HELICOPTER

HOT-AIR BALLOON

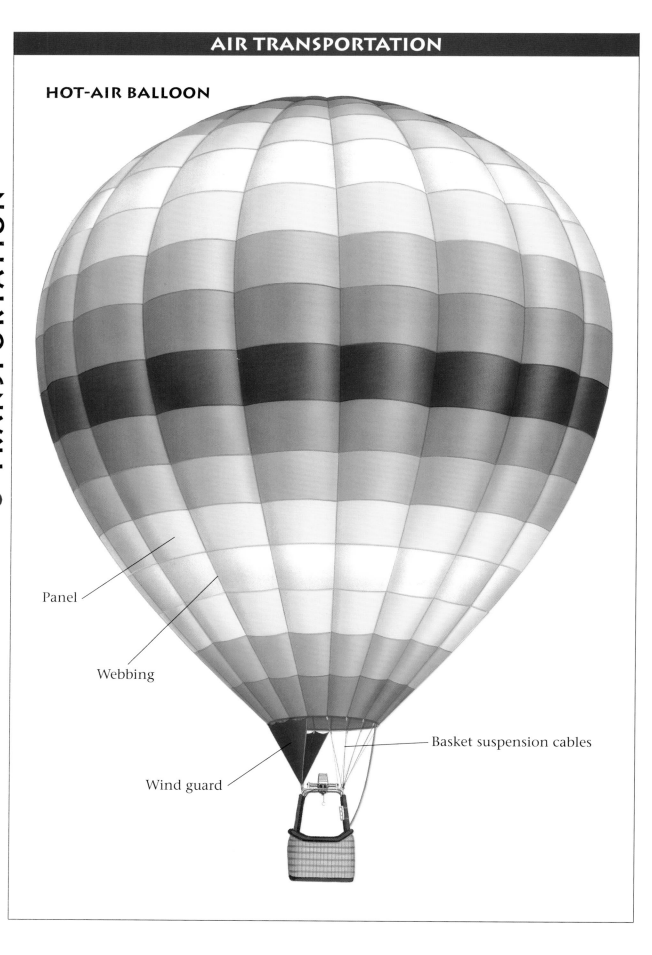

Panel

Webbing

Wind guard

Basket suspension cables

HOT-AIR BALLOON BASKET

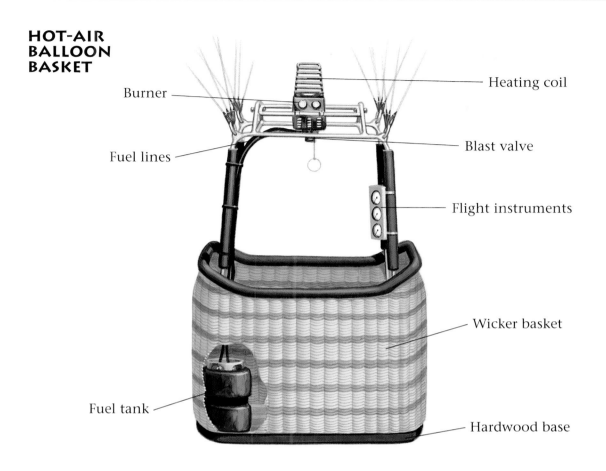

Burner

Fuel lines

Heating coil

Blast valve

Flight instruments

Wicker basket

Fuel tank

Hardwood base

BLIMP

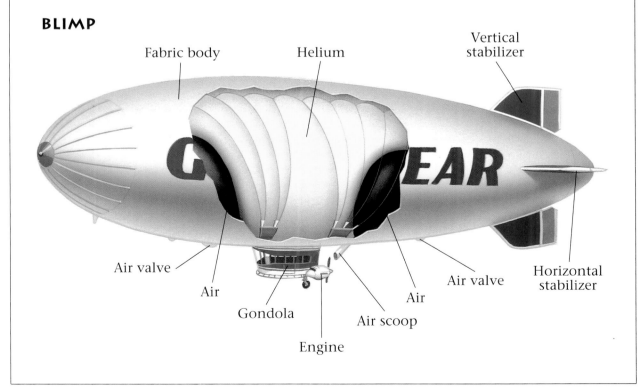

Fabric body

Helium

Vertical stabilizer

Air valve

Air

Gondola

Engine

Air scoop

Air

Air valve

Horizontal stabilizer

HANG GLIDER

GLIDER

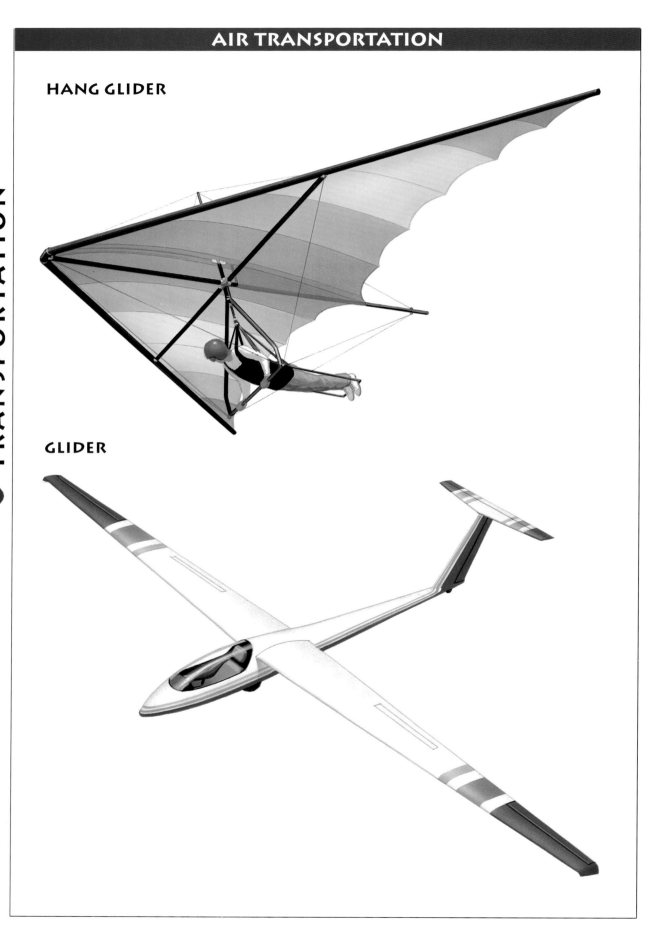

SAILBOAT

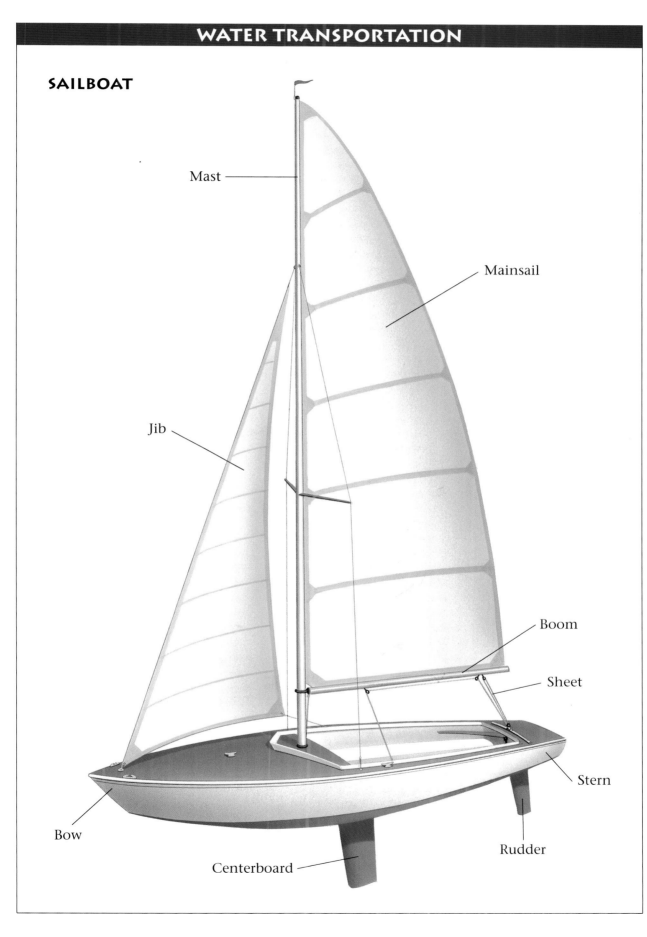

Mast

Mainsail

Jib

Boom

Sheet

Stern

Bow

Rudder

Centerboard

SHIPS AND BOATS

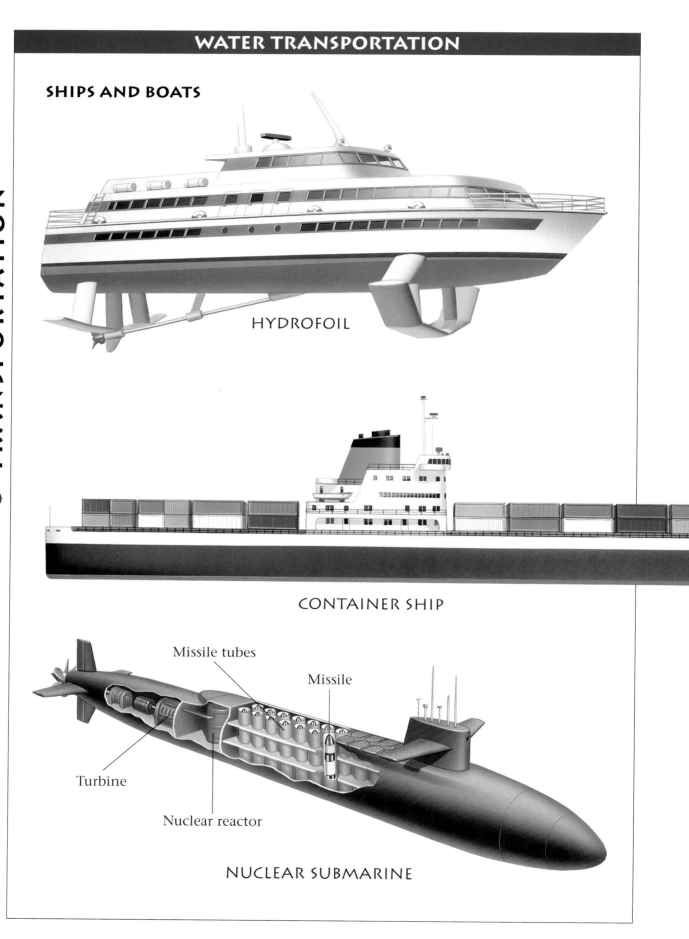

HYDROFOIL

CONTAINER SHIP

Missile tubes

Missile

Turbine

Nuclear reactor

NUCLEAR SUBMARINE

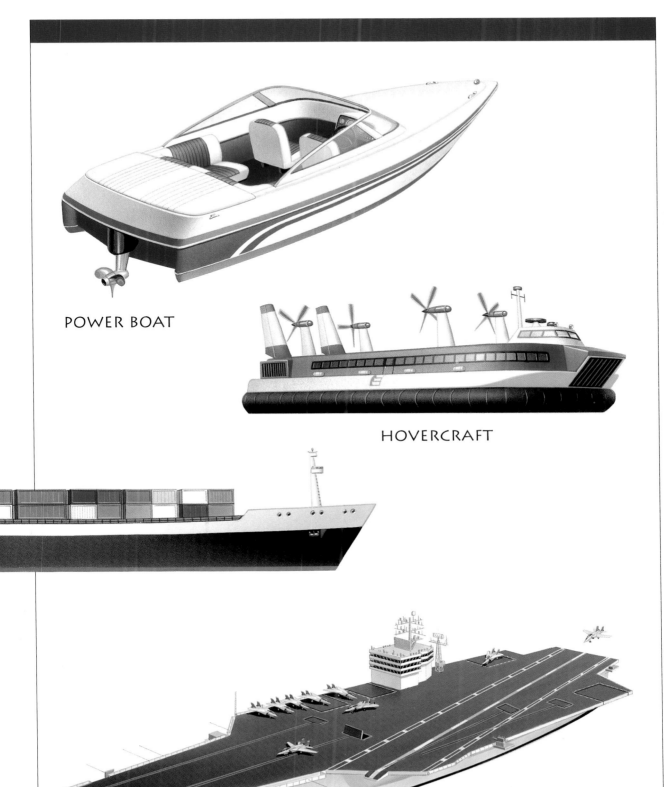

POWER BOAT

HOVERCRAFT

AIRCRAFT CARRIER

AUTOMOBILE

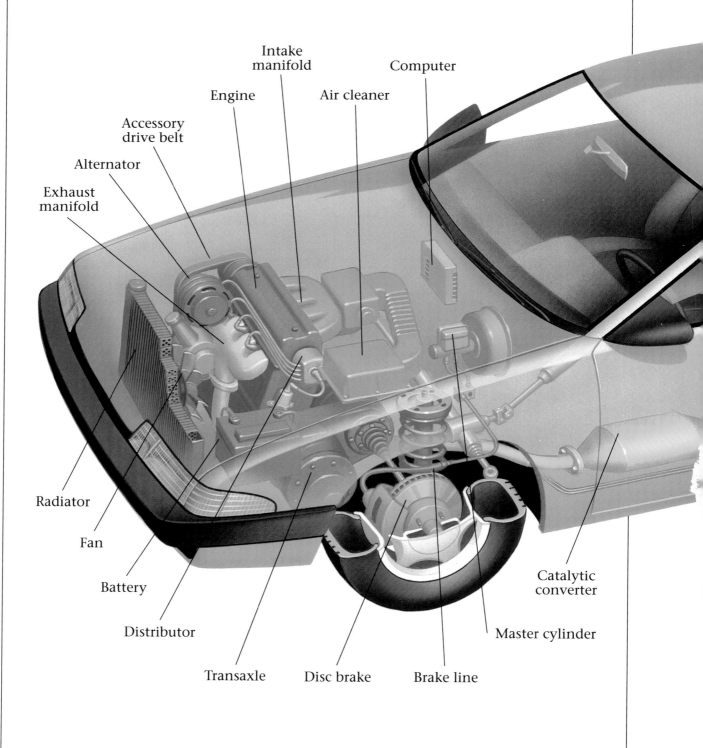

Intake manifold

Computer

Engine

Air cleaner

Accessory drive belt

Alternator

Exhaust manifold

Radiator

Fan

Battery

Distributor

Transaxle

Disc brake

Brake line

Master cylinder

Catalytic converter

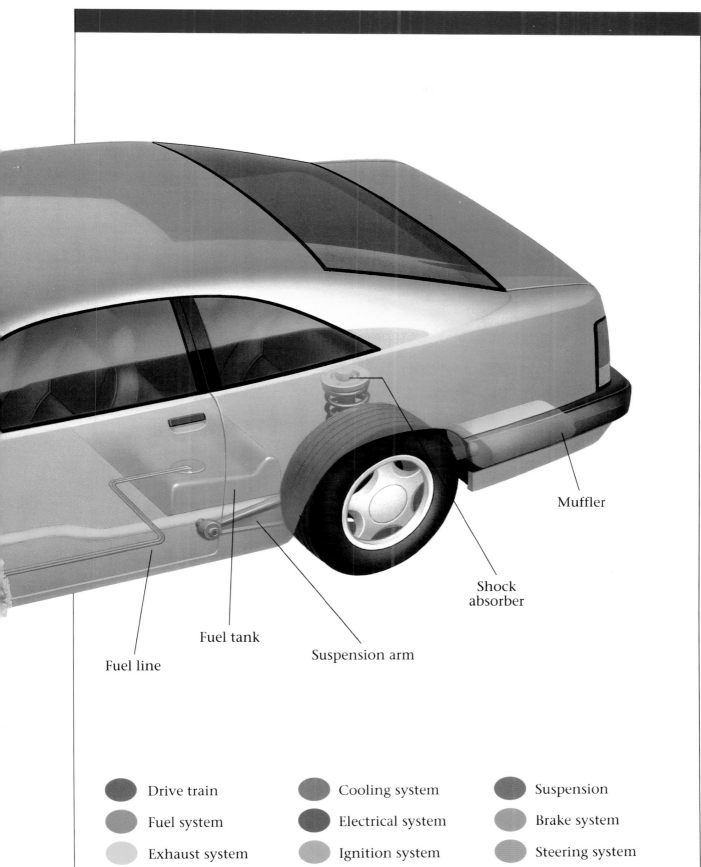

Muffler

Shock
absorber

Fuel tank

Suspension arm

Fuel line

Drive train

Fuel system

Exhaust system

Cooling system

Electrical system

Ignition system

Suspension

Brake system

Steering system

AUTOMOBILE BODY TYPES

TRANSPORTATION

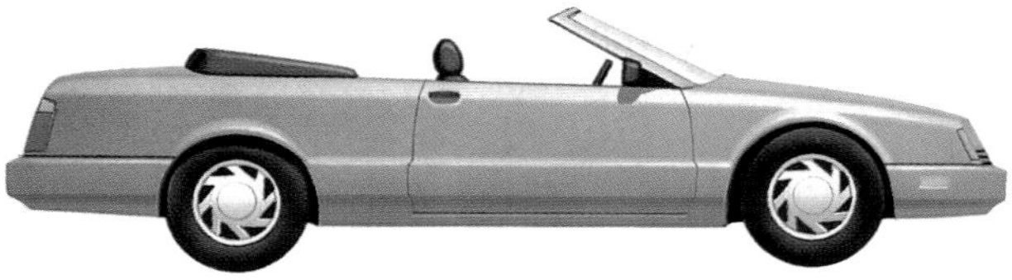

CONVERTIBLE

FOUR-DOOR SEDAN

SPORTS CAR

MINIVAN

HATCHBACK

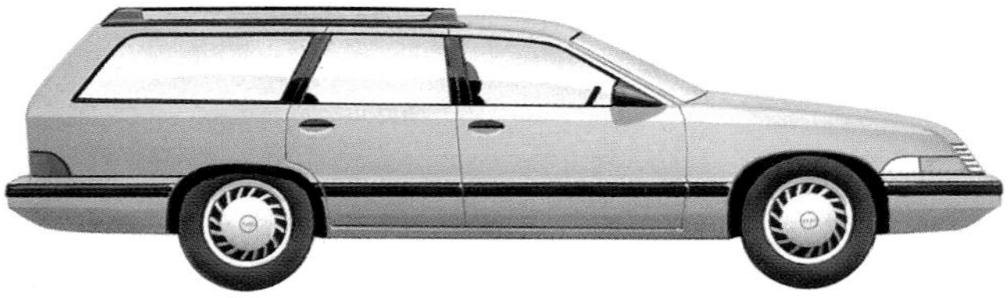

STATION WAGON

TWO-DOOR SEDAN

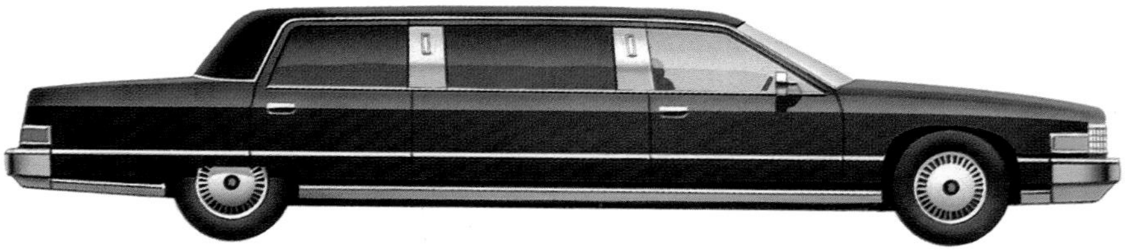

LIMOUSINE

BICYCLE

Shift lever

Handlebars

Brake lever

Brake cable

Caliper brake

Front derailleur

Toe clip

Pedal

Rear derailleur

Drive chain

MOTORCYCLE

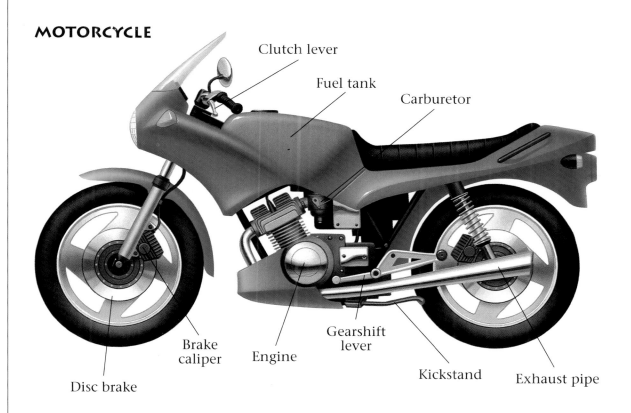

Clutch lever

Fuel tank

Carburetor

Gearshift lever

Brake caliper

Engine

Kickstand

Exhaust pipe

Disc brake

BUS

TROLLEY

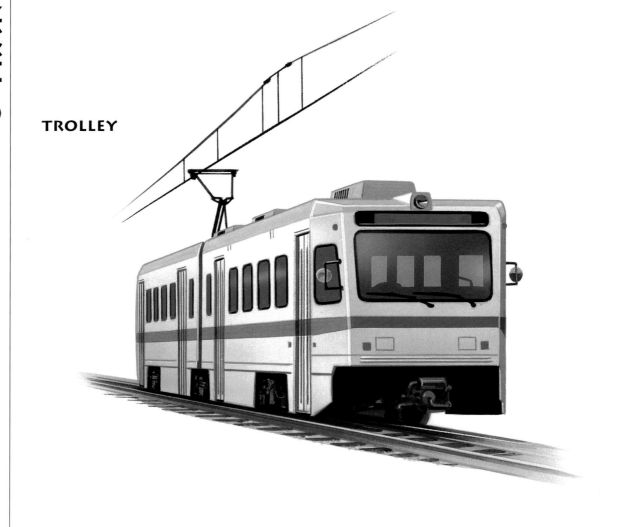

SUBWAY TRAIN

HIGH-SPEED TRAIN

DIESEL-ELECTRIC LOCOMOTIVE

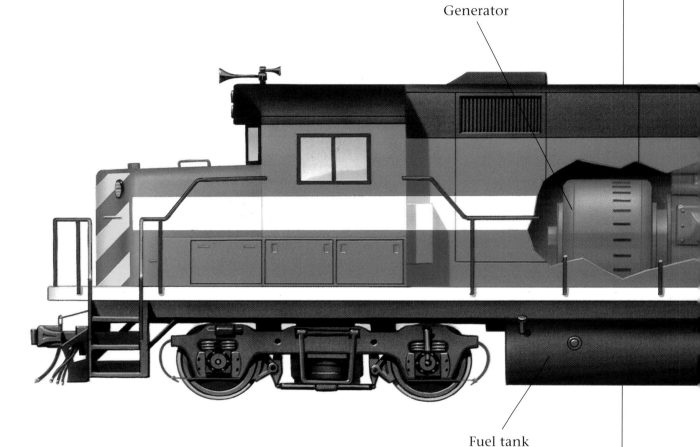

Generator

Fuel tank

TYPES OF FREIGHT CARS

HOPPER CAR

ENCLOSED HOPPER

BOXCAR

PIGGYBACK CAR

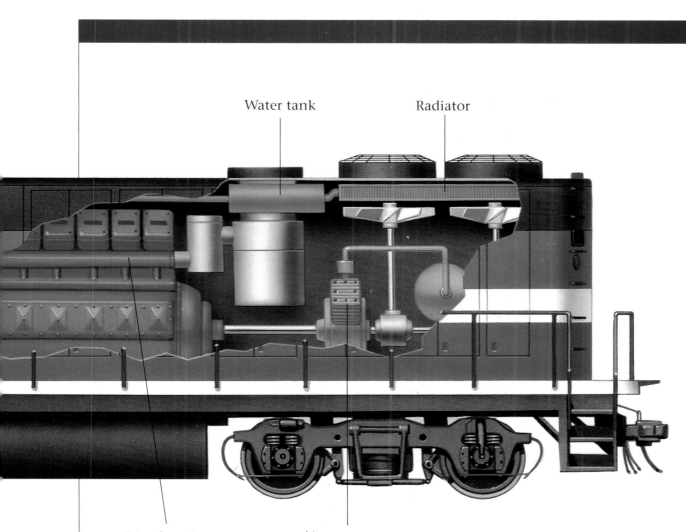

Water tank

Radiator

Diesel engine

Air compressor

AUTOMOBILE CARRIER

CONCRETE MIXER

TANK TRAILER

AUTO HAULER

SEMI-TRACTOR TRAILER

PICKUP TRUCK

VAN

DUMP TRUCK

CAB

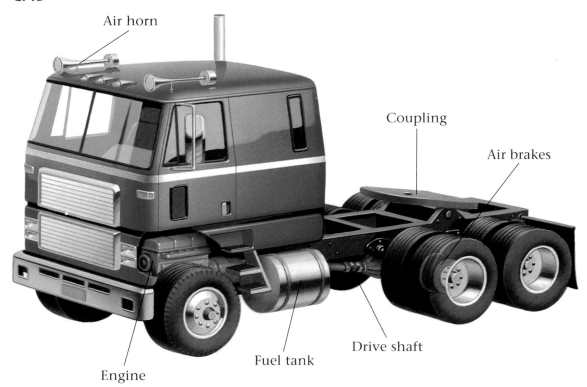

Air horn

Coupling

Air brakes

Engine

Fuel tank

Drive shaft

TRAILER

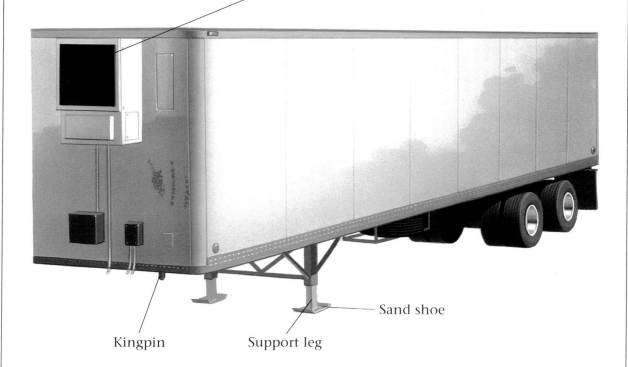

Refrigeration unit

Sand shoe

Kingpin

Support leg

HEAVY MACHINERY

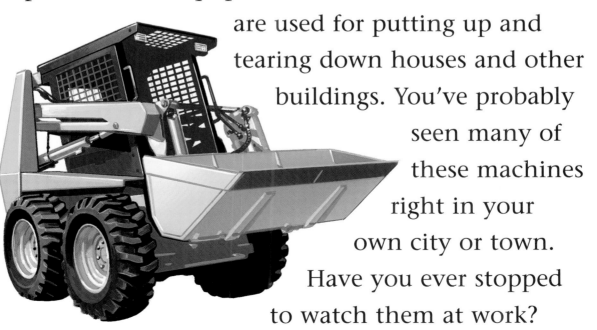

TODAY, PEOPLE RELY on machines to do many difficult jobs. The machines you'll see in the following pages are large and power-ful. Most of them can quickly perform tasks that would otherwise take many people and many hours to finish. Each of these machines is made to do a specific kind of work. Tractors and combines are important farm equipment. Bulldozers and cranes are used for putting up and tearing down houses and other buildings. You've probably seen many of these machines right in your own city or town. Have you ever stopped to watch them at work?

HEAVY MACHINERY

PUMPING TRUCK

Hydrant intake

Control stand

ELEVATING PLATFORM TRUCK

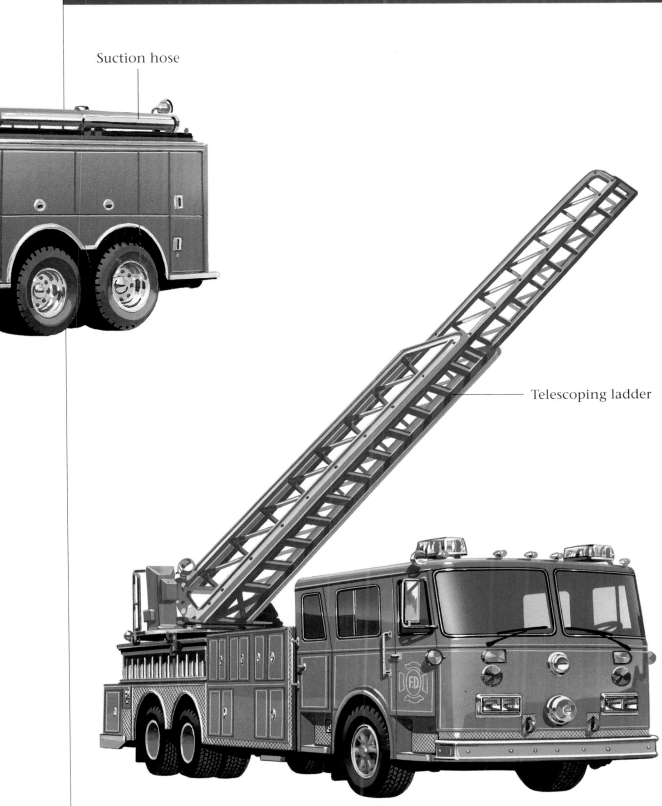

Suction hose

Telescoping ladder

AERIAL LADDER TRUCK

STREET SWEEPER

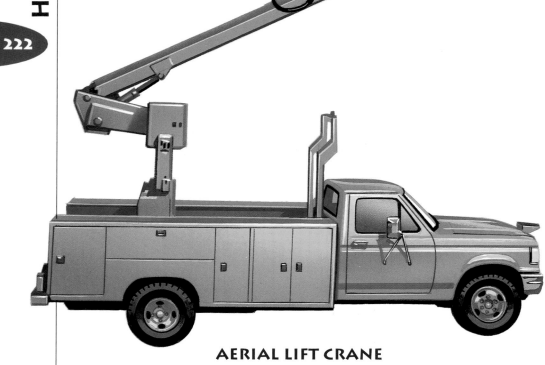

Work bucket

AERIAL LIFT CRANE

GARBAGE TRUCK

SNOWPLOW

TRACTOR

HAY BALER

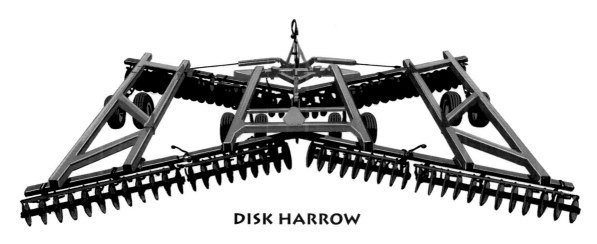

DISK HARROW

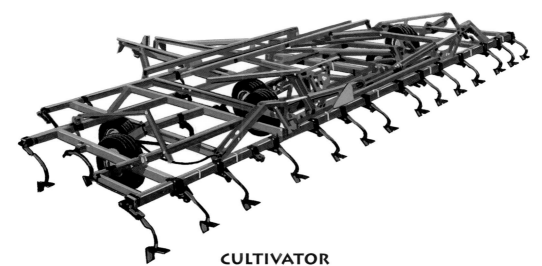

CULTIVATOR

Pickup reel

Divider

COMBINE

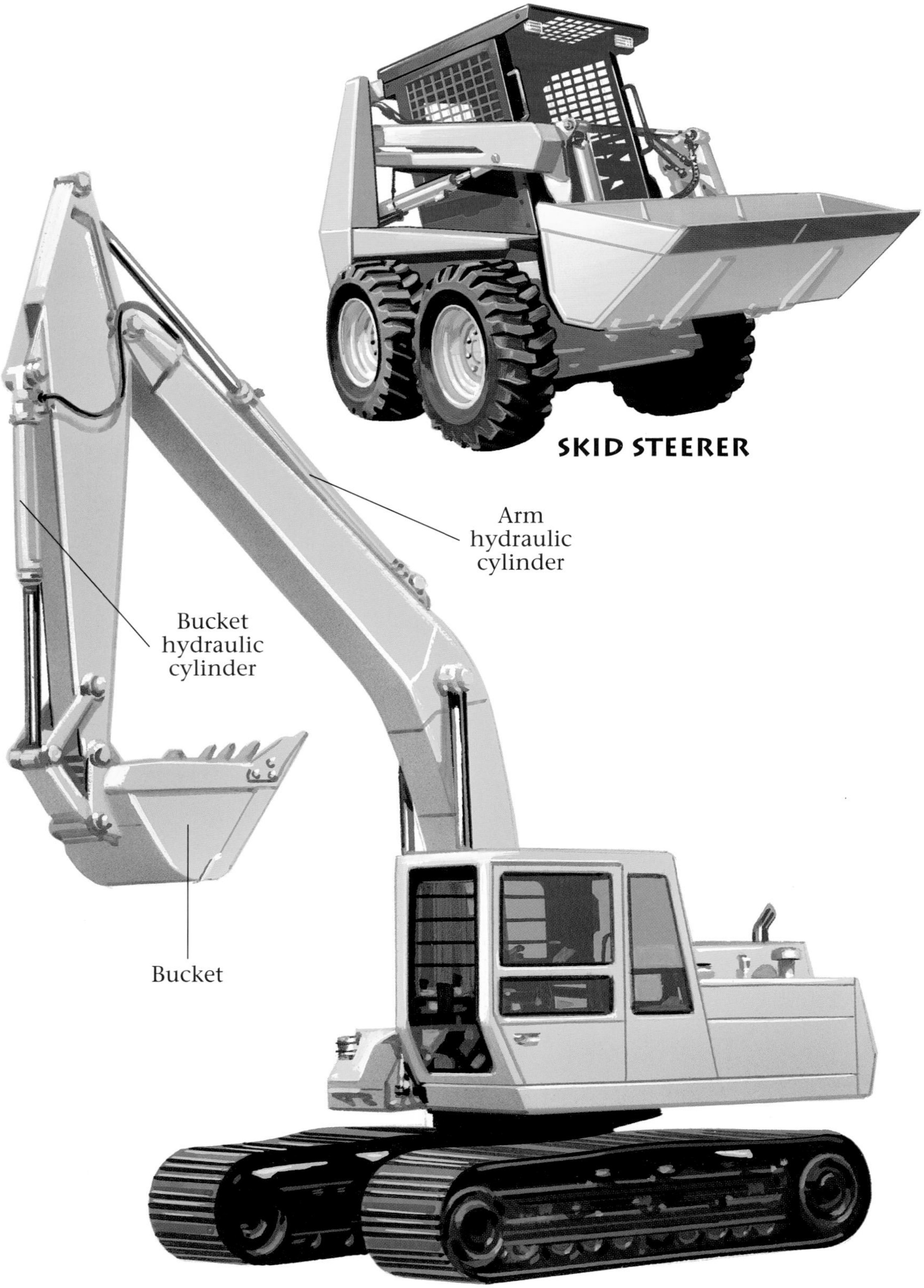

SKID STEERER

Arm
hydraulic
cylinder

Bucket
hydraulic
cylinder

Bucket

BACKHOE

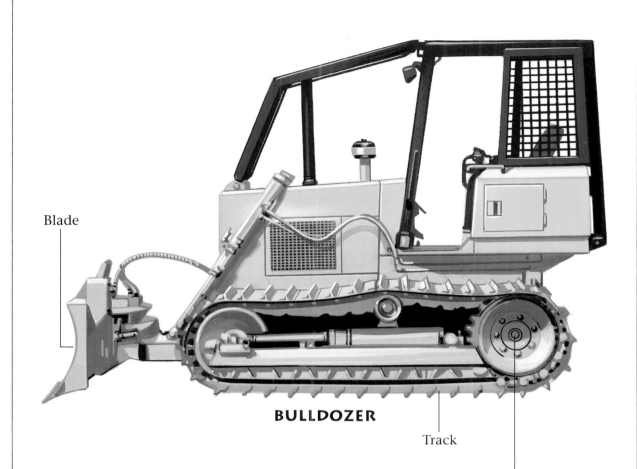

Blade

BULLDOZER

Track

Sprocket wheel

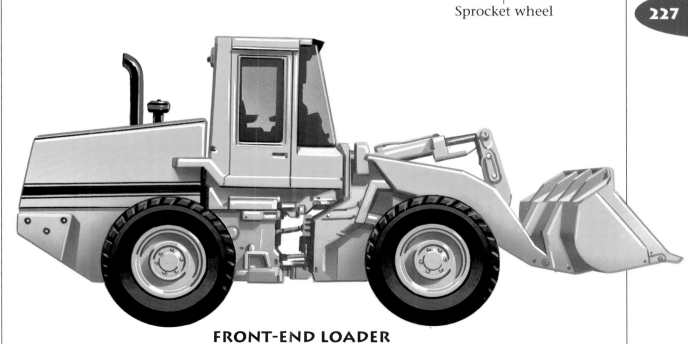

FRONT-END LOADER

HEAVY MACHINERY

TOWER CRANE

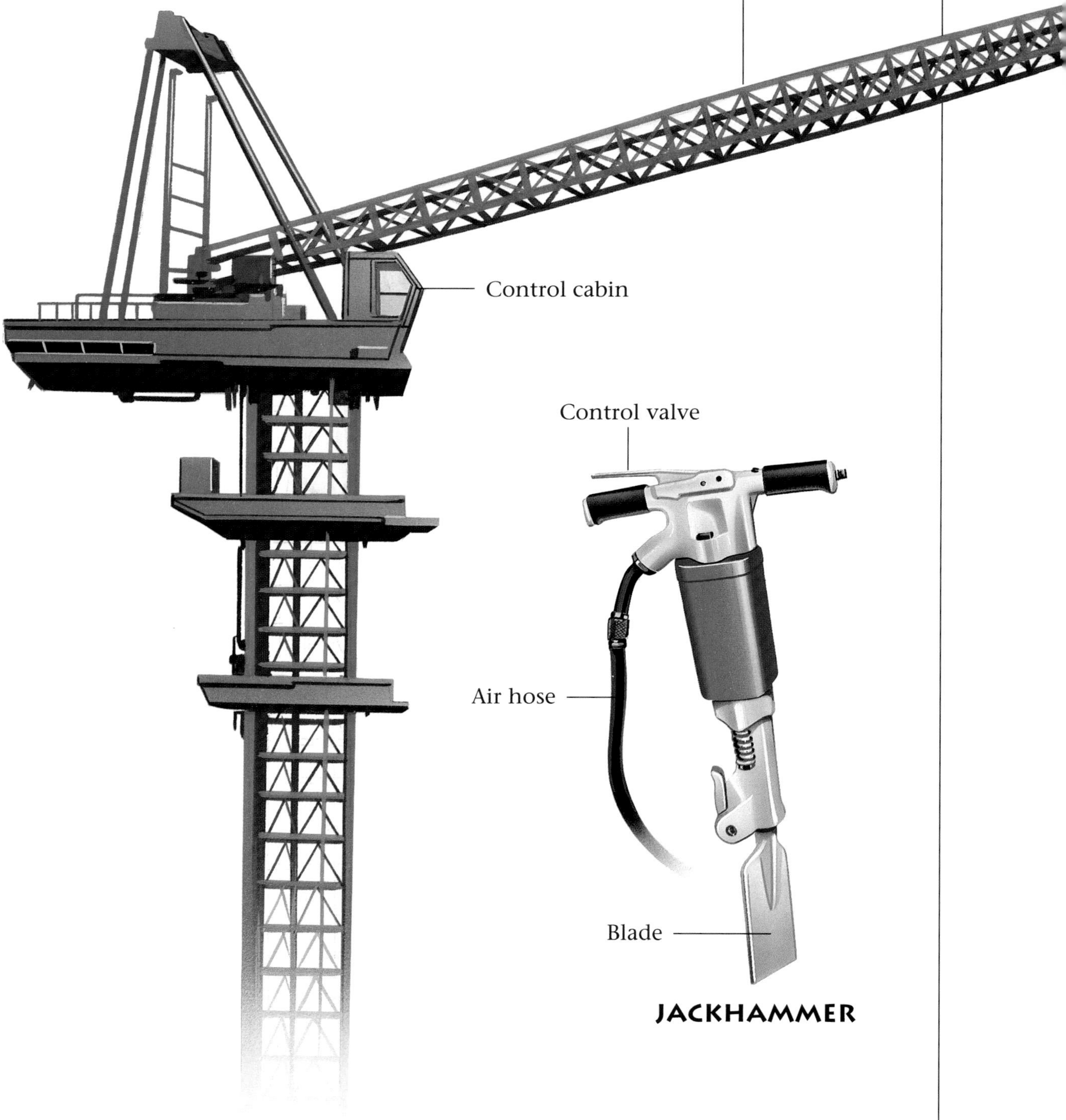

Boom

Control cabin

Control valve

Air hose

Blade

JACKHAMMER

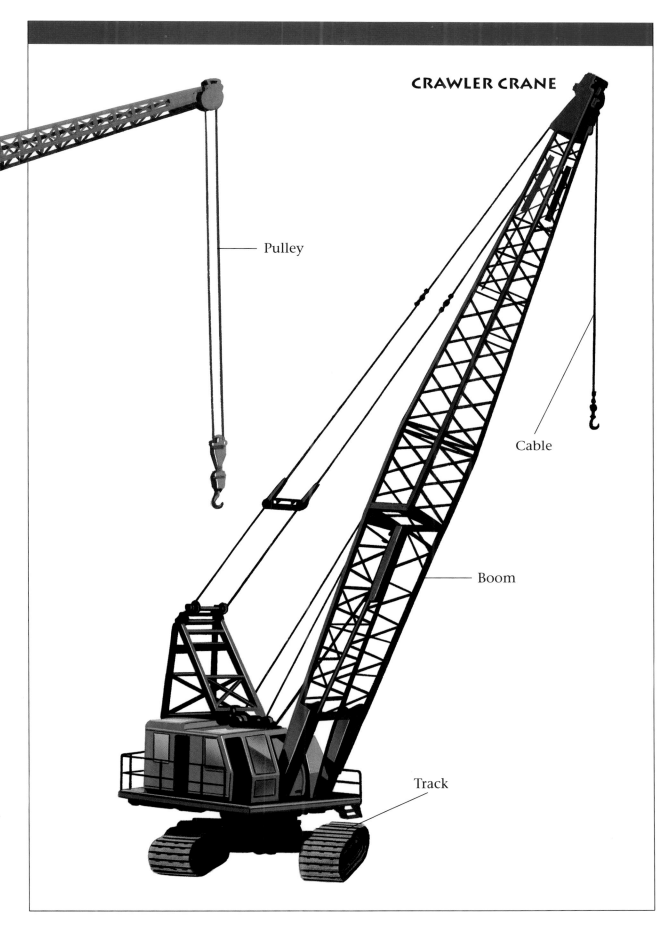

Pulley

Cable

Boom

Track

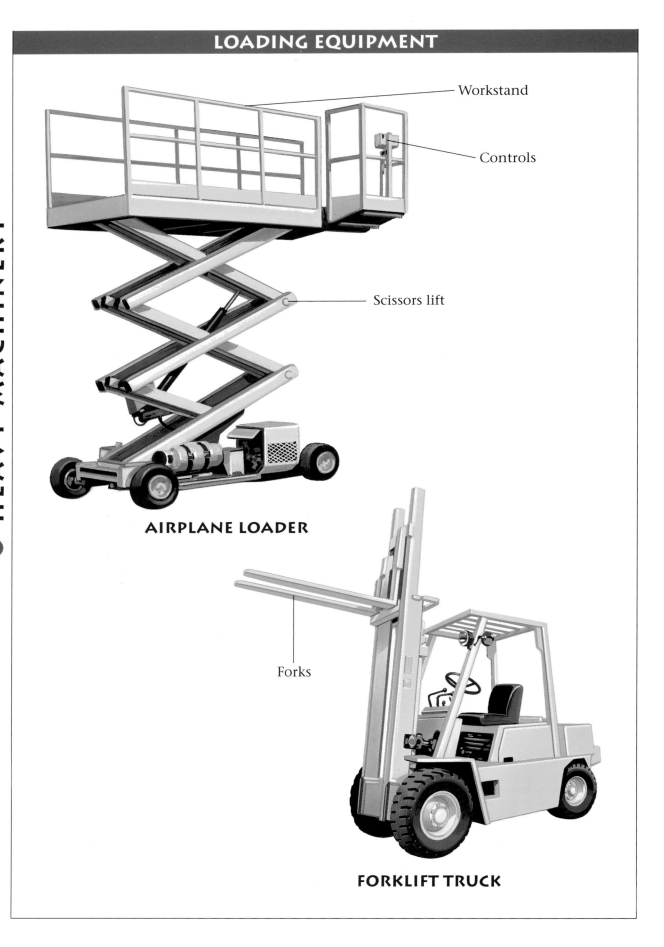

Workstand

Controls

Scissors lift

AIRPLANE LOADER

Forks

FORKLIFT TRUCK

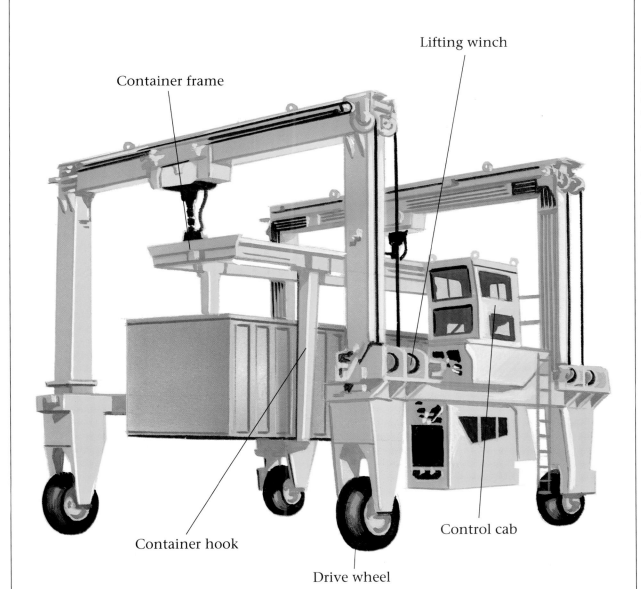

Container frame

Lifting winch

Container hook

Control cab

Drive wheel

STRADDLE CRANE

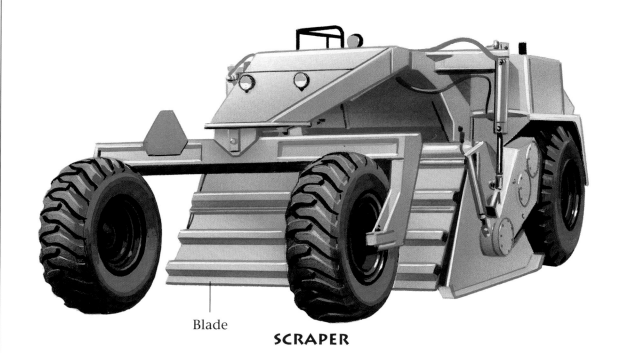

Blade

SCRAPER

ROLLER

COMMUNICATIONS

COMMUNICATION IS THE way that we express our thoughts, feelings, and ideas. Communication allows us to share information with each other. We use speech, writing, facial expressions, body language, and pictures to communicate. In this section, you'll find information about many of the devices we use to communicate today. Some of these devices have become available for us to use only in the last few years. Some will be familiar items you have in your own home. Others may be new to you. Which of the devices in this section do you use the most? How do these items make a difference in your life?

COMMUNICATIONS

234

CELLULAR TELEPHONE

CELLULAR TELEPHONE NETWORK

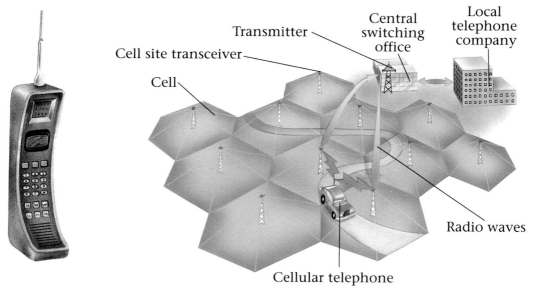

Transmitter
Central switching office
Local telephone company
Cell site transceiver
Cell
Radio waves
Cellular telephone

CORDLESS TELEPHONE

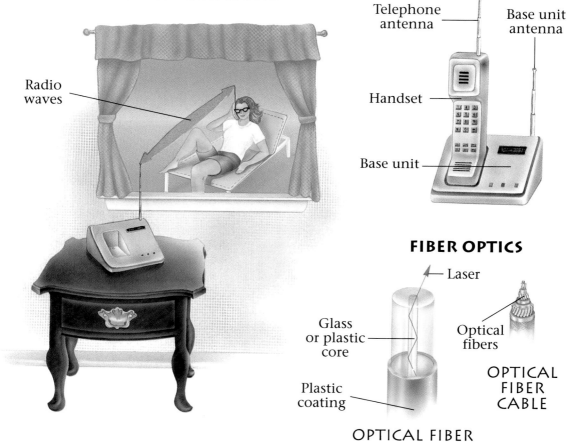

Radio waves

Telephone antenna
Base unit antenna
Handset
Base unit

FIBER OPTICS

Laser
Glass or plastic core
Optical fibers
Plastic coating

OPTICAL FIBER CABLE

OPTICAL FIBER

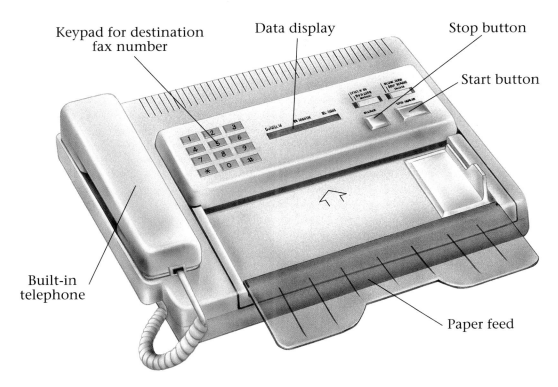

Keypad for destination fax number

Data display

Stop button

Start button

Built-in telephone

Paper feed

COMMUNICATIONS

235

SENDING

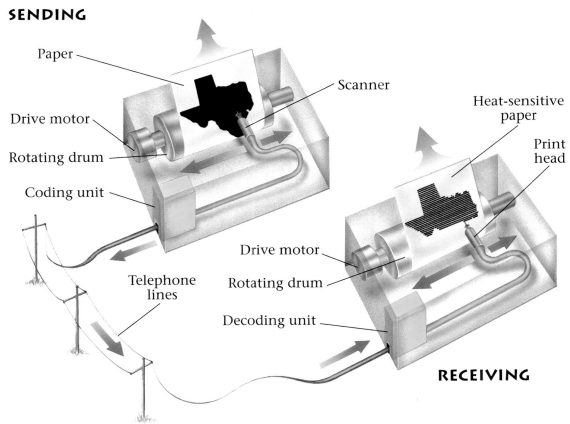

Paper

Scanner

Drive motor

Rotating drum

Coding unit

Heat-sensitive paper

Print head

Drive motor

Rotating drum

Telephone lines

Decoding unit

RECEIVING

COMMUNICATIONS

PERSONAL COMPUTER INTERIOR (MOTHERBOARD)

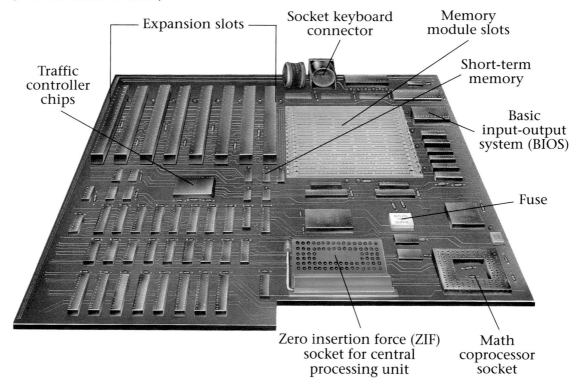

Expansion slots

Socket keyboard connector

Memory module slots

Traffic controller chips

Short-term memory

Basic input-output system (BIOS)

Fuse

Zero insertion force (ZIF) socket for central processing unit

Math coprocessor socket

PERIPHERALS

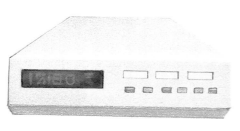

MODEM

SCANNER

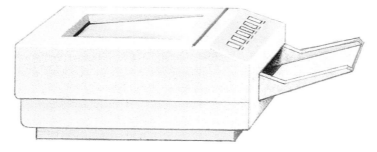

LASER PRINTER

236

PERSONAL COMPUTER

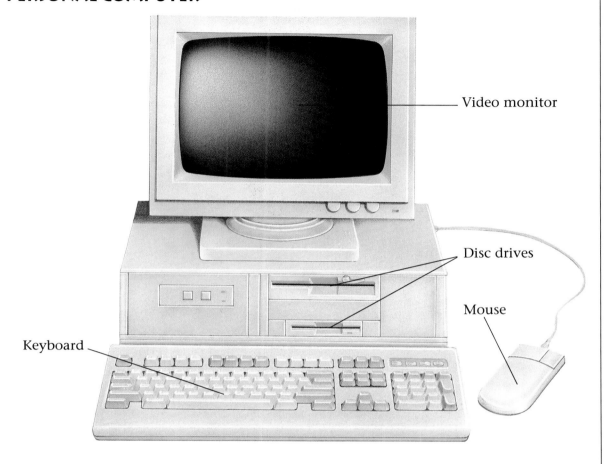

Video monitor

Disc drives

Mouse

Keyboard

OPTICAL DISC

OPTICAL DRIVE

DISKETTE

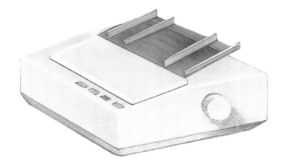

DOT-MATRIX PRINTER

CD-ROM DRIVE

POSSIBLE PATH OF AN ELECTRONIC MAIL MESSAGE

Router

Mainframe computer

Sender

Router

Internet backbone

Telephone lines

Mainframe computer

Telephone lines

Internet backbone

Router

Router

Mainframe computer

Receiver

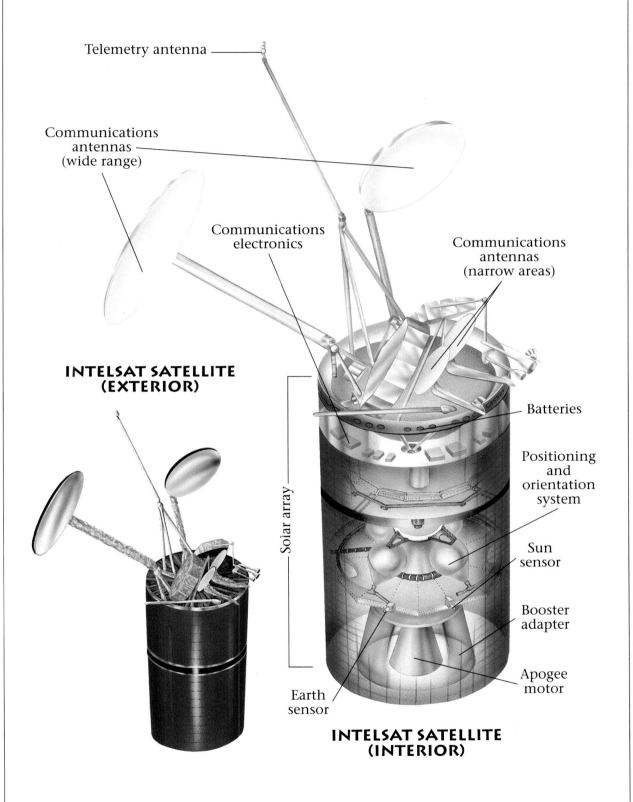

Telemetry antenna

Communications antennas (wide range)

Communications electronics

Communications antennas (narrow areas)

Batteries

Positioning and orientation system

Sun sensor

Booster adapter

Apogee motor

Earth sensor

Solar array

INTELSAT SATELLITE (EXTERIOR)

INTELSAT SATELLITE (INTERIOR)

COMMUNICATIONS

COLOR TELEVISION

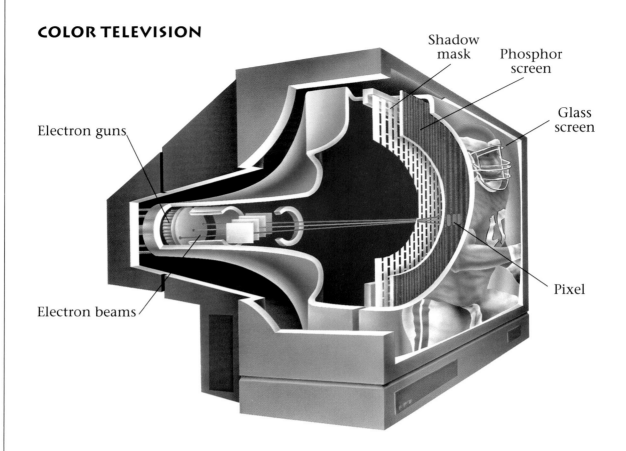

Shadow mask

Phosphor screen

Glass screen

Electron guns

Electron beams

Pixel

VIDEO CAMERA

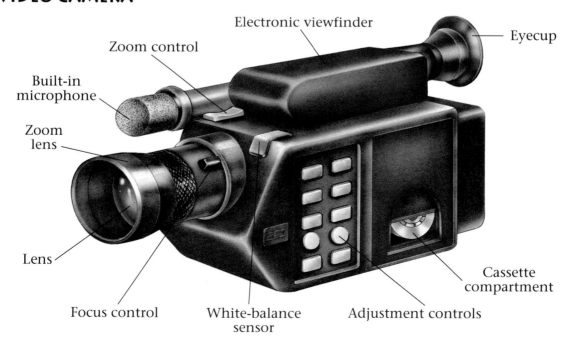

Electronic viewfinder

Eyecup

Zoom control

Built-in microphone

Zoom lens

Lens

Focus control

White-balance sensor

Adjustment controls

Cassette compartment

VIDEOTAPE PLAYER

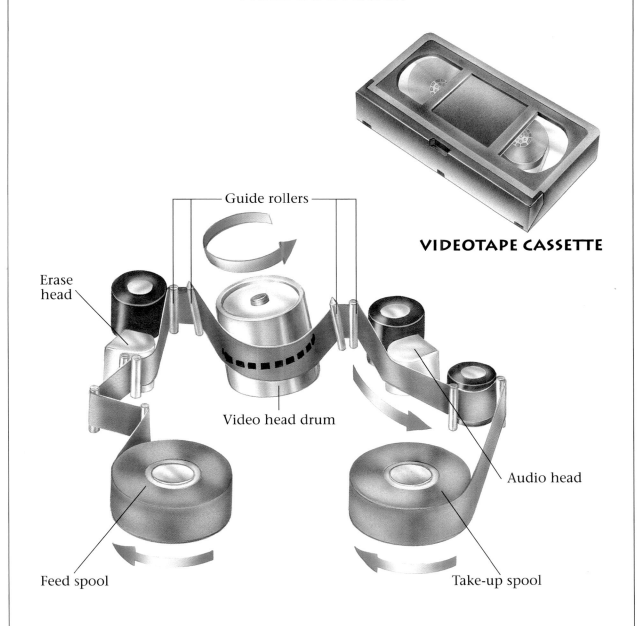

VIDEOTAPE CASSETTE

Guide rollers

Erase
head

Video head drum

Audio head

Feed spool

Take-up spool

COMMUNICATIONS

RADIO RECEIVER

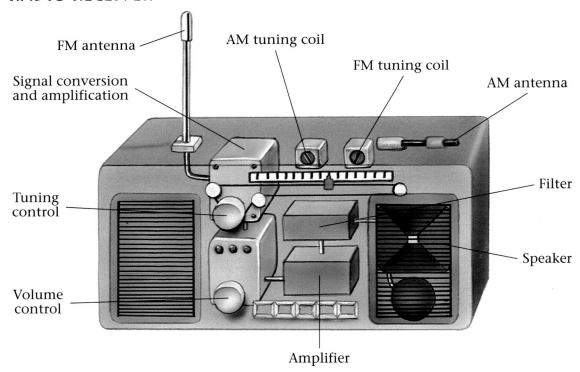

FM antenna

AM tuning coil

FM tuning coil

AM antenna

Signal conversion and amplification

Filter

Tuning control

Speaker

Volume control

Amplifier

RADIO TRANSMISSION

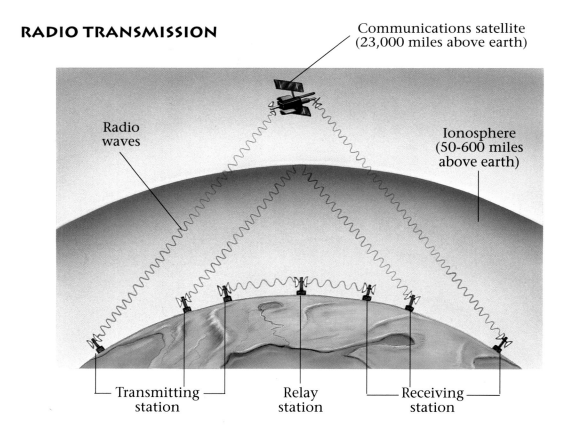

Communications satellite (23,000 miles above earth)

Radio waves

Ionosphere (50-600 miles above earth)

Transmitting station

Relay station

Receiving station

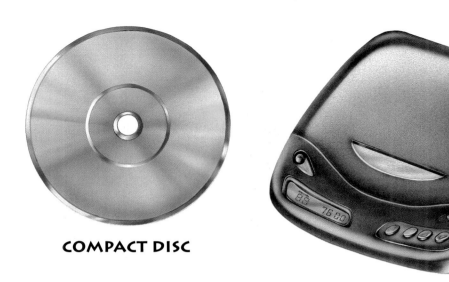

COMPACT DISC

COMPACT DISC PLAYER

COMPACT DISC PLAYER INTERIOR

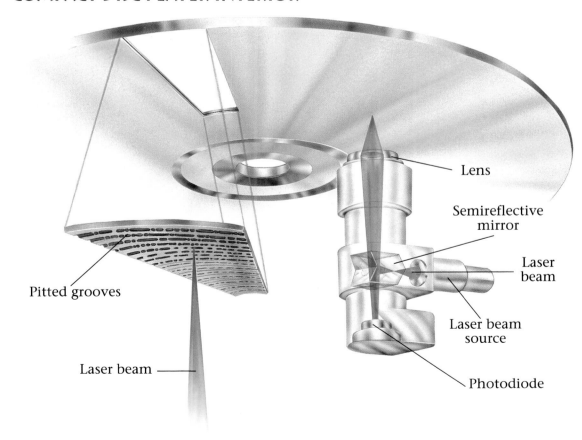

Lens

Semireflective
mirror

Laser
beam

Pitted grooves

Laser beam
source

Laser beam

Photodiode

GROUND STATION FOR TELEVISION BROADCASTING NETWORK

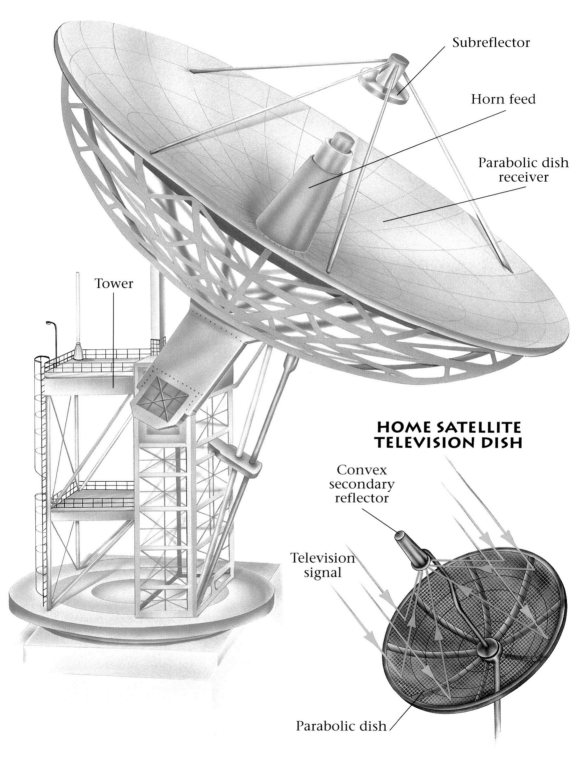

Subreflector

Horn feed

Parabolic dish receiver

Tower

HOME SATELLITE TELEVISION DISH

Convex secondary reflector

Television signal

Parabolic dish

ENERGY

EVERY TIME WE FLIP ON A light switch, cook on a stove, or ride in a car, we are using some kind of energy. The energy we use this way comes from many different sources. The movement of water and of wind can create energy for us to use. The heat of the sun is a great source of energy. We get energy from fossil fuels—coal, oil, and natural gas—and from chemical reactions in batteries. We also use the energy that is released by nuclear fission. What are some of the ways that you use energy in your life every day? Do you know where this energy comes from and how it gets to you to use?

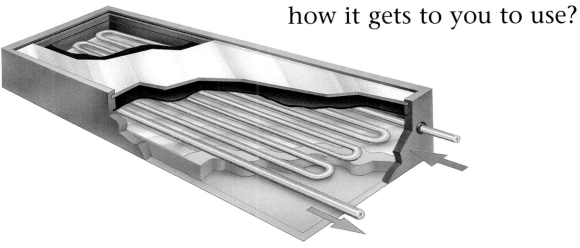

SOLAR WATER HEATER

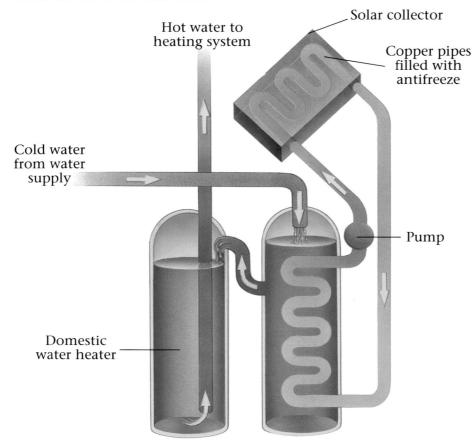

Hot water to
heating system

Solar collector

Copper pipes
filled with
antifreeze

Cold water
from water
supply

Pump

Domestic
water heater

FLAT-PLATE SOLAR COLLECTOR

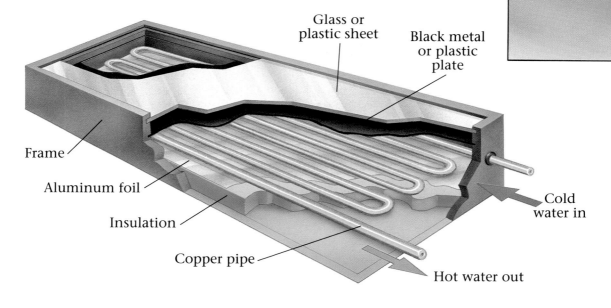

Glass or
plastic sheet

Black metal
or plastic
plate

Frame

Aluminum foil

Insulation

Copper pipe

Cold
water in

Hot water out

ENERGY

246

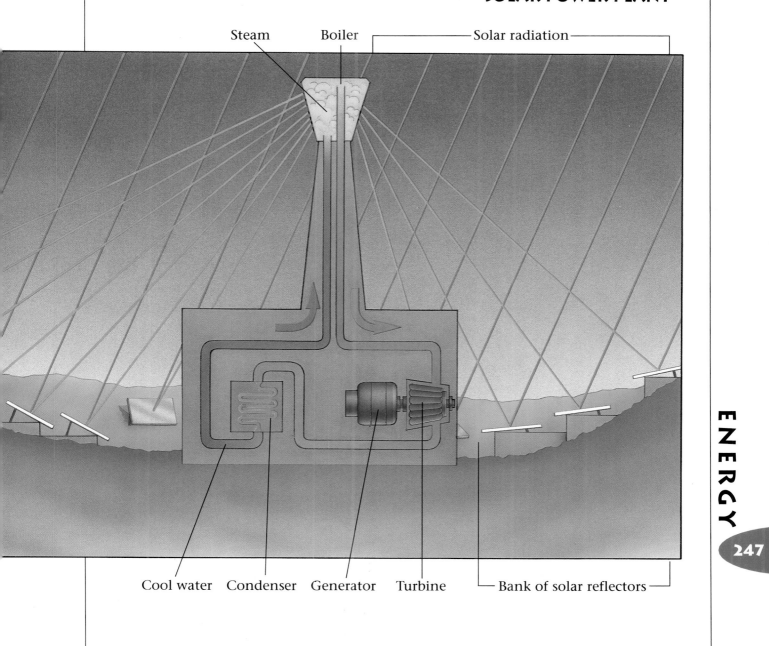

Steam   Boiler   Solar radiation

Cool water   Condenser   Generator   Turbine   Bank of solar reflectors

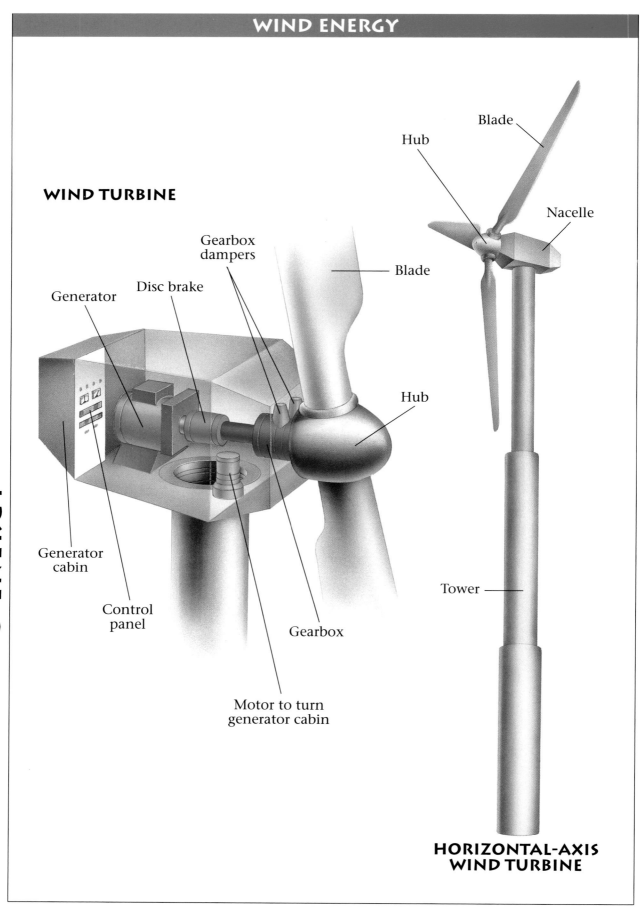

WIND TURBINE

Gearbox
dampers

Disc brake

Generator

Blade

Hub

Generator
cabin

Control
panel

Gearbox

Motor to turn
generator cabin

Blade

Hub

Nacelle

Tower

**HORIZONTAL-AXIS
WIND TURBINE**

ENERGY

248

TYPES OF WIND TURBINES

HORIZONTAL-AXIS

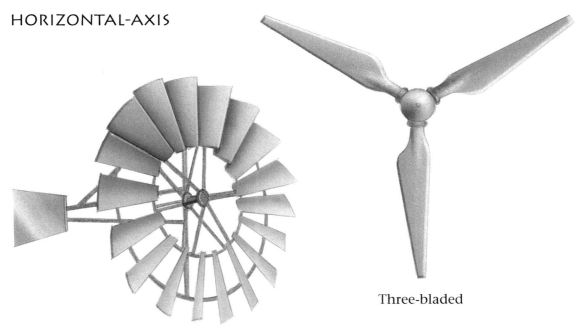

Multibladed farm
windmill

Three-bladed

VERTICAL-AXIS

Cross-arm rotor

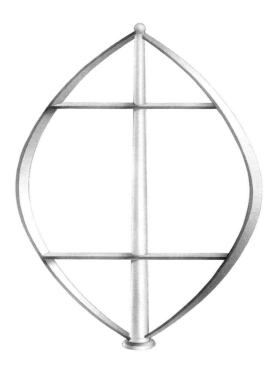

Darrieus rotor

OFFSHORE DRILLING RIG

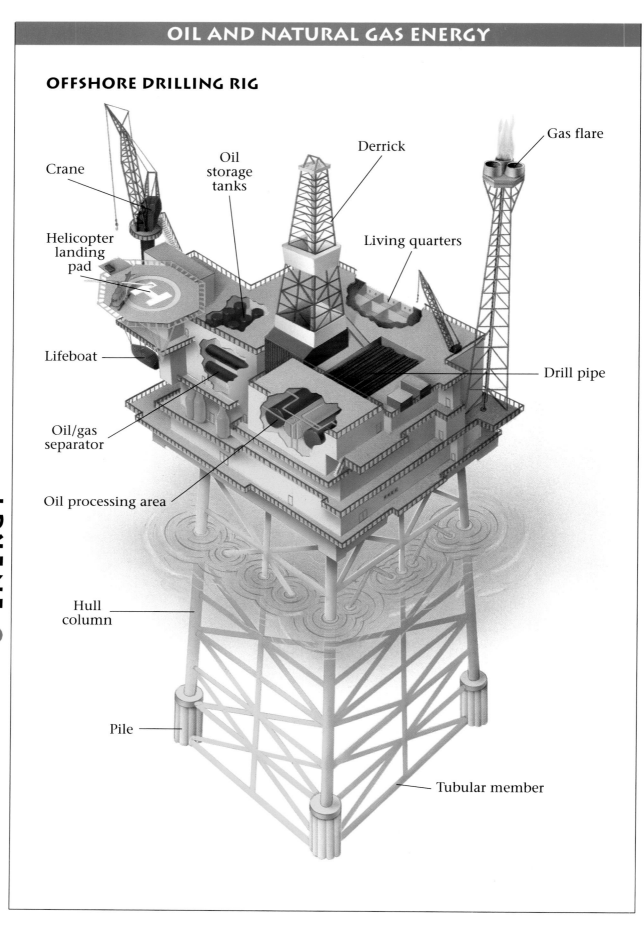

Crane

Oil storage tanks

Derrick

Gas flare

Helicopter landing pad

Living quarters

Lifeboat

Drill pipe

Oil/gas separator

Oil processing area

Hull column

Pile

Tubular member

PARTS OF AN OIL DERRICK

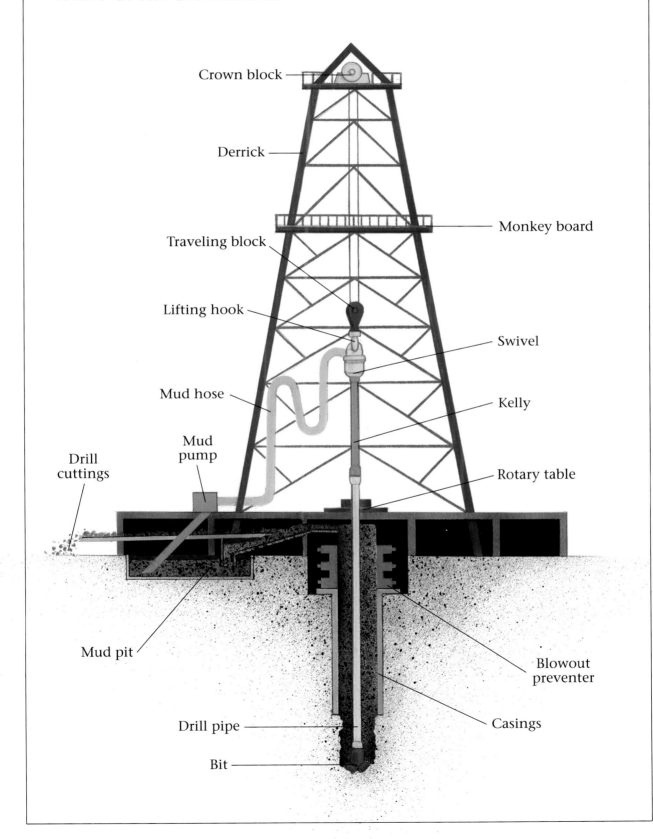

Crown block

Derrick

Traveling block

Lifting hook

Mud hose

Mud pump

Drill cuttings

Mud pit

Drill pipe

Bit

Monkey board

Swivel

Kelly

Rotary table

Blowout preventer

Casings

TYPES OF DRILLING RIGS

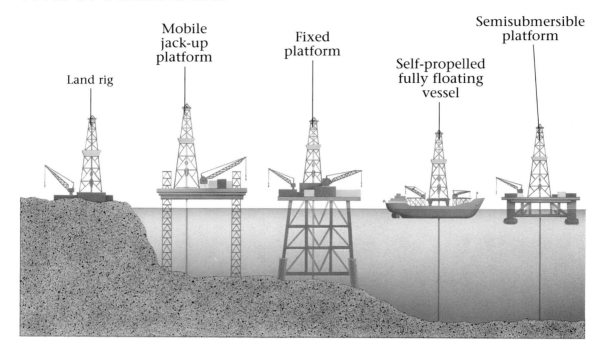

Land rig

Mobile jack-up platform

Fixed platform

Self-propelled fully floating vessel

Semisubmersible platform

DRILL BITS

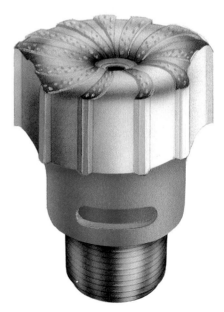

ROLLER BIT

DIAMOND BIT

COAL-FIRED POWER STATION

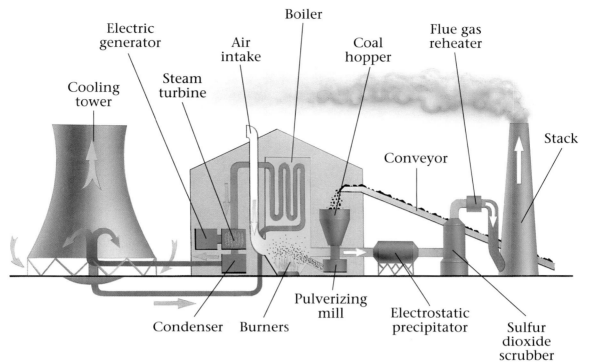

Cooling tower · Electric generator · Steam turbine · Air intake · Boiler · Coal hopper · Flue gas reheater · Conveyor · Stack · Condenser · Burners · Pulverizing mill · Electrostatic precipitator · Sulfur dioxide scrubber

MAJOR VARIETIES OF COAL MINES

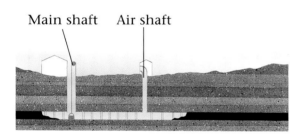

Main shaft · Air shaft

SHAFT MINE

DRIFT MINE

SLOPE MINE

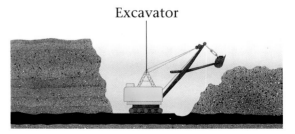

Excavator

SURFACE MINE

HYDROELECTRIC POWER STATION

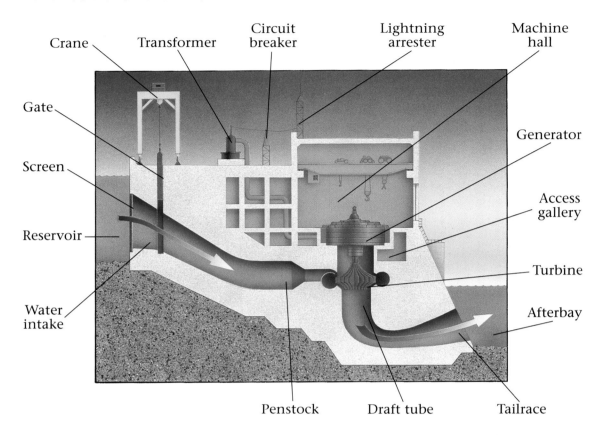

Crane — Transformer — Circuit breaker — Lightning arrester — Machine hall

Gate

Screen

Reservoir

Water intake

Generator

Access gallery

Turbine

Afterbay

Penstock — Draft tube — Tailrace

HYDROELECTRIC DAM

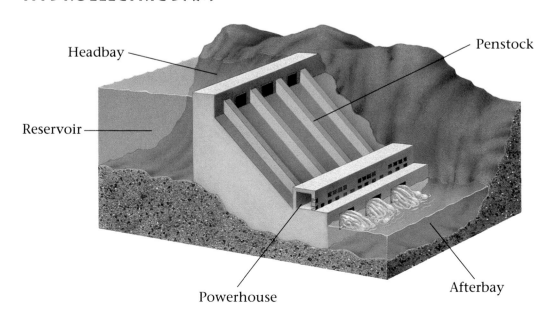

Headbay

Penstock

Reservoir

Powerhouse

Afterbay

ELECTRICITY DISTRIBUTION

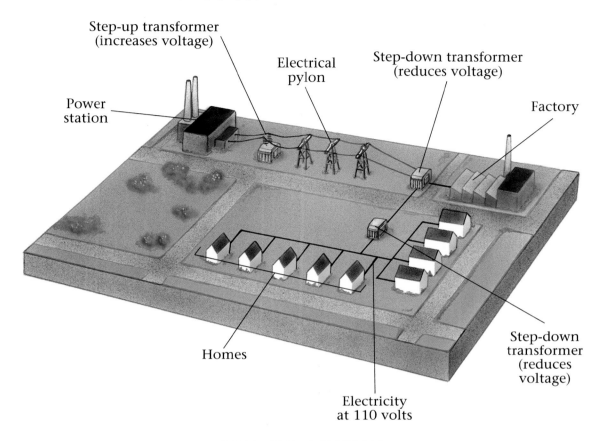

Step-up transformer (increases voltage)

Electrical pylon

Step-down transformer (reduces voltage)

Power station

Factory

Homes

Step-down transformer (reduces voltage)

Electricity at 110 volts

DRY-CELL BATTERY

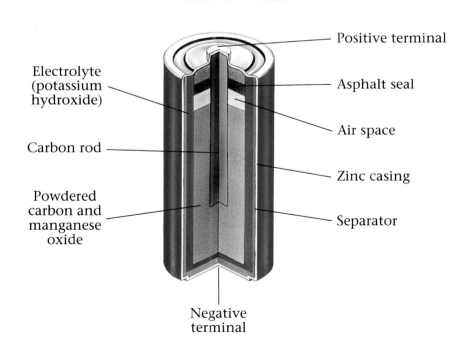

Positive terminal

Electrolyte (potassium hydroxide)

Asphalt seal

Air space

Carbon rod

Zinc casing

Powdered carbon and manganese oxide

Separator

Negative terminal

ENERGY

255

ENERGY

NUCLEAR POWER PLANT (PRESSURIZED-WATER POWER PLANT)

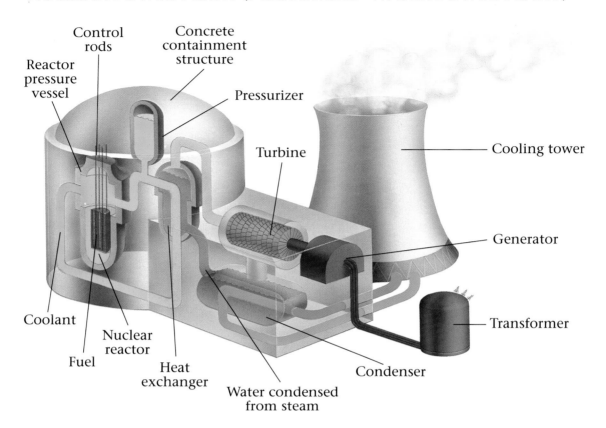

Control rods

Concrete containment structure

Reactor pressure vessel

Pressurizer

Turbine

Cooling tower

Generator

Transformer

Coolant

Nuclear reactor

Fuel

Heat exchanger

Condenser

Water condensed from steam

OTHER TYPES OF NUCLEAR REACTORS

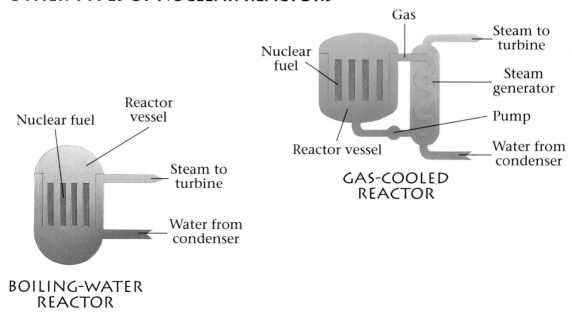

Gas

Nuclear fuel

Steam to turbine

Steam generator

Pump

Reactor vessel

Water from condenser

GAS-COOLED REACTOR

Nuclear fuel

Reactor vessel

Steam to turbine

Water from condenser

BOILING-WATER REACTOR

FOOD

ALL LIVING ORGANISMS NEED FOOD TO USE as energy and to help them grow. *Nutrients* are substances in food that our bodies need and use. *Fiber* is an important nutrient because it helps move the food through our bodies. *Carbohydrates* and *fats* give us energy. Our bodies use *protein, vitamins,* and *minerals* to grow and repair themselves. Different kinds of food contain different nutrients in different amounts. It's important that we eat many different foods so our bodies get all the nutrients they need. Your *diet* is the kinds of food you usually eat. The following pages will show you some foods that are high in certain nutrients and where those foods come from. The food pyramid in this section shows you how much of each kind of food you should eat to have a healthy diet.

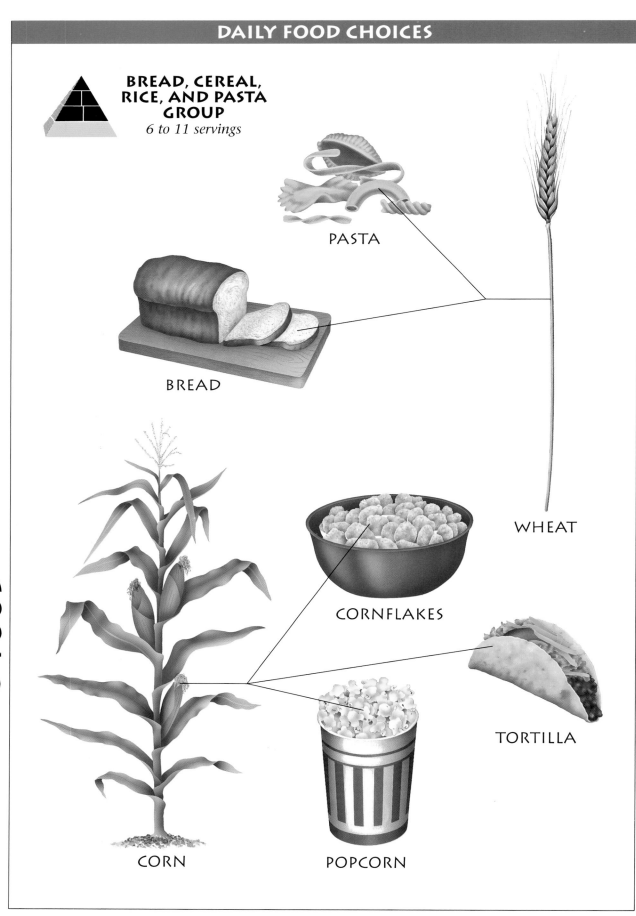

BREAD, CEREAL, RICE, AND PASTA GROUP
6 to 11 servings

PASTA

BREAD

WHEAT

CORNFLAKES

TORTILLA

CORN

POPCORN

FOOD

258

VEGETABLE GROUP
3 to 5 servings

KETCHUP

TOMATO
SAUCE

TOMATO

SALSA

FRUIT GROUP
2 to 4 servings

APPLE
JUICE

APPLESAUCE

APPLE

APPLE PIE

MILK, YOGURT, AND CHEESE GROUP
2 to 3 servings

MILK

COW

CHEESE

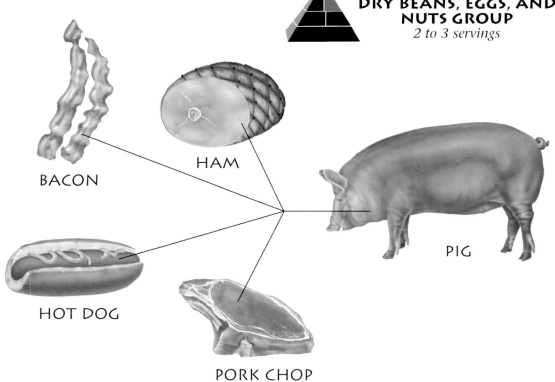

MEAT, POULTRY, FISH, DRY BEANS, EGGS, AND NUTS GROUP
2 to 3 servings

BACON

HAM

PIG

HOT DOG

PORK CHOP

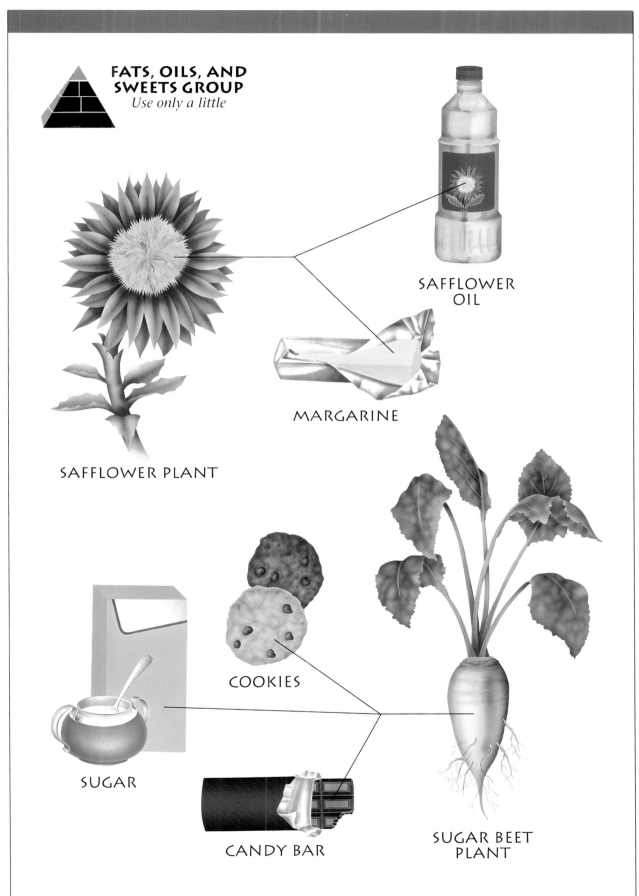

FATS, OILS, AND SWEETS GROUP
Use only a little

SAFFLOWER OIL

MARGARINE

SAFFLOWER PLANT

COOKIES

SUGAR

CANDY BAR

SUGAR BEET PLANT

Fiber and
carbohydrates

Vitamin A,
magnesium,
and folate

Vitamin C

Potassium

Calcium

Protein and iron

B vitamins
(thiamin,
riboflavin,
and niacin)

FOOD

262

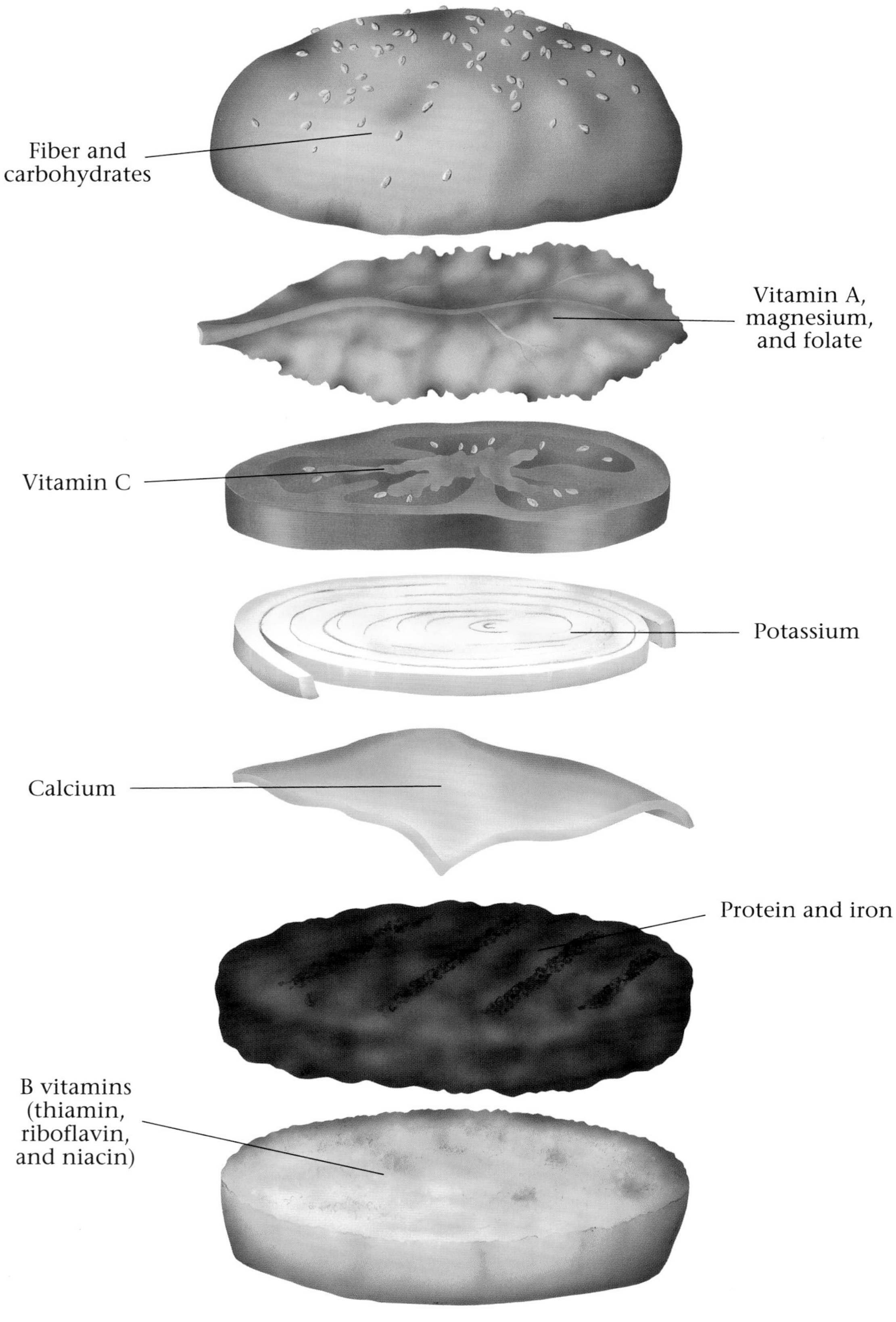

CLOTHING

YOU PROBABLY SPEND TIME each day thinking about clothes. You wear clothes, you buy clothes, you wash clothes, and you notice clothes that other people wear. We use clothes in different ways, and sometimes the way we use them affects what the clothes are like. Some clothes are made for practical reasons; down coats provide protection from weather, and sturdy work clothes are good to wear for messy chores. Other clothes are designed to help us express ourselves; T-shirts can have pictures or slogans that are important to us, for example. What kind of clothes do you wear? What kinds of clothes do your family and friends wear? What do the choices people make about clothing tell you about them?

BUSINESS SUIT

WORK CLOTHES

SPORTS CLOTHES

SHEATH DRESS

SUIT

PLEATED SKIRT

TURTLENECK

RUGBY SHIRT

T-SHIRT

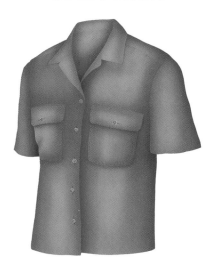

CAMP SHIRT

CREWNECK SWEATER

V-NECK CARDIGAN

JEANS

STRETCH PANTS

CLAM DIGGERS

SHORT SHORTS

BERMUDA SHORTS

CLOTHING

SAFARI JACKET

CAR COAT

BLAZER

TRENCH COAT

DOWN PARKA

DUFFLE COAT

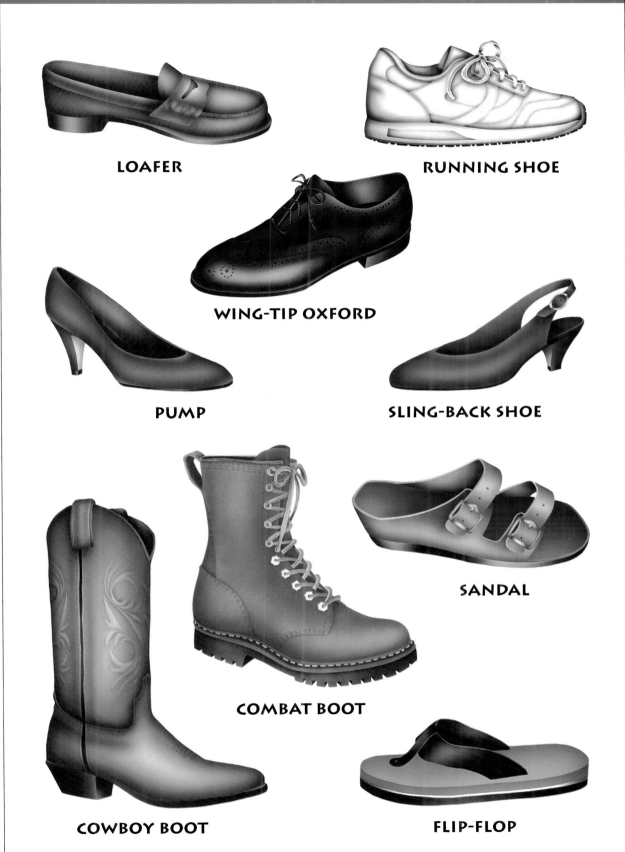

LOAFER

RUNNING SHOE

WING-TIP OXFORD

PUMP

SLING-BACK SHOE

COMBAT BOOT

SANDAL

COWBOY BOOT

FLIP-FLOP

CLOTHING

269

JOGGING SUIT

TENNIS SUIT

SWEAT SUIT

LEOTARD

SKI SUIT

HOUSEHOLD ITEMS

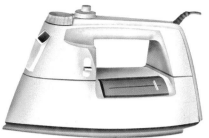

MOST OF THE ITEMS YOU'LL find in this section will be very familiar to you. You may have many of them in your own home, and you may have seen some of these items in other people's homes. Some are objects you use every day, like the refrigerator, the bed, or the toilet. Others are devices that someone else in your home uses, such as the iron or some of the kitchen utensils. If you look through these pages, you will probably learn new information about many objects you see every day.

HOUSEHOLD ITEMS

FLOOR LAMP

ARMCHAIR

Lampshade

Base

TABLE LAMP

SOFA

RUG

LOVE SEAT

END TABLE

COFFEE TABLE

DRESSER

CLOCK RADIO

NIGHT TABLE

DESK

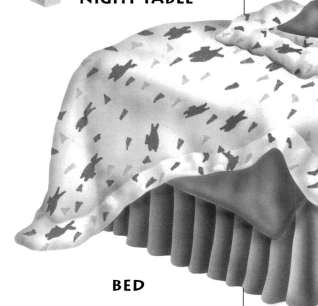

BED

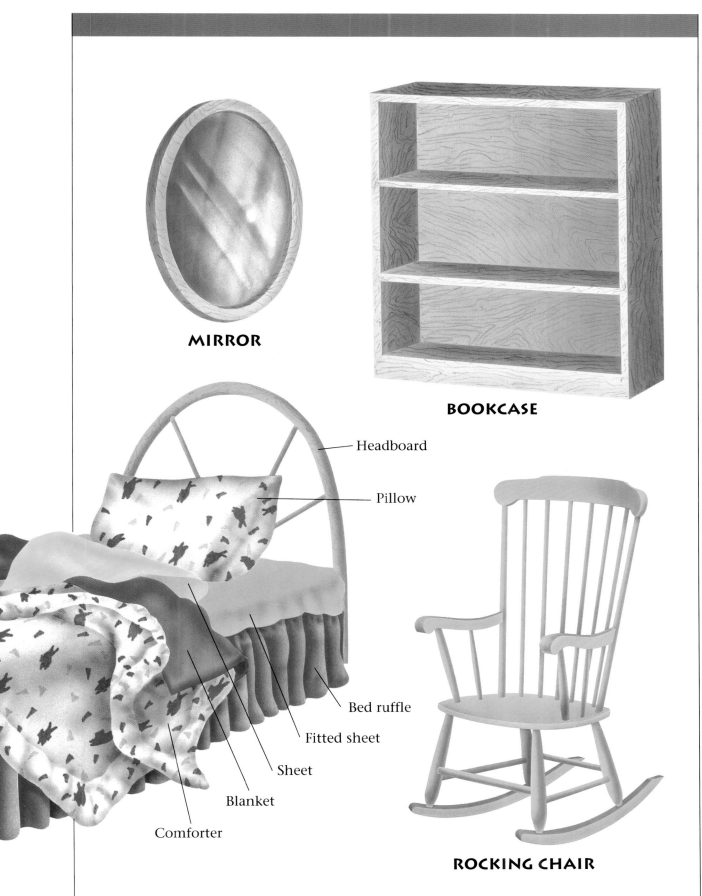

MIRROR

BOOKCASE

Headboard

Pillow

Bed ruffle

Fitted sheet

Sheet

Blanket

Comforter

ROCKING CHAIR

HOUSEHOLD ITEMS

TABLE

Extension

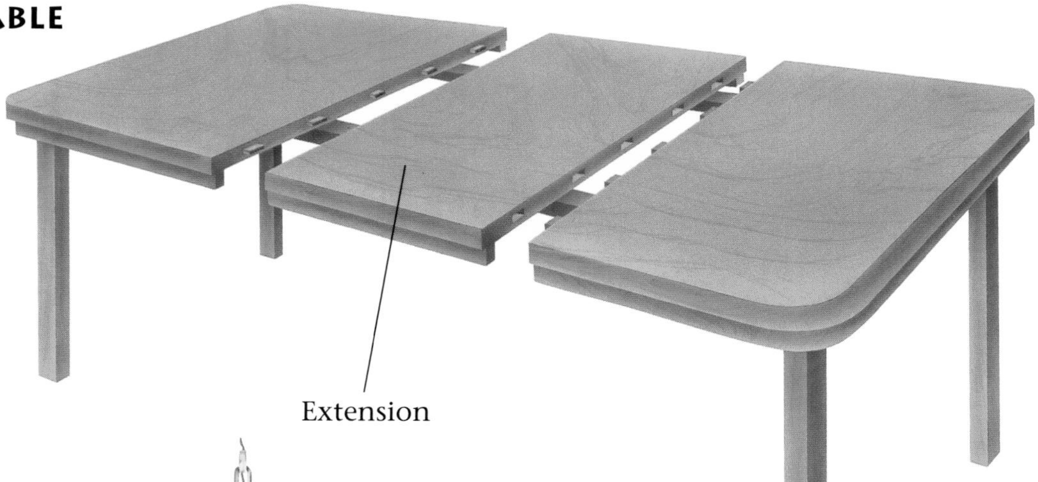

CHANDELIER

SIDE CHAIR

CHINA CABINET

BATHTUB ENCLOSURE

Showerhead

Water temperature control

Faucet

Bathtub

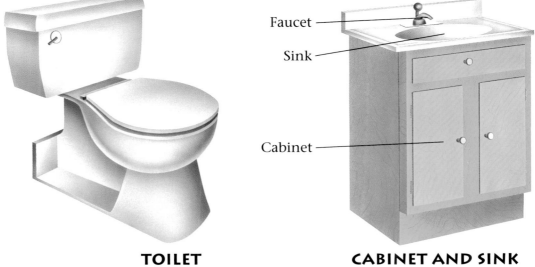

Faucet

Sink

Cabinet

TOILET

CABINET AND SINK

HOUSEHOLD ITEMS

UTENSILS

TURNER

KITCHEN
KNIFE

LADLE

ROLLING
PIN

WHISK

MEASURING CUPS

MEASURING
SPOONS

CAN OPENER

COLANDER

MIXING BOWL

POTS AND PANS

FRYING PAN

SAUCEPAN

DOUBLE BOILER

ROASTER

APPLIANCES

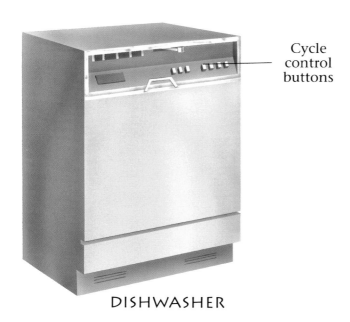

Cycle
control
buttons

DISHWASHER

HAND MIXER

FOOD PROCESSOR

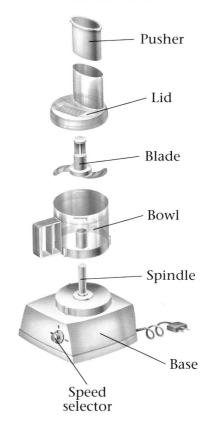

Pusher

Lid

Blade

Bowl

Spindle

Base

Speed
selector

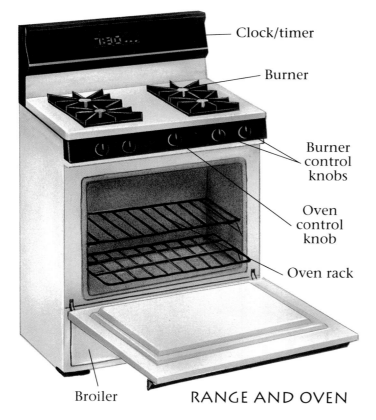

Clock/timer

Burner

Burner
control
knobs

Oven
control
knob

Oven rack

Broiler

RANGE AND OVEN

MICROWAVE OVEN

TOASTER

Thermostat

Freezer compartment

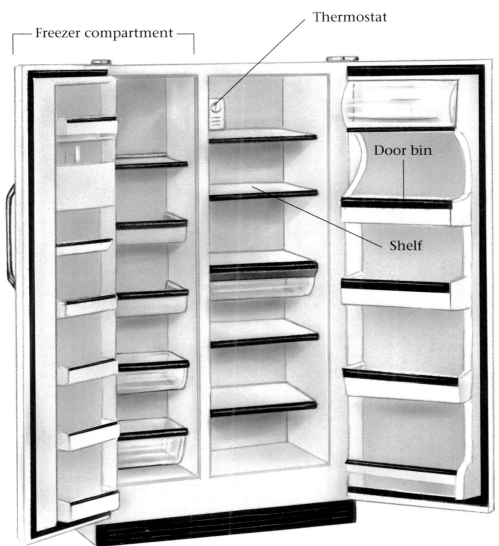

Door bin

Shelf

REFRIGERATOR

IRONING BOARD

VACUUM CLEANER

IRON

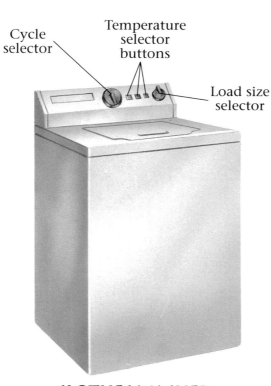

Cycle selector

Temperature selector buttons

Load size selector

CLOTHES WASHER

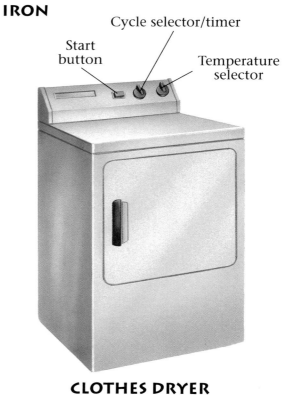

Start button

Cycle selector/timer

Temperature selector

CLOTHES DRYER

TOOLS

TOOLS ARE DEVICES THAT HAVE been specially made to help people do work. Making and using tools allows people to shape and use the world around them. The following pages show the kinds of tools that people use for basic jobs like plumbing, carpentry, and electrical work. Some of these tools can help with many different chores; hammers and pliers, for instance, have all kinds of uses. Other tools, such as lawn mowers and paint brushes, are made to perform one specific job. Does your family own tools like these? Have you ever used these kinds of tools to make a job easier?

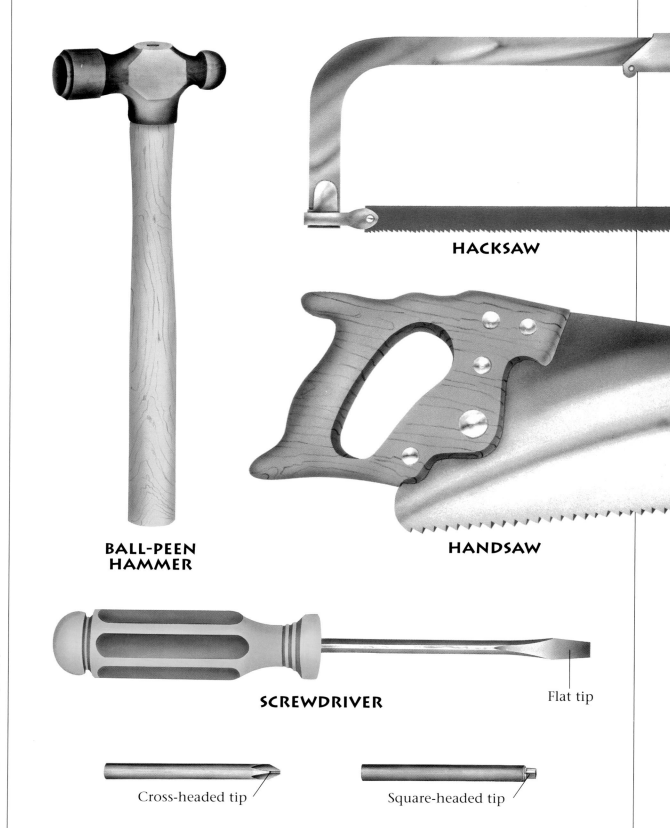

HACKSAW

BALL-PEEN HAMMER

HANDSAW

SCREWDRIVER

Flat tip

Cross-headed tip

Square-headed tip

TOOLS

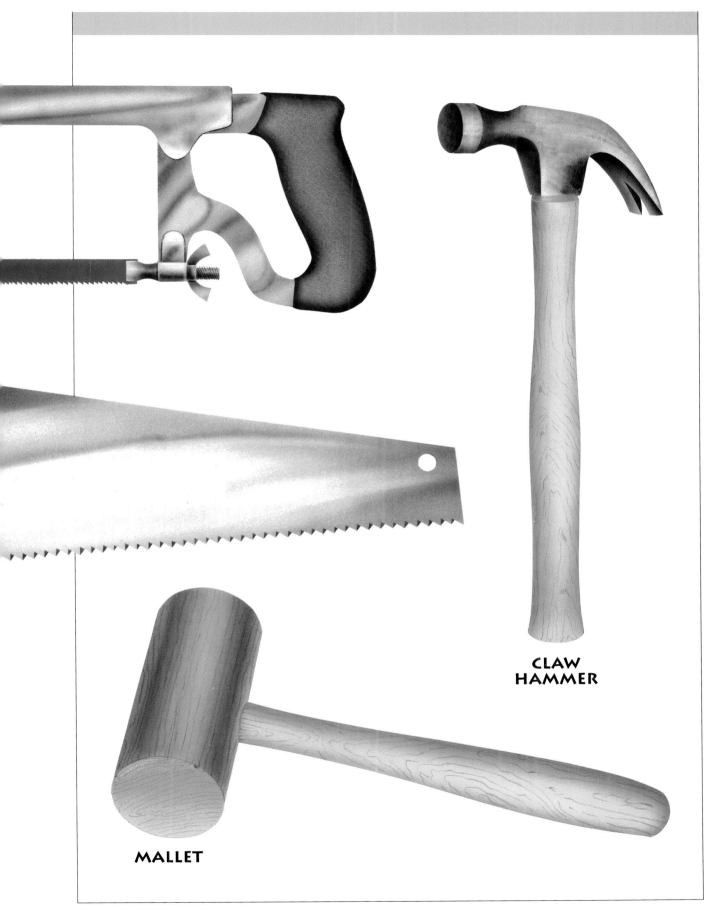

CLAW HAMMER

MALLET

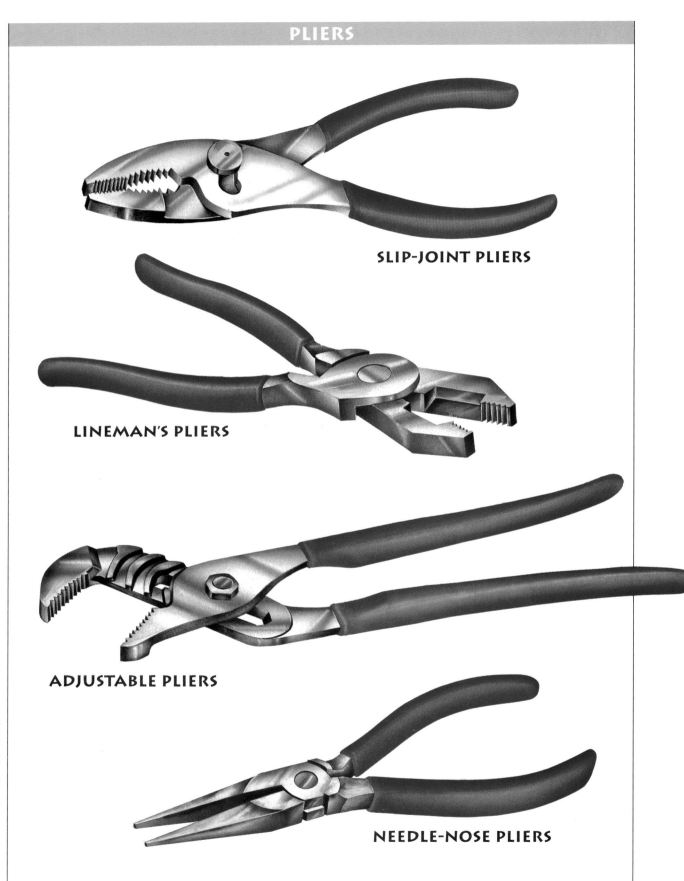

SLIP-JOINT PLIERS

LINEMAN'S PLIERS

ADJUSTABLE PLIERS

NEEDLE-NOSE PLIERS

TOOLS

286

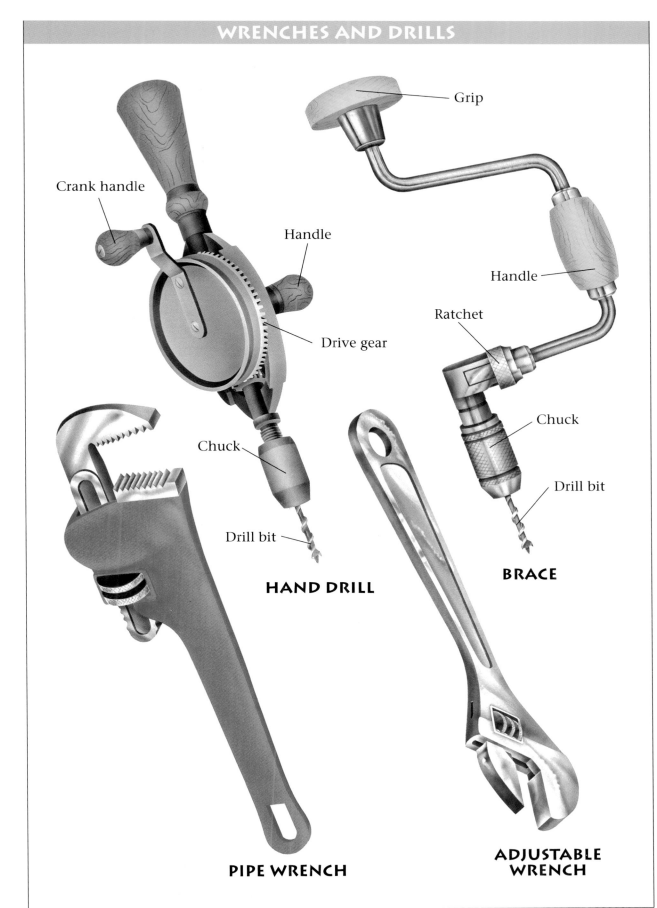

Crank handle

Grip

Handle

Handle

Ratchet

Drive gear

Chuck

Chuck

Drill bit

Drill bit

HAND DRILL

BRACE

PIPE WRENCH

ADJUSTABLE WRENCH

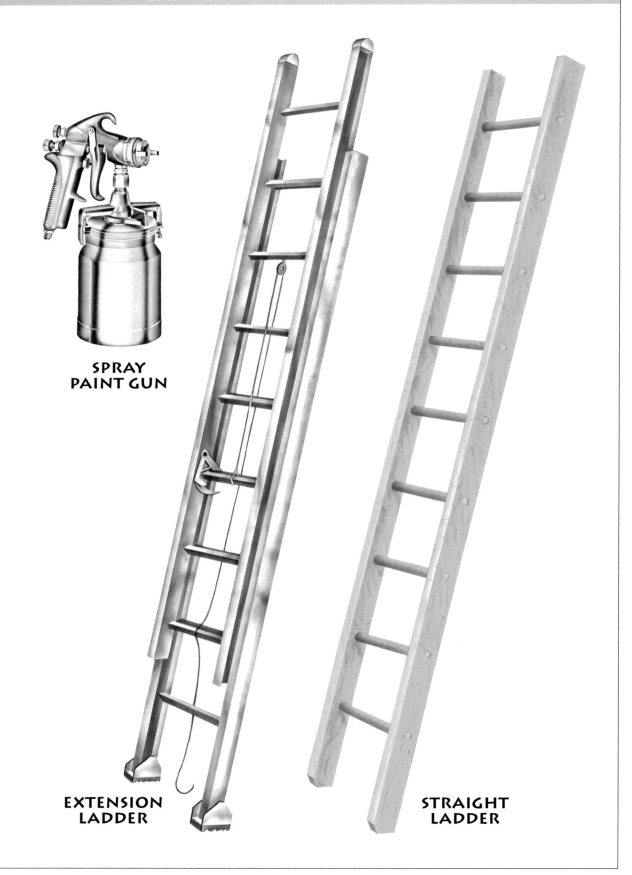

SPRAY
PAINT GUN

EXTENSION
LADDER

STRAIGHT
LADDER

PAINTBRUSH

PAINT ROLLER AND ROLLER TRAY

STEPLADDER

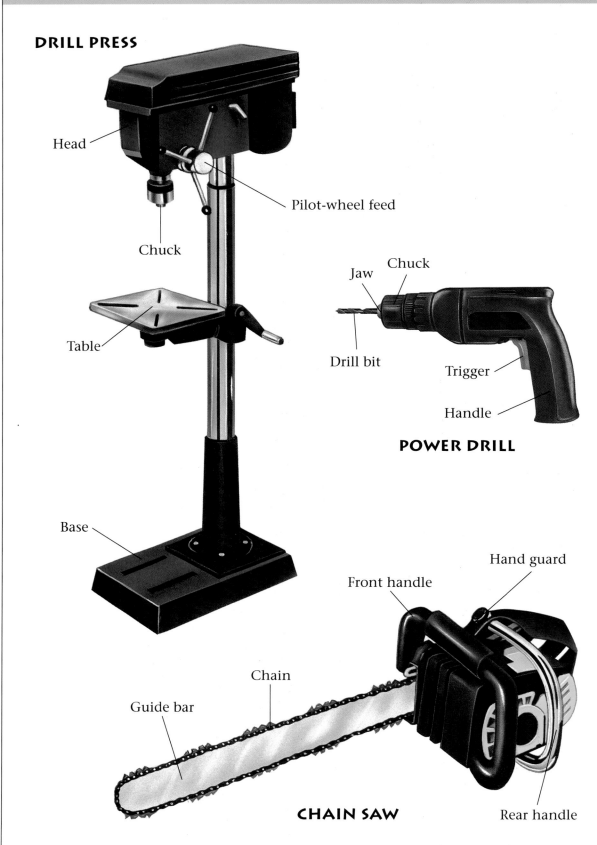

DRILL PRESS

Head

Pilot-wheel feed

Chuck

Table

Base

Jaw

Chuck

Drill bit

Trigger

Handle

POWER DRILL

Hand guard

Front handle

Chain

Guide bar

Rear handle

CHAIN SAW

CIRCULAR SAW

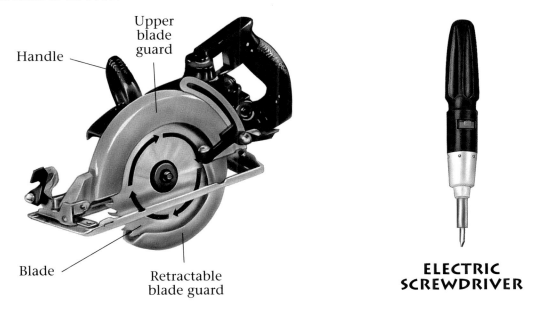

Handle

Upper blade guard

Blade

Retractable blade guard

ELECTRIC SCREWDRIVER

TABLE SAW

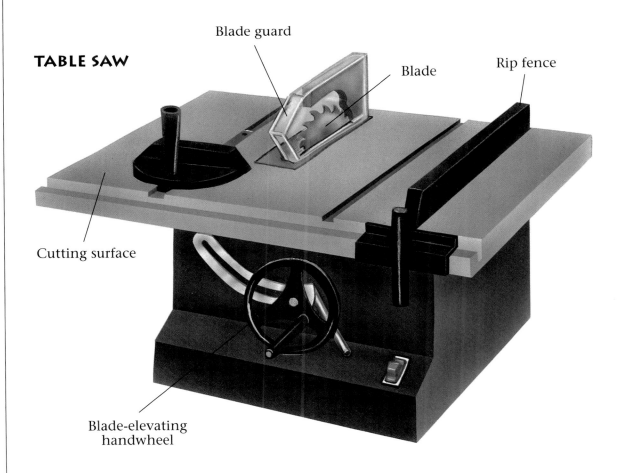

Blade guard

Blade

Rip fence

Cutting surface

Blade-elevating handwheel

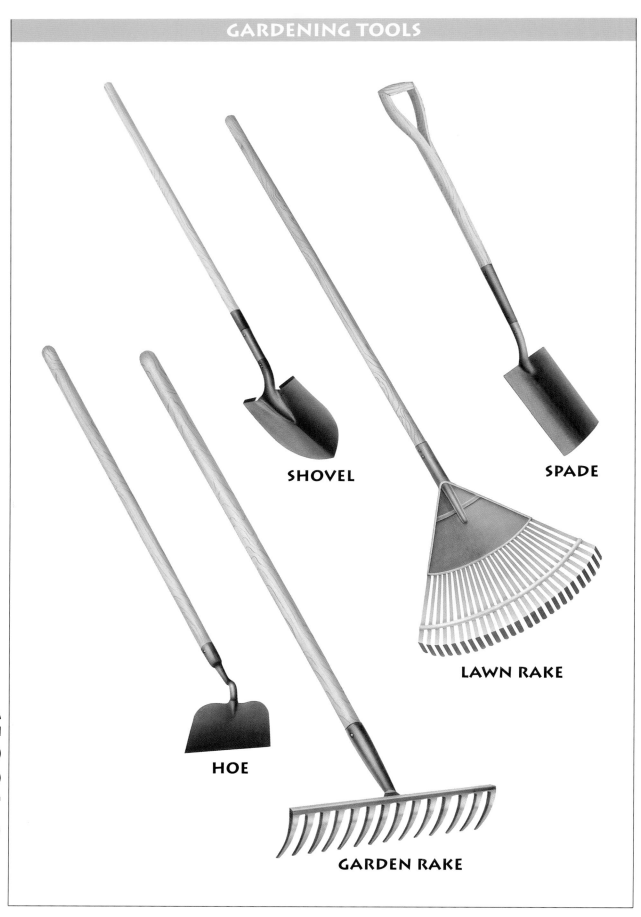

SHOVEL

SPADE

LAWN RAKE

HOE

GARDEN RAKE

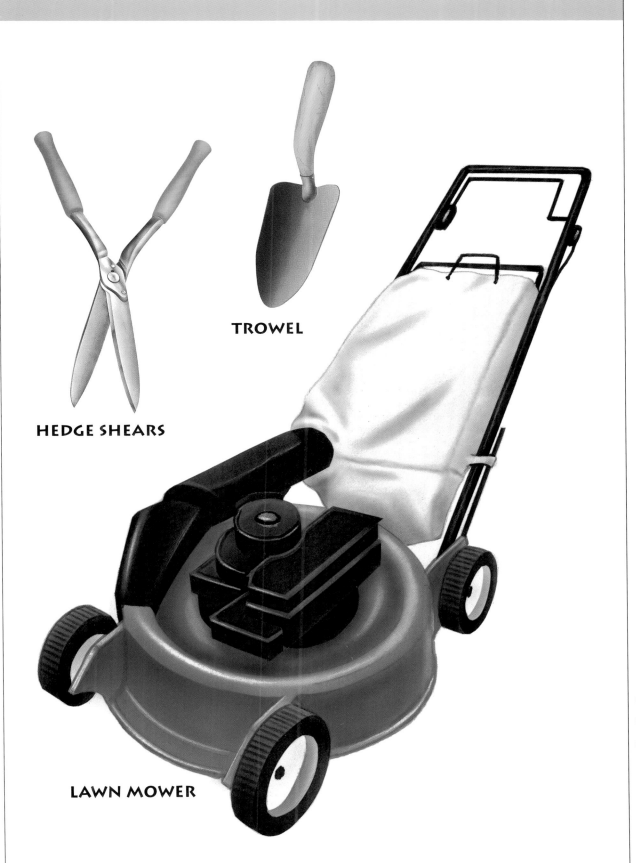

HEDGE SHEARS

TROWEL

LAWN MOWER

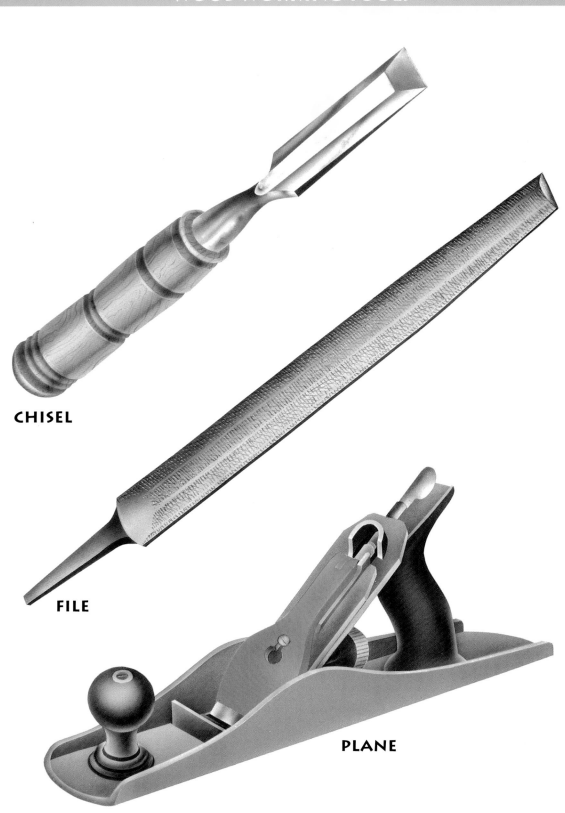

CHISEL

FILE

PLANE

INDEX